# PROMISED LAND

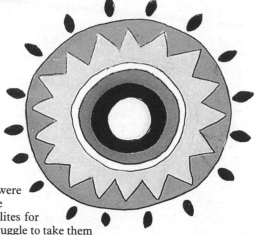

'What made me first realize the
path of our farmworkers' union was
when I compared the conditions we were
living in with those that I saw in the
Scriptures; the situation of the Israelites for
example, . . . where Moses had to struggle to take them
to the Promised Land . . . Our struggle is the same; Moses
and his people had to cross the desert, as we are crossing one
right now; and for me, I find that we are crossing a desert full of
a thousand hardships, of hunger, misery, and of exploitation.'

Vidal, Salvadorean peasant

## Acknowledgements

A great many people have contributed to this book. First and foremost, I would like to thank those Salvadoreans, whom I cannot mention by name, but without whose collaboration this book could not have been written. Some risked their lives taking me into guerilla held territory. Others gave me hours of their time, despite the many tasks the war demanded of them, to recount their experiences. Others have provided information, read drafts and discussed with me the themes of this book. To the people of El Salvador, and in particular my friends in Chalatenango, I dedicate this book.

I would also like to thank the following people for their help: Jutta Blauert, Catherine Matheson, Sally O'Neill and Brian McKeown of Trócaire and my editor Neil MacDonald. Bambina Carnwath, Pilar Bohórquez and Steve Lewis transcribed the testimonies. Special thanks to Gavan Duffy for the graphs and much else, and our son Dick, who delayed his arrival to enable me to complete the manuscript.

Jenny Pearce
Maternity Ward, Whittington Hospital, London
September 1985

# PROMISED LAND

## PEASANT REBELLION
## IN CHALATENANGO
## EL SALVADOR

JENNY PEARCE

First published in Great Britain in 1986 by Latin America Bureau (Research and Action) Limited, 1 Amwell Street, London EC1R 1UL

Copyright © Latin America Bureau (Research and Action) Limited 1986

Published with the assistance of Trócaire.
The views expressed, however, are those of the author.

*British Library Cataloguing in Publication Data*

Pearce, Jenny
    Promised land: peasant rebellion in Chalatenango, El Salvador.
    1. Peasantry — El Salvador — Political activity — History    2. Revolutionists — El Salvador — History
    I. Title
    322.4'2'097284      HD1339.S3

    ISBN 0-906156-21-1

Written by Jenny Pearce
Maps by Michael Green © Latin America Bureau
Cover illustration by Valeria Varas
Cover design by Chris Hudson
Typeset, printed and bound by Russell Press, Nottingham
Trade distribution in UK by Third World Publications, 151 Stratford Road,
        Birmingham B11 1RD
Distribution in the USA by Monthly Review Foundation

# CONTENTS

**List of figures**

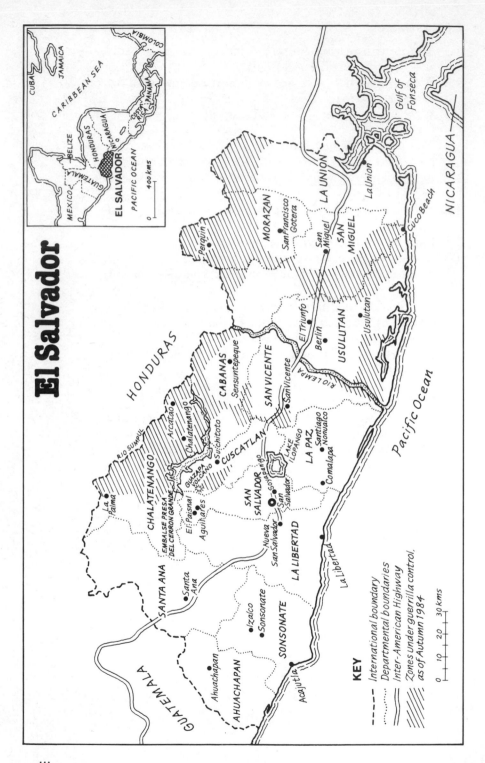

# El Salvador

**KEY**

- – – – International boundary
- ········· Departmental boundaries
- ═══════ Inter-American Highway
- ///////// Zones under guerrilla control, as of Autumn 1984

# PROLOGUE

Any talk of El Salvador's recent history simply repeats the same old history. It helps us explain and justify our tragedies and our heroic moments. Yesterday, today, tomorrow, our lives are enriched by experiences that have taught us not to let ourselves die, even in the direst conditions, to go on living through the toughest circumstances.

Our history is not very different from that of other Latin American peoples. However, the characteristics of each country do help explain the origins of the transcendental struggle which every region is engaged in. This applies to both El Salvador and Central America.

Let me briefly look through the window of the past in order to spy out the future. In the background, as always, will be Chalatenango, Morazán, San Miguel, Usulután, Cuscatlán, San Vicente. This small world, unknown even ten years ago, now impinges on the fate of peoples and nations. Because we have not been alone, nor will we be alone during these dangerous hours when open military intervention offers extermination as the way to resolve the struggle we are caught up in. To some extent, the whole world is involved when a regional conflict is being waged in defence of the interests of the multinationals, which is tantamount to saying the interests of the manufacturers of arms, whether conventional or non-conventional.

Yet we should persevere in our hope that those of us who believe in humane solutions are in the right. We have survived, and we must continue to survive. In spite of the centuries' old history, written in blood, pain and tears (to parody the English statesman). The history of our peoples will win out over the madness of over-weening materialism. The history of all those who have fought and suffered under the weight of obscurity and humiliation.

It is a history which has varied little through the centuries, until uprisings and revolts began to force their way in. But the violent face of power showed itself to those begging for a fairer society. Four centuries of unending violence.

An army and the National Guard were formed. Advisors and technical aid were invented. In other words, arms were sold and people instructed in how to use them to their full efficiency. These forces were installed to protect the minority landowners from internal unrest: meaning the vast mass of the exploited and dispossessed. The army was

1

built as an occupying force. When the former ambassador of the United States to El Salvador affirmed in 1980 that this country boasted perhaps the most bloodthirsty army in the world, he was referring to its actions within national boundaries. His evidence draws on real-life experience: the army's conduct when faced with its own people. When those who voice the policies of the multinationals speak of foreign intervention in El Salvador and Central America, they are referring to this majority, made up of peasants and the oppressed, even though their speeches are trying to prove something else.

The sector that for centuries held the weapons has always known who should fire them. Against those who dreamt of a land that once was theirs: against those who sought to express themselves in poetry and architecture in which centuries earlier they had proved their skill. Until now the only thing that no tyrant has managed to overcome has been dreams. And there are dreams which last for centuries. The awakening after so long is all the more beautiful. This awakening is called awareness. Awareness not as an abstraction but as a concrete truth translated into organized action.

These Chalatenango peasants are the children and grandchildren of those who succumbed in the dye factories, in the sugar cane, coffee and cotton plantations. Yet they are not the same. Their new awareness is the dream come true. They are already half-way down the road: the remainder is held in the hands of the world's oppressors. This half is what yet remains to be fought for. Inhuman practices must be defeated. All of us must put our faith in humanity's own grandeur. The dream is one of coexistence, justice, and happiness. The dream lies within our grasp; it is awareness throughout the world which must play its part in helping us Salvadoreans see our dream come true.

*Manlio Argueta*

# INTRODUCTION

In 1984, I visited a number of areas of El Salvador which were under the control of the FMLN guerilla forces (Farabundo Martí National Liberation Front). I spent my time primarily in the department of Chalatenango, but passed through Guazapa and the department of Cabañas.

The objective of the trip was to collect oral histories from the peasants in the areas under guerilla control. I was interested in the development of El Salvador's peasant movement, the relationship of the peasantry to the guerilla forces and the forms of popular organization in the zones of control.

The journey to guerilla-held territory was not easy to make. Travel was mostly by night and through territory still under the control of the Salvadorean army. Our passage was only made possible by the collaboration of peasants who risked their lives to act as our guides through clandestine guerilla corridors in enemy territory. Once inside the guerilla zones, the hazards were mostly from the air. We were bombed every day and sometimes machine-gunned, often fleeing for cover to survive, but this has become a way of life for the men, women and children who live there. Bombardment which had been relatively sporadic during 1983, intensified dramatically at the beginning of 1984. Unable to defeat the guerillas in ground battles, the Salvadorean army, advised and supplied by the US government, had taken the war into the air.

The targeted areas were the guerilla controlled zones. The victims were the civilian supporters of the guerilla army and not the guerillas themselves, who are mobile and in my experience rarely present when the bombs fall. It was in any case evident that the pilots dropped bombs where they saw any sign of daily life: clothes on a line, a cooking fire, or a dwelling just visible in the trees. There was no attempt to identify military targets. The bombing contravenes the Geneva conventions of 1949, signed and ratified by both El Salvador and the US, which defines a civilian as someone who does not carry arms and is intended to protect them in times of war. As the March 1985 Americas Watch report, *Draining the Sea*, explained:

3

'When terror tactics are used against civilians, pursuit of this strategy violates international law. The Geneva conventions of 1949 which have been signed and ratified by El Salvador and the United States, and Protocol 11 of 1977 which has been signed and ratified by El Salvador, were intended to protect civilian non-combatants against such tactics. Because the evidence shows that the use of such tactics is systematic and, apparently, a deliberate practice, we believe that the government of El Salvador may be fairly charged with committing war crimes.'

The box below records my experience of being under bombardment.

---

### Days Under Fire

**Monday, 23 January 1984:** About 9.30 pm we hear the sound of a low plane. It circles around, buzzing like a lethal mosquito one can never quite catch. It has no lights. We think it has gone and go back to our sleep. But the buzz returns, relentless. It now seems inevitable it will drop its bombs. But for some time it just circles around, invisible in the night sky. Then suddenly a bright orange light descends slowly from the sky, lighting up the area below. A parachute flare! It's the most menacing sight I've ever seen. Such a premeditated act of murder to light the path of your bombs, ensure you have human targets, most of whom, like us, would be in bed for the night. We hasten down the slopes for cover, slipping in the darkness and the tangled twigs and branches. We can't see a thing and end up in some kind of pit in the undergrowth, clinging to each other as the bombs fall all around us . . . It's very frightening, I feel quite helpless. The people here have to deal with this almost daily. In the four days we have been here there have been two serious bomb attacks in our vicinity. With considerable relief, we are told the plane has gone and we return to the house. We are woken up again at 4 am by the sound of the plane. But this time it doesn't bomb. We are beginning to get used to the tightening of the stomach each time we hear the sound of a plane.

**Tuesday, 24 January 1984:** At about 11 am we hear the buzz of the plane. I'm writing this in the *tatu*, the air raid shelter that the peasants have hewn out of the hillside. Two bombs have already fallen, and now the A-37 plane which drops the heavier bombs has come. We are four young children, a teenage girl, an old woman and a man. The atmosphere is tense. They have been bombing this area a lot recently, since we arrived in fact. I feel some fear at the bottom of my stomach, no panic, relative calm, but quite vulnerable. Most of all I feel choked with anger looking around at the faces of the peasants with whom I share this shelter and thinking of the objective of that plane. Everyone keeps a calm, if tense, dignity . . .
. . . The planes have now passed. I can hardly keep up with this diary. Every time I write about one bombardment, I am caught in another.

**Wednesday, 25 January 1984:** I wake up in the middle of the night to the sound of the giant mosquito circling round above us. I hold my breath, but

it passes on. I wonder what it was up to, just trying to cause panic? . . .
. . . About 1 am two A-37 planes appear. We slide down a bank for cover. They fly in formation, almost jauntily it seems, savouring their power over the people below. They drop about 12 bombs, the explosions seem very near. I can see brown smoke rising up from one of the 'hits' . . .
. . . It's 8.30 pm. We prepare to lie down for the night when one of the *compas* asks if we want to see the results of the day's bombing. We rush out and in the night we make out a convoy of people carrying two small figures in hammock stretchers. It's a dramatic and sombre sight. We learn that the children are Alfredo López, seven years old, with a bad shrapnel wound in his leg, and his five-year-old sister, Maritsa, who has a lump of flesh taken out of her behind. Their three-year-old brother, Lito, has been killed in the attack and both their parents are badly wounded. The convoy is taking the children to the 'hospital'. We follow them. The 'hospital' is just a converted peasant *adobe* dwelling, and the operations are carried out by candlelight. The mother arrives while we are there. She has heavy bleeding from a shrapnel wound in her leg and is in great pain. But it's not just her own pain that makes her suffer, it's the loss of her child and the sound of her other sick children crying . . .
. . . Once again, I feel a great anger. This is US policy at work. These peasants I am living with have nothing. They might possess the worn clothes they stand up in and at the most, one change of clothing; some have a stone for grinding corn, a few plastic plates perhaps, and there might be a wooden bench and table in their huts, but nothing much else. And here is the US government, pouring thousands of dollars into planes and bombs to wound, kill and destroy the little they have. I feel heavy with the reality of this war.

*Seven-year-old Alfredo López being carried to guerilla hospital in a hammock stretcher*

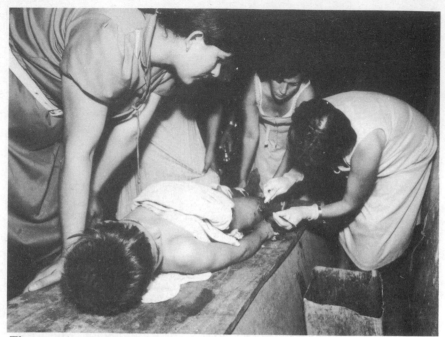

*The operation on Alfredo's leg wound*

I spent most of my time with this civilian population – widows, orphans and poor peasant farmers – whose children were often in the guerilla army. They had opted to stay in the guerilla controlled zones, where they were building new forms of democratically elected local government, called *Poder Popular Local* (Local Popular Power). Through the PPLs, the peasants were solving some of their most immediate material problems as well as participating more actively than ever before in the organization of their communities. They were attending to the health and educational needs of the population, so neglected by the Salvadorean government, establishing popular clinics and literacy classes. Production was organized to guarantee all members of the community a basic diet as well as to grow food for the guerilla army. The peasants had few resources and little outside technical help and depended mostly on their own collective efforts and creativity in solving the many difficulties they encountered. But through the experience, many had deepened their commitment to the revolutionary process which was bringing some real changes to their lives.

Their commitment was tested not only by the daily bombardment from the Salvadorean army but also by the numerous army sweeps through the zones in an effort to dislodge the guerillas and their supporters. During these invasions, the army had slaughtered their cattle, burnt their crops and houses, and murdered anyone unable to run as they approached. These invasions and the mass retreats of the population, called *guindas*, haunt the population. Their experiences, some of which are recounted in this book, are amongst the most harrowing of any recent war.

This book is inevitably profoundly influenced by my experience with the peasants. It convinced me that the media emphasis on the military side of the guerilla struggle in El Salvador has neglected some fundamental questions about the nature of the Salvadorean civil war. In a country as small and densely populated as El Salvador, with no isolated mountain redoubts to conceal a guerilla army, the very existence of guerilla controlled territory is remarkable and contrary to most classic guerilla theory. In this situation, popular support is essential for survival. The early history of the guerilla army in El Salvador shows how local peasants fed and protected the first small guerilla camps set up in the very midst of enemy army posts.

But the importance of the Salvadorean civil war does not lie just in the degree of popular support for the military effort, but in the extent of popular mobilization and organization which preceded the civil war. Thousands of Salvadoreans reached their own political conclusions through experience in organizations, such as rural and urban unions, set up during the 1970s to win improvements in their living conditions. It was these experiences which brought many Salvadoreans into political activity for the first time and ultimately into the guerilla army.

My visit to the controlled zones confirmed the belief that the Salvadorean struggle is one of the most politically significant in twentieth-century Latin American history. The extent of popular mobilization and organization, the emergence of a number of outstanding peasant and worker leaders, and the experience of popular democracy in zones of control are some of the features of that struggle which distinguish it from other Latin American revolutions. It is the strength of the popular movement which has helped sustain the guerilla war, despite the adverse geographical conditions of the country and the hostile international climate in which it has arisen.

Unlike the Cuban and Nicaraguan revolutions, for instance, the Salvadorean revolution has had few temporary political advantages. For instance, the former were both able to win support or acquiescence from a fairly wide range of social forces alienated by corrupt and decadent dictatorships, personified in the figures of Batista and Somoza respectively. The US was then unable to respond when successful revolutions went beyond the overthrow of the dictators and embarked on a process of social transformation. But both revolutions generated their own post-revolutionary psychosis in the US. In the wake of the Cuban revolution the US developed an effective range of counter-revolutionary strategies designed specifically to prevent neighbouring countries from taking the same path. In 1979, the Nicaraguan revolution precipitated the same response. Since then, US counter-insurgency methods have been employed with renewed vigour against the Guatemalan and Salvadorean opposition.

In 1982 the Guatemalan army succeeded in halting the momentum of the guerilla struggle through a brutal counter-insurgency war. Though the guerilla movement there is by no means destroyed, it no longer constitutes an immediate threat to the ruling order. The FMLN, however, has sustained a war which has lasted for five years, in territory much more inhospitable to guerilla warfare than in Guatemala, and where US involvement has increased steadily over the years. The political history of the popular movement in El Salvador in the 1970s provides some explanation for this, and is a major theme of this book.

This theme is illustrated here through a study of the peasant movement in El Salvador, focussing on the department of Chalatenango. This is only one area where the peasant movement developed in the 1970s. There were also interesting experiences around Aguilares and Guazapa (recorded by Carlos Cabarrús in *Génesis de una revolución*), Suchitoto and San Vicente. The guerilla organizations, the RN (National Resistance) in Suchitoto and the FPL (Popular Liberation Forces) elsewhere, established strong influences in these areas. Another organization, the ERP (People's Revolutionary Army) gained wide support in Morazán, but the peasants in this department were organized more directly in support of the military struggle. Chalatenango was chosen for this study partly because of its history of peasant organization in the 1970s but also because by the early 1980s, it had become one of the strongest zones of guerilla control, where the political experiment of local popular government (PPLs) advanced more rapidly than elsewhere. Many of the peasants involved in the PPLs were activists of the peasant union, and I could trace through interviews, not only the history of the peasant movement in the area but also the nature and extent of their participation in the revolutionary process taking place in the guerilla controlled zone. These interviews are reproduced in bold type throughout the book.

There are a number of other themes in this book which try to relate the experiences of the peasants in Chalatenango to the wider context of the Salvadorean civil war. The first two chapters give the background necessary to understand the forces which have erupted in El Salvador. Chapter 1 outlines the historical roots, the dispossession of the people of rural El Salvador and their separation from their land. This lies at the heart of the misery of the people of El Salvador and this chapter makes clear that a solution to this problem is not available inside the present political order. Chapter 2 gives an account of the fundamental economic factors which set the parameters for the present struggle and the possibility of change in Chalatenango. It also gives a picture of life in rural El Salvador today. Chapter 3 recounts the earlier attempt, in 1932, to establish a just social order, its subsequent bloody repression and the establishment of a system of brutal control which lasted for 50 years. Also in this chapter, more subtle methods of rural control which emerged in the latter part of this period are dealt with. These involved the creation of organizations under US direction, including unions favourable to the existing order which would pre-empt the independent organization of local people. These examples are instructive for understanding the less-observed aspects of US policy throughout Central and Southern Latin America and perhaps elsewhere in the world. Against this background we recount the early stirrings of those forces which grew to oppose the existing order; in particular within the Catholic Church. Together, these three chapters provide an understanding of the causes and issues of the war. Readers already equipped with this material may prefer to skip to Chapter 4.

Chapter 4 deals in detail with those catalytic agents which allowed the growth of a new popular movement in the countryside. It was the new pastoral methods of the church which first awoke the peasantry to their plight, broke the fatalism and passivity which had gripped so many and encouraged the first independent peasant organizations. Subsequently, the revolutionary organizations began to attract support from those peasants who had gained experience in the peasant unions and realized that the Salvadorean ruling class was not going to allow them access to the means to life as a result of peaceful pressure. Chapter 5 tells the story of the growth of these peasant unions, largely in the words of those involved. Chapter 6 follows the evolution of events leading towards revolution and open warfare, and subsequent chapters deal with the military and political aspects of the revolution in rural Chalatenango.

This is not an isolated peasant war but an extraordinary mass movement of people fighting to replace misery by a humane existence. The testimonies in this book demonstrate that it is ludicrous to see this movement in East-West terms. The voices of these Salvadorean people are not solely those of people engaged in a war or fighting an ideological battle but of people with hope and a desire that all Salvadoreans can gain a better way of life.

Christian Poveda

# 1
# THE COLLAPSE OF THE PEASANT ECONOMY

The roots of the Salvadorean revolution lie in the failure of the Salvadorean economy to provide the majority of the country's people with a means of survival. Nor has the ruling class implemented the structural reforms which might enable it to do so. The Salvadorean economy today creates misery rather than a means to life. This chapter traces how this has come about and why.

Since the last quarter of the nineteenth century, a series of changes in El Salvador has led to the gradual destruction of the peasant economy and hence of the ability of the people to meet their basic needs from the land. The Salvadorean rural population is no longer a peasantry in the classic sense, with family labour providing the major part of the household income through direct production. Instead, El Salvador's rural cultivators have been transformed, particularly over the last thirty years, into a proletariat or semi-proletariat wholly or partially dependent on wage labour for survival.

During this period a growing number of peasants have lost access to land altogether and become totally dependent on wage labour; others who previously paid for their plot of land in labour have had to pay money rent. Tenant farmers and peasant smallholders alike have seen the size of their plots reduced as pressure on the land has intensified. They overwork tiny plots on the most marginal land and rely on fertilizer to make anything grow. Unable to generate sufficient income from the land to meet their needs, the land-poor as well as the landless have come to depend on cash wages for all or part of family subsistence. The large estates have been unable to absorb this growing labour surplus in the rural areas, while relatively few of those who migrated to urban areas have found jobs in the industrial sector.

While the population grew, the people were dispossessed. This process can be seen in three phases: the introduction of cattle and indigo in the colonial period, the rise of coffee in the *laissez-faire* period of the late nineteenth century, and the cotton boom of the twentieth century. These each took over different sections of El Salvador's land area. There are fundamental similarities in each phase. In each, production moved from answering the direct needs of the producers to a cash crop capable of realizing a surplus. This was seen as 'progressive'

11

in that this surplus would become available for investment and economic change, but in fact the changes brought the immiseration of those displaced. The phases differ significantly in that the pace of the process accelerated. The first covered a period of two hundred years under a colonial administration with mixed attitudes to the change, while the last took less than twenty years.

The following sections show this process of dispossession after reviewing the pre-Conquest relation of the people to the land. This is followed by an analysis of the present situation and the failure to provide solutions. A series of figures illustrates the structure of the problems.

## The Indian and the Land

*'The concept of the community of man with the soil, weather and plants was the basis of attitudes towards the use and ownership of land. To the Indian, private and individual ownership of land was as meaningless as private ownership of the sky, the weather, or the sea. Land, like the plants that grew on it, was for man's use and could not be claimed under exclusive individual ownership.'* [1]

The time when the Indians lived in harmony with their natural environment in El Salvador and the land could sustain a large population has long passed. Human settlement in the area dates back to some years before the birth of Christ, and for hundreds of years before the Spanish arrived the land supported relatively high population densities, particularly in the highland areas. The arrival of the Spanish heralded the introduction of a new concept of land and its use centred on its exploitation for personal gain through the labour of others.

The western part of Cuscatlán, the area known today as El Salvador, was originally inhabited by the Mayans. But El Salvador was never a centre of Mayan culture. The Indians whom the Spanish encountered at the time of the Conquest were mostly Pipil, Nahuatl-speaking Indians related to the Aztecs who migrated from Mexico in the eleventh century. They first settled in the area to the south and west of the river Lempa, but they came to control some three-quarters of the country. The rest was occupied by a number of different Indian groups: the Pokoman, related to the Mayans, settled the north-west of the country; and the Lenca, the area to the north and east of the river Lempa.

Archaeological evidence suggests an extensive pattern of human settlement at this time which included the eastern district and coastal lowlands. These were subsequently depopulated under the Spanish as a result of the introduction of diseases which made the area unfit for human habitation.

The staple crop of the Indian groups was maize, which can be grown in a variety of climates and can support a fairly dense population

12

using primitive technology. Indeed, the yields of maize per hectare far exceeded those of wheat grown in Europe at the time. The Indians used fire to clear the *milpa* (maize field) and a sharpened stick to dig and plant. Apart from maize, they also domesticated several types of beans and squashes, pumpkins, chilli peppers, cocoa, tobacco, cotton, honey and wax. But it was maize which occupied the central, almost mystical place in the Indian cosmos (see box).

The most populated areas of El Salvador at this time were the intermontane valleys of the country's central volcanic chain which contains the most fertile soils, enriched by volcanic ash and lava deposits. The Indians settled mostly on the valley bottoms which they irrigated and farmed intensively. But they complemented this lowland

---

### Children of Maize

Today, as many centuries ago, maize forms the central element of the daily life of the Salvadorean peasantry. Maize flatbreads *(tortillas)*, roasted or steamed cobs *(mazorca)*, fermented spirit *(chicha)* and a beverage *(atole)* are some of the maize-derived products which feature in the Salvadorean diet. The daily grinding of the maize, and the twice-yearly maize harvests, dominate life in the rural areas. Salvadorean sorghum, a grain similar to millet, is often used as a cheaper substitute or addition to maize products.

The importance of the *milpa*, the small maize field, for the peasants today, is rooted in the traditions and culture of the Mayans which were carried on by the Pokoman, Lenca and Pipil Indians. For the Mayan ancestors of the Salvadoreans, maize was a dominant factor of their lives, both in agriculture and in their religious culture. Maize was a sacred plant, given by the gods, a living being from which the mould of life was made. Stored beneath mountains of rock, the seed of the maize was discovered, according to legend, by ants which carried the grain on their backs. Man found out about it but could not retrieve it from the rocks. So he asked the rain gods for help, but they could not blast the rock apart. As a last resort, the oldest god sent a woodpecker to find a weak spot then blasted it with thunder. The Popul Vuh of the Guatemalans extends this mythology to man and woman being created out of a paste of maize. The yellow and white ears of the maize are also said to come from mythical places in Tabasco and Chiapas in southern Mexico, where temples were built to the maize goddess, Imix, to appease her and enrich the soil for a better harvest.

Traditional agriculture was based on this mythological view of maize which was seen as the god's special food for man, a precious means of sustenance and the foundation of the world. Certain rituals always surrounded the preparation of the *milpa* and the sowing and the harvesting of the crop. An offering was made, for instance, to Tlaloc, the rain god, at the beginning of the rainy season when the seed was planted. During the weeks of early growth prayers were made to Cinteotl, god of the young maize plant, and Xilonen, goddess of the growing maize, while the harvest was protected by Tozi, goddess of the ripened maize.

farming with periodic migrations to the more extensive land available on the surrounding highlands, where they applied slash-and-burn techniques. It was a farming pattern worked out through experience of centuries of dependence on the land for survival, and therefore carefully adjusted to the nature of the terrain, the soil and the plants.

Social organization amongst the largest indigenous group, the Pipiles, probably followed that of the Aztecs. The basic territorial unit was the *capulli*, which consists of several families of a clan group under a local chief. Individual families were given a plot of land to use but not to own and the same was true of Mayan society where the basis of social organization was the *chinamit*. Tribute to the priest was seen as part of the essential rituals of appeasing the gods and ensuring sunshine and rainfall at the right times of the year, while the nobility received tribute by virtue of their social status.

## Losing the Land I — the Colonial Period

*'The Indian before the Conquest had been a cultivator, a seedplanter. The conquering Spaniard became a mining entrepreneur, a producer of commercial crops, a rancher, a merchant . . . He wanted to convert wealth and labour into saleable goods, into gold and silver, hides and wool, wheat and sugar cane. No Spaniard could count himself wealthy as a mere recipient of maize, pieces of jade or cocoa beans. Wealth to him meant wealth invested in Spanish goods, capital multiplying miraculously in the process of exchange. He had not braved the hardships of the Indies merely to come into the inheritance of his predecessor; he wanted to organize and press the human resources under his command, to pay his debts, to enlarge his estate, to take his place among the other men grown rich and powerful in the new utopia.'*[2]

The land of Cuscatlán was first sighted by the Spanish in 1522. The first expedition of conquest was led by Pedro de Alvarado in 1524. Not until a third expedition in 1528 was Indian resistance finally overcome, though the Indians continued to fight back sporadically and the area was not completely pacified until 1539.

The land had little mineral wealth to attract the Spaniards; its main attraction was its fertility and the large Indian population who knew how to work it. Between 1525 and 1530, the labour power of this population was granted to the soldiers and priests of the Conquest in the form of *encomiendas*. Indians were literally 'recommended' into the charge of a Spaniard who was responsible for their conversion to Christianity and who could receive tribute or work from them on his estate. The Indians kept control of their lands and many Spaniards sought land near the Indian villages in order to make use of the labour services they were entitled to, encouraging an early mixing in the races

14

and cultures.

The powers granted to the Spaniards over the Indians were virtually limitless. Laws introduced by the Spanish Crown to protect the Indians were rarely enforced. A typical example of these powers was the grant to a Spanish soldier called Miguel Díaz:

*'By this instrument you, Miguel Díaz, are put in possession of the town of Nahuizalco . . . with the lords and chief men and with all the lands and villages and inhabitants thereof and subject to it, for you to use them in your house and farms in conformity with the ordinances of New Spain.'*[3]

For most of the sixteenth century, the only exportable wealth from the region was generated by traditional Indian products, mostly cocoa and balsam. The Spaniards encouraged the expansion of production but this was increasingly left to independent Indian villages, notably in the south-western part of the country known as *Los Izalcos*. Indian communities and traditions are said to have survived much longer in this area as a result of this early period of semi-autonomy. Few Indians enriched themselves however, as tribute payments were very high.

Shortage of labour began to affect cocoa production by the end of the sixteenth century. By this time war and disease had decimated the indigenous population and the crown still limited the import of negro slaves. Competition from Guayaquil and Venezuela also gradually eroded the external markets for Salvadorean cocoa. It was the search for new wealth-generating products which was to change dramatically the relationship of the Indian to the land and production in El Salvador. Gradually, the colonial economy shifted from the commercialization of Indian produce to direct Spanish control over production and a considerable expansion in Spanish demand for land and labour. Already, by the late sixteenth century, cattle raising had become a source of conflict between Indians and settlers. Cattle threatened the unfenced Indian plots and the Spanish landowners made claims to all the land over which their cattle roamed, forcing many Indians to leave their villages.

But the crop which came to dominate the colonial economy was a blue dye, indigo (*añil*), in growing demand in Europe as a replacement for woad in textile manufacture. The main centre for indigo production was the valleys and slopes of the central highlands, though unlike coffee which came to dominate the economy two centuries later, indigo could be grown on a wide variety of physical locations. The area around San Salvador was gradually devoted to indigo, while San Vicente, San Miguel and to a lesser extent Santa Ana, came to be important producers, combining indigo with other crops, mainly sugar and tobacco.

Cattle raising and indigo production were carried out on large estates, called *haciendas*. The *hacienda* was an individually owned,

almost self-sufficient economic unit, which included a large expanse of
land given over to a combination of commercial farming and
subsistence agriculture. Subsistence agriculture was carried out by
tenant farmers who paid for their land in labour rent or with a
proportion of their crop.

Whereas the *encomienda* system did not encroach on the land of the
Indian villages, the commercial estates which began to emerge in the
period 1590 to 1630 required large tracts of land and much of the
suitable land was already inhabited by Indian villages. These years saw
the first wave of pressure on Indian lands. Indigo cultivation also
imposed heavy labour demands, exacerbating the shortage. The
harvesting and processing of indigo required a large permanent labour
force and even more seasonal labour. Considerable amounts of the
green plant had to be harvested in order to extract a small amount of
dye. Initially, forced labour was used on the *haciendas* under the
*encomienda* system. Later, the crown itself arranged the distribution of
Indian labour to the landowners who needed it *(repartimiento)*,
expecting them to pay a small amount for the Indians' services. This
was abolished in 1600 and in 1603 inspectors were appointed to impose
a ban on the forced labour of Indians in the indigo mills, where working
conditions were particularly harsh and unhealthy.

Gradually, new ways of guaranteeing a labour supply were
introduced, though coercion remained an important element.
Sometimes day labourers or *jornaleros* were employed on the estate for a
wage, though this was not very common. Another arrangement sought
to tie the Indian to the estate through the loan of money which he was
unable to pay back out of his wages. He then became permanently
indebted to the estate owner, a system known as debt peonage.
Elsewhere an Indian would be given a plot of land on an estate in
exchange for labour services for the owner; he was known as a *colono*.

With the rise of indigo production, commercial farming came into
competition with the traditional subsistence agriculture of the Indian

villages. It was both encroaching on Indian land and its labour demands were affecting village life. In some areas, the villages were just absorbed into the *hacienda*. In others, particularly in the densely populated central highlands, the *hacienda* continued to exist alongside the village but the village gradually lost its population to the estate.

In this situation the traditional village community began to lose its importance for the Indian population. It ceased to reflect their needs and interests and became an instrument of the landowners and the colonial government, used by the former to guarantee their laboursupply and the latter to raise taxes. Exploitation and ill-treatment of Indians was now widespread in the villages, despite legislation to prevent it.

Many Indians began to leave their villages and sought a plot of land anywhere where they could be left in peace, forming a migratory population which filled the seasonal labour needs of the indigo estates. They were soon distinguished from the Indians who remained, taking on a social identity more akin to the Spanish and adopting their language and dress. By the end of the colonial period *ladinos*, neither Spanish nor Indians but combining features of both, constituted some half of the population. In this way the traditional Indian village slowly declined and the population dispersed.

But despite the decline of the villages, many did manage to survive alongside the *hacienda*. This may have been due to the Spaniards' desire to maintain certain villages as sources of labour or agricultural produce.[5] They acknowledged indigenous forms of land tenure in legislation which recognized the right to claim ownership to land on the basis of occupation and use. The Spanish also created communal land structures *(ejidos)*, which usually referred to the lands granted to the municipal council which administered the Indian villages, and the *tierras comunales* which was the farm land reserved for the Indian communities. The Spanish recognized that existing communities had rights over lands they had always held.

Until 1700, land grants and unregulated land seizures for indigo cultivation and cattle ranching were the basis of land settlement. But with the growth of the *hacienda*, attempts were made to give land titles and determine boundaries for both the *haciendas* and the Indian communities. But the process was heavily stacked against the Indians. Title was on the basis of occupation and as the Spanish had already seized much land during the Conquest and used their cattle to claim more, the Indians were unlikely ever to recover their original landholdings. An additional problem for the communities was the uncertain status of the *ladino* squatters who lacked any legal rights to land and who often settled on land that the village communities considered their own.

The granting of land titles was never a systematic exercise which could have given some security to the Indian communities, but a rather ad hoc process which depended on the initiative of the prospective owner in seeking a survey to determine ownership. This mostly happened in the central highland areas where land disputes became increasingly common as the estate owners sought to extend their control over the fertile region. The Indians rarely succeeded in their efforts to secure legal title, and by 1770 there were 440 well-established colonial *haciendas* in the country. These covered quite a large expanse of land. In 1807 the five largest of the estates totalled almost 19,000 hectares.[6] By the close of the colonial period the Spanish had come to control almost one third of the colony's land area.[7]

---

## The struggle for the land: San Pedro Perulapán

The case of the village of San Pedro Perulapán illustrates the continuity of Salvadorean history. Already in the eighteenth century the Indian villagers were facing growing insecurity over access to land. More than two and a half centuries later their descendants' attempts to gain access to the land are met with harsh repression.

**1705** In November 1705 the *alcaldes* (mayors) of the Indian villages of San Pedro Perulapán and San Bartolomé Perulapía made a joint petition to the colonial authorities for a formal survey to be made of their common lands, a legal title to this land to be given to them, and the allotment of further lands to be made for their growing needs. The petition prepared by a Spanish lawyer acting on their behalf as their *defensor*, stated:

*'Both our villages hold certain land in which we have had our milpas and cultivated plots since time immemorial; but we have no title to them. Because of this we are troubled and intruded upon by our neighbours. Thus our lands have become inadequate for our needs and, as our numbers are increasing . . . we ask you to order that sufficient lands be allotted to our villages in proportion to their population.'*[8]

**1978** In March 1978 there was a huge coordinated military operation, in which ORDEN played a major role, in the area of San Pedro Perulapán. This area is a centre of strike action and land occupations by peasant unionists and we were told that the operation was to curb the growth and activities of (the peasant organizations) FECCAS and UTC. We were told how the military and para-military forces searched and looted houses, arbitrarily arrested many workers, assaulted inhabitants and caused many others to flee in fear of their lives . . . Another woman told us that on 17 March 1978 about 35 members of ORDEN arrived at her house. They hit her and her husband with machetes and threatened to kill them for being members of FECCAS. She was taken to prison in San Pedro Perulapán, where she was again beaten . . . the ten-day reign of terror left 68 people missing, dozens injured and at least six dead — two of them decapitated.[9]

# Losing the Land II — Independence and the Coming of Coffee

*'On the one hand we see our virgin fertile lands that are calling for the application of capital and labour to reap the wealth that is promised; while on the other, we see the majority of the inhabitants of our villages content to grow crops of maize and beans that will never raise this miserable people above their sorry position, but will remain in the same wretched state as they endured in colonial times . . . the government is determined to transform the Republic, to make each one of the villages, yesterday sad and miserable, into live centres of work, wealth and comfort.'* (Editorial, *Diario Oficial*, 23 March 1880)[10]

El Salvador became an independent nation in 1839 after a long process of struggle which had begun in 1811 and been followed by the short-lived Central American Federation. The immediate post-independence period was marked by social and political unrest and economic decay, resulting initially in the decline of commercial agriculture. But, in the long term, export-oriented agriculture expanded under the new commercial freedom arising from political independence. Coffee, El Salvador's 'grain of gold', was to accelerate radically the process of dispossession.

Under Spanish rule, trade had been controlled by merchants in Guatemala City and Cádiz. With independence, El Salvador was able to open up its own ports on the Pacific coast. Foreign ships, particularly from Britain, now came to El Salvador with a range of new manufactured goods. As imports grew, so did the search for a way to expand export earnings to pay for them.

The government at this time was in the hands of the country's most powerful landowning families, increasingly influenced by imported *laissez-faire* economic theories. The names Regalado, Orellano, Escalón, Prado and Menéndez appear frequently as signatories to early legislation; many of them are still major landowning families in El Salvador. Up until the 1870s, indigo was still the country's most important export crop, even undergoing a period of quite rapid expansion in the mid-nineteenth century when production became increasingly concentrated in the north and east of the country. But some landowners began to experiment with other crops as competition from alternative sources and the development of synthetic chemical dyes threatened the indigo market. Coffee was originally just one of these experimental crops, having been introduced on a small scale in the 1820s for local consumption. Indigo, however, is a low-cost crop with quick returns, and many landowners were reluctant to make the investment necessary to diversify production. The state therefore took the initiative and began, under the reforming Liberal government of Gerardo Barrios and his successors, to offer incentives in the form of tax exemptions and lower export duties in order to encourage diversification.

Whereas indigo could be grown in a range of climates and soils, coffee, it was discovered, was best suited to the fertile volcanic soils on land above 1,500 feet. By the 1850s, coffee plantations were emerging in a number of areas, notably in Santa Ana, Sonsonate, Ahuachapán, Santa Tecla, San Salvador and later on the lower slopes of the San Miguel volcano and in the area to the west of San Vicente. As its commercial value became apparent, so railways and roads were built and the search for suitable land began in earnest. Between 1860 and 1880, the expansion of coffee production was very rapid; by the latter date it had overtaken indigo in value and acreage. It was mostly undertaken by the wealthiest landowners and some rich urban professionals, such as lawyers and doctors. These were the only people with access to capital and credit who could afford to wait the three-year minimum before the plant gave fruit.

The legal situation of landholdings in El Salvador was still confused. The post-independence government had initially continued the practice of recognizing both communal and individual forms of land-ownership, but efforts were made to define the areas under private ownership. With the rapid growth of coffee production the pressure on existing agrarian structures reached new levels of intensity.

Coffee required more land, more time, more labour and more capital than indigo. The best land for coffee, the upper slopes of the valleys and basins of the central plateau and the sides of volcanoes, were also areas traditionally densely populated by Indian communities. The gradual encroachment onto Indian communal lands which had begun in the colonial period now became an onslaught. A government survey of common lands in 1879 found that Indian villagers regarded over one quarter of the country as theirs, much of it in the fertile central highlands. It was noted from the survey that much of this land was under-utilized, while that which was cultivated was used only for subsistence crops. The very concept of communal ownership, concluded the country's commercially-minded ruling elite, was not only inefficient but it was also a disincentive to peasants to give their labour to the new coffee estates. While they were able to meet their basic needs from subsistence farming, it was argued, peasants were unlikely to increase production or become labourers on the farms of others.

Some landowners began to seize common lands illegally, but by the latter part of the century, the government was convinced that it was its responsibility to bring about the necessary changes in the use of common lands, and that only by abolition could these changes be achieved. A series of laws were passed between 1879 and 1882 which reflected the view that the expansion of commercial agriculture required that all land be held by individuals as private property.

A decree of 26 February 1881 abolished the *tierras comunales* and instructed the *administrador* of each community to divide up the common land among the members of the community who would now be regarded as the owners of the land they used. A year later the *ejido* was abolished, and those that occupied or cultivated land on the *ejido* became the legal owners and received a legal title on the payment of a sum of money. The owner was then subject to a land tax for the first six years of legal ownership.

Considerable confusion surrounded the complex legislation and procedures dealing with the land claims that resulted from the decrees. It was a situation which greatly favoured the wealthier landowners who could hire lawyers and bribe *alcaldías* who were responsible for submitting details of ownership of land not claimed by private individuals. Much of the common land was actually cultivated by villagers who lived in a village rather than on their land, and this enabled others to claim the land as theirs.

The laws radically altered the pattern of land tenure in the country and enabled wealthy landowners to incorporate many common lands to expand their coffee plantations. The process was uneven. In some areas unsuitable for coffee, small and medium sized farms did emerge as villagers who lived and worked on their plots claimed ownership by right of possession. But across the central highlands, coffee expanded at the expense of the common lands and led to a rapid increase in the landless peasant population. Despite this, the ruling elite felt it was necessary to introduce legislation, such as anti-vagrancy laws, to guarantee a labour supply for the plantations, particularly at harvest time. (A number of these laws were later grouped together in the Agrarian Law of 1907). In 1881 rural justices of the peace were appointed in each village with the power to force peasants to work on the estates when labour was required, and to punish them if they left the estates before completing their tasks. A rural police was created in 1884, and by 1889 the key coffee-growing departments of Ahuachapán, Sonsonate and Santa Ana, had set up a mounted police force which was extended to the entire country in 1895. But the end of the nineteenth century saw a period of rapid population growth. Between 1878 and 1931, the population increased from 554,000 to 1,493,000. This increased pressure on the land and the number of peasants forced to rely on the landowners for work or for a subsistence plot in exchange for work grew as a result. As time passed, therefore there was less need to invoke anti-vagrancy laws to guarantee a labour supply.

The permanent labour on the plantations was at first provided by *colonos*, who worked on the estate in return for a small subsistence plot of land. But as the profitability of coffee increased, all the land was required for planting and the *colono* became more frequently a worker who received a small wage and a wooden hut on the estate. The *colono*

## 'A Brilliant Future'

The perspective for the future of Salvador seems brilliant. The political and social conditions are decisively improving and the prosperity of the republic, with its fertile soil and hardworking population, seems secure. The progressive spirit of the governing classes and their rapid absorption of foreign ideas provide cause to believe that the control of economic life of the country by foreign interests, which are becoming more and more noticeable in these regions, can be avoided here. The introduction of foreign capital is, naturally, very necessary for the development of the country, as is the immigration of foreigners of a better class. But it is to be hoped that this can be effected without causing the impoverishment and collapse of the families of the national leaders. If the best people of the republic can continue in the future playing the role which they play at the moment in politics and agriculture, then the small country promises to remain as one of the most prosperous and most civilized states of tropical America.
(Dana G. Munro, 1918)[11]

and his family could be called upon to carry out any tasks the landowner demanded, whenever he wanted. It was the dramatic fall in real wages of coffee workers in the west of the country in the late 1920s which was to provoke El Salvador's first major peasant uprising in 1932 (see Chapter 3).

The expansion of coffee production was prodigious once the way had been cleared to provide the necessary land and labour. By 1901, coffee made up 76 per cent of all exports. Between the first world war and the depression of 1929, the area dedicated to coffee increased by between 60 and 90 per cent above the 1860 level. Foreigners who visited the country at this time sang its praises, comparing its prosperity and the productivity of its labour force very favourably with other Central American countries. Most of these observers failed to see that a whole sector of the population was excluded from this progress, only a few isolated voices drawing attention to the plight of the growing numbers of rural poor (see box above).

This was the period when a further concentration of land took place in El Salvador. The first world war and the consequent dislocation in world trade severely depressed coffee prices. This affected particularly the small coffee producers of which there were still a number at this time. Most of them had had to borrow from the larger landowners at high interest rates with short payment periods. As the Civil Code allowed the confiscation of mortgaged properties in cases of failure to repay the loan, the result was a transfer of land to the larger landowners.

The fall in coffee prices also convinced many landowners of the need to introduce more efficient and modern production methods.

Only the larger producers could afford to do this and they were able to consolidate further their hold over the industry. Production soon recovered and 70,000 hectares of land were planted with coffee by 1919, rising again to 96,500 by 1933. By that date coffee represented 95 per cent of exports and production was in the hands of a mere 350 producers. As coffee production expanded, food production declined. Between 1922 and 1926 there were dramatic rises in maize, rice and bean prices. Maize and rice imports, which were negligible before 1928, began to grow significantly.[12]

Another effect of the expansion of coffee and increasing land scarcity was migration to the urban centres. A rural exodus was apparent in the 1892-1930 intercensal period, when some 18,400 people migrated to the urban centres, accounting for 11.2 per cent of the total urban growth in the period.[13] This increased almost seven times in the next 20 years. Emigration, particularly to Honduras, became significant by the end of the 1920s. An estimated 12,000 Salvadoreans were living in Honduras at the end of the decade, almost ten per cent of the host country's labour force at the time.[14]

The dispossession and impoverishment of the Salvadorean peasantry which had begun with the *hacienda* system in the colonial period thus accelerated with the rise of coffee. The modernization of infra-structure that came with coffee could have led to real development of the country's resources. Instead it resulted in a rapid concentration of land ownership and created an enormously rich and powerful elite with a voracious appetite for increasing its personal wealth. Although the decrees of the 1880s laid the basis for the expansion of coffee, production was concentrated initially in the central highlands. But as prices rose in the 1920s, it began to extend into other suitable land where basic grains were previously grown.

---

### Divided Country — El Salvador in the 1940s

As one travels through the rural districts almost never does one see the *casa grande* (mansion) of a coffee planter. Their homes are in the exclusive districts of San Salvador, Santa Ana etc. If the proprietor does have a house on the land for his own use, it is generally a place to which he may go to spend a weekend.

Almost nowhere in the republic does one find evidence of communities of small-scale, independent farmers. The coffee planters, the *hacendados*, and the peons are the social classes in El Salvador's rural population. There is very little evidence of any intermediate stratum, of any small-scale farmers, of a genuine middle class of agriculturalists . . . The Indians have lost their lands. Also they have almost ceased to remember that their progenitors once were land owners.[15]

---

23

Soon maize production was excluded altogether from the coffee-growing areas. As a result the Salvadorean economy came to depend almost exclusively on coffee exports, and peasants growing subsistence crops were forced onto the worst soils, without access to credit or the means to invest in improving the land and its productivity. The interests of the coffee elite now determined the course of national life; the *Asociación Cafetalera* (Coffee Growers Association) became, in the words of one writer, a 'second state'.[16] Coffee was the grain of gold for only a very few Salvadoreans.

## Losing the Land III – Modernization and the Cotton Boom

Pressure on the land intensified in the 1940s post-war period when landowners made efforts to diversify production and lessen their dependence on coffee. While indigo had taken over the valleys and lower slopes of the central highlands and coffee had occupied the upper slopes, the coastal areas, the country's last agricultural frontier were lost to peasant agriculture through the expansion of cotton. Later, particularly in the 1960s, the central belt, which is too low for coffee and too high for cotton, was incorporated into the export sector with the planting of sugar cane.

This expansion was devastating for small peasant farmers in the subsistence sector. The growth of export agriculture occurred at the expense of land which provided not only a means of livelihood for the small farmer but which was also the source of much of the country's food. The expansion of cotton production took place in the regions of best farmland in the departments of La Libertad, San Miguel, Sonsonate and San Vicente. Between 1935 and 1965 the land under cotton grew a hundred-fold (from 1,100 hectares to 110,000), with major consequences for food production. There is a close correlation between yearly totals of land licensed for cotton production and the rise of maize imports from 1930 to 1971.[17] Sugar cane too, displaced the cultivation of basic grains in the central valleys and in some parts of the coastal plain of La Paz and Sonsonate. The total area planted with sugar cane increased almost fourfold between 1960/61 and 1974/75 (from 8,500 hectares to 33,200). By the 1960s export crops accounted for some 42 per cent of the area cultivated in major crops.

The labour for the large agro-exporting estates in El Salvador has traditionally been provided by the subsistence sector. Originally, the landowners ensured their supply through the *colono* system; smallholders and tenant farmers would provide the extra labour required during harvest time. Until the 1960s the majority of El

Salvador's rural population had access in this way to at least some land however small the plot. This situation began to change in the 1950s under the impact of the strategies to modernize and diversify the agro-export sector and the consequent cotton boom. The decline of the *colono* system of land tenure and non-wage labour relations, together with population pressures, contributed to a massive growth in landlessness and land poverty, a trend which accelerated in the 1960s and 1970s.

The shift towards wage labour which had begun on the coffee estates fairly early in the century accelerated in the 1950s with the expansion of cotton. The 1950 and 1961 censuses show first of all a marked reduction in the size of *colono* plots. During that period all *colono* plots over ten hectares disappeared, while there was a striking increase in units of less than one hectare (an increase of 85 per cent) and from one to two hectares (an increase of 52 per cent).[18] The total area of land in *colonato* was halved in the intercensal period from 82,000 to 41,500 hectares. Many *colonos* were evicted at this time from cattle ranches on the Pacific lowlands as a result of the expansion of cotton.

By the 1960s the *colonato* had almost disappeared as a significant form of land tenure. From 55,000 landholdings with *colono* forms of tenancy in 1961 the number had fallen to 17,000 by 1971.[19] The process was hastened by the minimum wage legislation of 1965 which sought to abolish all semi-feudal forms of labour relations. This legislation, although often ignored, encouraged planters to reduce the number of *colonos* on their estates. A study in 1971 published by PROCCARA (Peasant Training Programme for Agrarian Reform) explained the impact of the legislation on the *colonato*, particularly in those areas where it was already a form of wage labour:

'*Under the former system of wages, the owner paid 1.50* colones *and three meals. The system was attractive for the owner because the food was cheap, coming from the estate's own crops and probably from the payment he received in kind from his tenants. In monetary terms that complement to the paid salary was relatively low. With the fixing of the minimum salary at 2.25* colones, *the monetary cost increased considerably and the owner reacted by ending his workers' right to a parcel of land. For the* colono *the situation has meant a fall in his real income and instability in terms of job opportunities.*'[20]

As the legislation also included women and children, who used to work alongside the men on the estates throughout the year, many plantation owners no longer saw the employment of family labour as worthwhile. The owners now reduced their *colono* labour force to what was needed at the slackest time of year and relied on the increasing numbers of landless temporary labourers for non-harvest work and specific tasks on the estate.

25

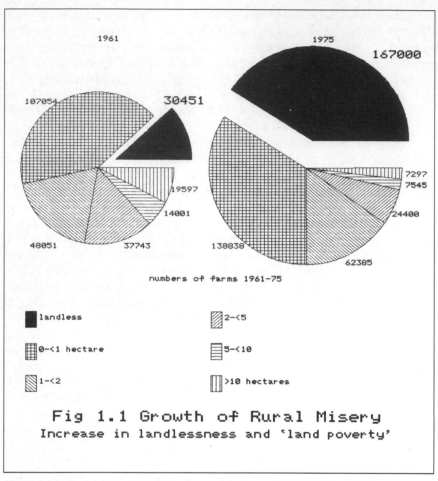

Source: United Nations Development Project (UNDP) *Realidad Campesina y Desarrollo Nacional*, 1976, No.5 in Burke 1976

## Landless . . .

'*Everywhere the landscape provides evidence of a growing landless and unsettled population. In any part of the country, the sight of dispersed huts of sticks and straw indicates the temporary residence of peasants, either seeking to plant a crop of maize on a nearby piece of land, or waiting for the opportunity to work in neighbouring plantations.*

*Along the coastal plain where subsistence farmers have lost the right of access to lands previously owned and worked under tenuous claims, groups of huts have appeared by the sides of roads, along the valleys of rivers, on little-used cart tracks and on any other stretch of land that is regarded as accessible to all. Cotton plantations there are invaded and permanently settled unless the owners remove the huts, though wide areas of land are often*

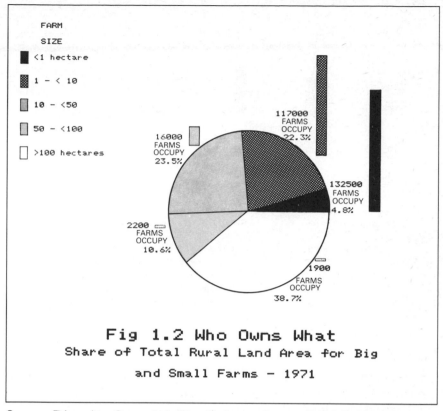

FARM
SIZE
■ <1 hectare
▨ 1 - < 10
▨ 10 - <50
▨ 50 - <100
□ >100 hectares

117000
FARMS
OCCUPY
22.3%

16000
FARMS
OCCUPY
23.5%

132500
FARMS
OCCUPY
4.8%

2200
FARMS
OCCUPY
10.6%

1900
FARMS
OCCUPY
38.7%

## Fig 1.2 Who Owns What
Share of Total Rural Land Area for Big
and Small Farms - 1971

Source: Dirección General de Estadísticas y Censos (DEGC): *Censo Agropecuario* 1950, 1961 and 1971 (El Salvador, 1950, 1961 and 1971) in Deere & Diskin 1984, table 8, page 17

*more effectively protected against illegal settlement by the constant aerial spraying of cotton by toxic chemicals throughout the growing season.*

*Across the heavily populated central highlands, though the coffee and sugar plantations are generally effective in excluding squatters, the erection of temporary huts and the cultivation of maize and sorghum on any piece of available land, however unsuitable, continues everywhere. On the most inaccessible steep and rocky slopes, a straw hut, a scratched patch of earth and the bent backs of a squatter family tending their maize are a common sight.*

*In the mid-Lempa valley, where extensive cattle* haciendas *are the characteristic unit of farming, the widespread invasion of large and often ill-defined properties by squatters, tenants, and sharecroppers continues as in previous centuries; but now, as the numbers involved become greater, so too does the challenge to the validity of property titles and the rights of land use. In many* haciendas *intrusion has been encouraged by landowners who seek to increase their income by renting out parts of their estates which because of relief, soil or drainage conditions are unsuitable even for rough grazing; in*

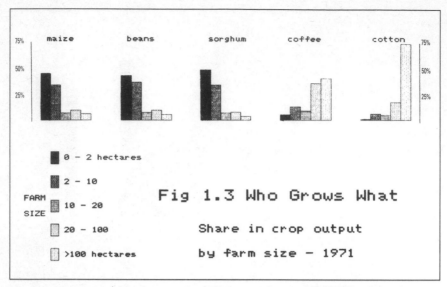

Fig 1.3 Who Grows What

Share in crop output

by farm size – 1971

FARM SIZE:
- 0 – 2 hectares
- 2 – 10
- 10 – 20
- 20 – 100
- >100 hectares

Source: Dirección General de Estadísticas y Censos (DEGC): *Anuario Estadístico* 1978 (San Salvador, 1978), table 311-05 in Deere & Diskin 1984, table 11, page 21

*others, the* hacendado *has sold his property to its illegal occupants.'*[21]

Competition for land became acute in the 1960s and created great insecurity for the rural poor. Figure 1.1 on page 26 shows the growth in landlessness and land poverty in El Salvador from 1961 to 1975. In contrast to the situation of land scarcity facing the rural poor, Figure 1.2 on page 27 shows the large amount of land in the hands of El Salvador's landowning elite. By 1971, 1.5 per cent of the farms occupied 50 per cent of the cultivated area, while 70 per cent of the farms occupied only 10 per cent of the land. The country's most profitable production – that of coffee and cotton, takes place on the large estates, particularly those over 100 hectares (see Figure 1.3, above).

These large farms under-utilize much of their land, leaving it fallow for periods or as natural pasture. A considerable portion of land in El Salvador is given over to cattle raising, about 22 per cent of total agricultural land, of which 75 per cent is natural unimproved pasture. The cattle estates tend to be the most technologically backward in El Salvador and the largest farm units, corresponding to the more traditional *latifundia* of Latin America.

The most intensive land use takes place on the small farms dedicated to basic grains. Productivity in this sector has been seriously affected by the declining size of plots due to competition for land and the poor quality of land available. Intensified pressure on the land has had serious ecological consequences which in turn affect production.

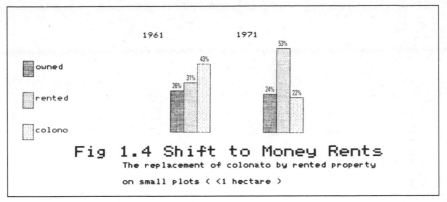

Fig 1.4 Shift to Money Rents

The replacement of colonato by rented property

on small plots ( <1 hectare )

Source: *Censo Agropecuario* 1961, 1971, in T.J. Downing 1978 table 11, page 41.

Small cultivators are forced to over-farm their land. By 1979 farms smaller than one hectare were leaving only 3.5 per cent of their agricultural land fallow, compared with 44 per cent in farms larger than 200 hectares.[22] Soil erosion has become severe under the pressure of this intensive farming on the small plots, with the government estimating in 1965 that 190,000 hectares of land needed immediate protection against erosion.[23]

In the 1960s many landowners began to rent out land they could not use for commercial crops but for money rent rather than in exchange for labour or produce. This brought major changes to the peasant economy. Figure 1.4 above shows the growth in rented land between 1961 and 1971 for smaller farms. By 1977, 50 per cent of all farms in the country were rented farms of less than two hectares.[24] Already by the 1960s, rental payments reached as much as 30 per cent of the gross value of production on these small farms and this figure must have increased in the 1970s as competition for plots to rent pushed rents up.[25] Peasants were forced to search each year for a small plot to rent and for temporary work to pay for the rent, agricultural inputs and basic necessities. The many who could not find land formed a migrant population constantly in search for jobs in either the countryside or city.

## . . . and Jobless

Figure 1.5 on page 30 shows that by 1975 the landless and land-poor had come to depend on wage labour for between 30 and 50 per cent of their income. But as demand for jobs grew, so the rural population came up against a major problem of the rural economy: the inability of the agro-export sector to absorb the labour supply except in November and December, peak harvest months for the cotton and coffee crop. In

29

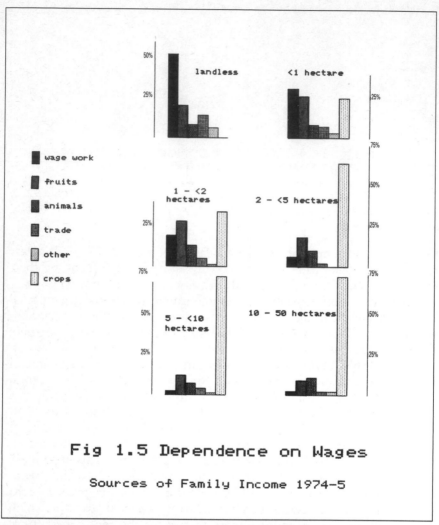

# Fig 1.5 Dependence on Wages

## Sources of Family Income 1974-5

Source: United Nations Development Programme (UNDP): *Realidad Campesina y Desarrollo Nacional.* Project ELS/73/003, Vol.7 (San Salvador, 1976) p.83, in Deere & Diskin 1984, table 2, page 6

these months five times as many people as normal are employed. Given the labour requirements of the estates and the availability of labour, each rural worker in El Salvador only has the possibility of working 140 days out of the 260 working days available in the year.[26]

El Salvador has one of the highest rates of labour under-utilization (open unemployment as well as under-employment) in the Americas.[27] The majority of family labour is superfluous on farms of four hectares or less. This is a result, not of seasonal factors, but structural factors such as lack of land.[28] But the larger farms are unable to offer sufficient employment to absorb the surplus from the small farm sector except

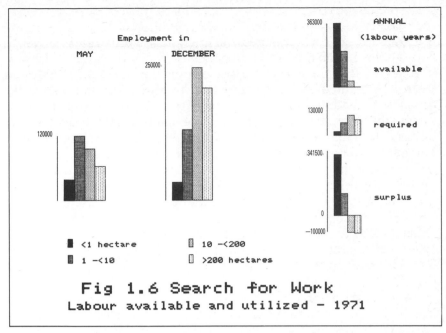

**Fig 1.6 Search for Work**
Labour available and utilized — 1971

Source: ILO-PREALC, 1977, Vol II, tables 89 and 94, and Burke 1976, table 6, page 478

during the harvest season. Figure 1.6 above illustrates this seasonality of labour demand in rural El Salvador and shows that there is a labour surplus of 466,000 people in the small farm sector, 45 per cent of which (273,000 people) are unable to find work on the larger farms over ten hectares.

The enormous reserve army of landless migrant labourers has kept wages very low in the rural sector. Real wages for permanent agricultural employment have declined in the 1965-79 period, and although the minimum harvest wage has steadily increased in real terms (particularly the coffee harvest wage), it has not compensated for the reduction of rural incomes resulting from decreasing access to land for the majority of the rural population.

Job opportunities were also affected in the 1960s by the increasing level of mechanization, particularly on the cotton and sugar estates. Permanent wage labour grew by only 0.3 per cent during the 1960s.[29] In 1965 there were 1,600 tractors, representing one tractor for every 480 hectares of cultivated land; by 1971 there were 2,500 or one tractor for every 200 hectares of cultivated land, although the process of mechanization slowed down considerably in the 1970s.[30]

Given the difficulties of surviving in the rural areas, many peasants began to migrate to urban areas in search of jobs. There is a direct relationship between migration patterns in El Salvador and land scarcity. Rural/urban migration began quite early in the 1890s

31

corresponding to the first post-independence wave of dispossession of the peasantry from the land.[31] The concentration of coffee holdings in the 1920s led to a further increase in migration to urban areas as well as to neighbouring Honduras. On the basis of W. Durham's calculations, it appeared that for every two persons on the move in El Salvador between 1932 and 1972, one migrated to Honduras and one to the urban areas within El Salvador, suggesting that the reasons for the migrations were related to the same problem of resource scarcity and poverty. In 1969 between 60 and 70 per cent of the Salvadoreans in Honduras were poor peasant farmers, the majority from the impoverished border departments of Chalatenango and Cabañas.[32]

When war broke out between Honduras and El Salvador in 1969, some 130,000 of the emigrants to Honduras were forced to return to El Salvador, creating further pressure on the land and ending northern emigration as a safety valve for this pressure. But in the 1970s other outlets for migration were found. By the end of the 1970s as many as 500,000 Salvadoreans were living in Guatemala and many thousands in the US.[33]

Most of the migrants to the urban areas of El Salvador first move from the countryside to the small towns, and from there to the bigger provincial towns and the capital. The department of San Salvador has received the largest percentage of migrants. The majority of migrants are young (between the ages of 15 and 44) and female. Most people migrate for economic reasons, and many come to the urban areas in search of employment, particularly after the promotion of manufacturing industry in the 1960s.

In 1950 70 per cent of the population were still engaged in agriculture which provided 70 per cent of GDP. Employment outside seasonal picking and processing of coffee and cotton was minimal. Only limited manufacturing had developed during the world crisis of the 1930s where there was some advantage over foreign imported goods such as heavy, bulky products like cement and bricks as well as drinks, soap, and textiles. But state technocrats could not fail to appreciate the economy's poor long-term growth prospects while it remained dependent on primary products and external markets. A few recognized the need to diversify exports and activities. At the same time, the US desire to avoid second Cubas in the region led it to promote policies of moderate reform and economic modernization. One result was a treaty of regional integration to establish the Central American Common Market in 1961 and the launching of an industrialization strategy. By 1963 new private investment, particularly foreign, was moving into manufacturing, mainly into traditional industries such as foodstuffs, drinks, textiles and footwear, but also some intermediate products like chemicals, petroleum products and minerals.

Manufacturing became the most dynamic sector of the economy in the 1960s and production doubled between 1959 and 1969. But the proportion of manufacturing output in the total product remained very low at about a fifth of value added. Many of the enterprises set up with foreign investment were simply 'assembly' plants, using local labour to package imported components for the regional market or re-export, using imported technology and having little multiplier effect in the rest of the economy.

But the most obvious failure of the process of industrialization was that it did not generate a significant expansion in employment opportunities. T.J. Downing used the figures available for the regions where industry was concentrated and found that employment in manufacturing grew by only an average five per cent a year compared with a growth of manufacturing value added (in real terms) of ten per cent over the same period. By 1972 manufacturing employment in these regions accounted for only three per cent of the total permanently employed labour force in the country, compared with 53 per cent employed in agriculture. Official figures put the unemployment rate at this time at 20 per cent of the rural population and 16 per cent of the urban population (a figure which excludes the vast numbers of underemployed). It is evident that employment generated by industrialization did not keep pace with the growth in the urban population.[34] At its peak in 1977, manufacturing only employed 59,000 workers.[35] Over half of the men who migrate to San Salvador end up as construction workers, and the majority of women as domestic servants.[36] Many of the migrants find no fixed employment but are forced into the informal sector (prostitution or street vending), which by the early 1970s accounted for 40 per cent of the occupied non-agricultural labour force.[37]

It is not surprising that migration to San Salvador began to decline in the 1960s as the migrants encountered as much poverty in the urban as in the rural areas. A 1974 study of urban households found that a third of San Salvador households earned poverty-level incomes while 20 per cent earned less than the income necessary to meet the minimum subsistence food budget.[38]

## The State and the Rural Sector

If the 1960s saw the deepening of a structural crisis for the poor majority of El Salvador, the 1970s were to reveal the incapacity of the system to introduce the necessary reforms to prevent a major social upheaval. The changes already outlined drew the poor peasant further into the money economy. Money rent now replaced rent in labour and kind and this rose while demand for land increased. Wage labour, which had previously been a seasonal complement to subsistence farming for the majority of peasants, now became an essential means of survival.

The government began to show some concern with the situation in the rural sector as increasing landlessness and unemployment threatened to create social unrest. But the incapacity of the modern sector to generate more employment made this problem intractable within existing economic structures and policy priorities. A more immediate concern was the need to increase food production for the country's growing population and reduce food imports, a problem which affected the economy as a whole.

By the end of the 1960s the government began to pay some attention to increasing basic grain production. The changes in land tenure during the previous decade had increased the number of small farmers and hence food producers, but they worked highly fragmented plots of land on poor soils. There was some government encouragement to larger farms to grow basic grains, most successfully during the mid-1960s, when a temporary decline in cotton productivity obliged some larger landowners to shift production. On these large estates in the low-lying areas, where mechanization was already fairly advanced in cotton production, the technology could be applied to basic grains.

During the 1960s small farms were encouraged to apply fertilizer to their plots. In 1965 the United States launched a project with the Salvadorean government to promote the use of improved seed, fertilizer and insecticide. Maize yields can be increased by a factor of three by such inputs, and from 1967-1970 and 1971-1973 they increased by 17 and 13 per cent respectively.[39] The war with Honduras had ended maize and bean imports from that country and forced the government to increase investment in domestic agriculture, which stimulated production. It has been estimated that 80 per cent of the increase in maize production in the 1960s was due to increased productivity compared to 20 per cent due to the increase in land area planted.[40]

The country became, just for a while, self-sufficient in maize production. But rising productivity did not check the falling living standards of the rural poor. Most basic grain production is carried out on rocky ground frequently on awkward slopes and hillsides where it is difficult to use machinery. The overwhelming majority of small farmers continued to use traditional techniques of cultivation, without adequate preparation of the land, or input of fertilizer, insecticides, herbicides and pesticides.

The small farmers also remained largely dependent on intermediaries for the marketing of their crops and for the supply of agricultural inputs. They often had to sell their harvest in advance to the intermediary in order to pay for these inputs and for clothes and rent. Lack of direct access to markets meant the small producer had no control over pricing. Speculation by intermediaries caused the prices of all basic grains to fluctuate widely on the internal market in the 1960s and 1970s. In 1973, the Ministry of Agriculture Department of Agroeconomic Studies revealed that in 1970-71 the basic grain crop of 12,367,000 *quintales* was worth 124 million *colones* on the market, of which only 62 million went to the farmer.[41] The institution established to regulate prices in the 1960s, the IRA (Institute for the Regulation of Supplies), proved ineffective. It lacked storage capacity and credit, and although these were improved somewhat in the 1970s, it was commercial producers, not small peasant farmers, who benefited.

From the late 1960s on, the Salvadorean state attempted to stimulate diversification of crops, modernization of production methods and infrastructure more systematically. The impetus came from a major study in 1968 by USAID, (the *Nathan Report*), and a subsequent Ministry of Agriculture/AID review in 1971. In 1972 the government embarked on a recognizable modernization plan compared with the uncoordinated efforts of the previous decade. It included a considerable increase in state investment in infrastructure (roads, water supply, energy, irrigation and ports), and in large-scale basic industries, such as cement.

In agriculture the state promoted technical research, improved marketing and storage facilities, credit policies, irrigation and drainage schemes, crop diversification and the establishment of cooperatives (see Chapter 3). But the main impetus for the policies was US-inspired strategies for modernizing agriculture, the so-called 'green revolution'. Part of the strategy was to promote non-traditional exports, amongst them meat, which as a result of high meat prices in the US became an exportable product. This was made possible by the development of a modern ranching sector, with improved breeds of cattle, veterinary control and pasture. The state gave considerable support to investment in silos and sheds for beef and milk cattle. However, as a result, internal prices for meat rose dramatically, eventually forcing the government to control exports.

Government support to these activities benefited the large and medium-sized landowners, who alone could afford the necessary investment, and it was they who reaped the profits. State as well as private credit shows a marked imbalance in favour of the larger landowners (see Figure 1.7, page 36). Many coffee producers also own commercial banks. In contrast, the majority of small farmers depend for credit on intermediaries who often charge higher interest rates than the banks.

An important part of government plans for agricultural developments in these years was a series of large scale irrigation projects. An estimated 512,000 hectares of land in El Salvador is irrigable, though by 1971 only 20,000 hectares had actually been irrigated. An OAS study in 1974 stated that irrigation projects could double the area available for cultivation by bringing land into use in the six-month dry season. Another 120,000 hectares of land, subject to flooding or poor

35

drainage in the wet season, could be brought into production through drainage schemes. The study proposed the improvement of some 116,700 hectares of land over the period 1970-1990.[42] By 1980 there were some 110,000 hectares of irrigated land in El Salvador.

The Zapolitán scheme was begun in 1970 and the Aticoyo scheme on the Upper Lempa river in 1973. Another irrigation and credit scheme was launched in 1976 as part of a short-lived project for land distribution. The government's financial burdens hampered the irrigation projects considerably. But the real problem was the system of land tenure and distribution which restricted the benefits of such projects to large-scale commercial farmers. The government saw the projects' main objectives as increasing and modernizing production and reducing imports, rather than dealing with the urgent problems of the rural poor.

# The Failure to Reform

*'The cause of all our ills is the oligarchy — that handful of families who care nothing for the hunger of the people, but need that hunger in order to have cheap, abundant labour to raise and export their crops'.*
(Archbishop Romero, 1979, quoted in M.M. Rodríguez, *Voices from El Salvador*)

The 1976 project of land distribution is a good example of the limits to

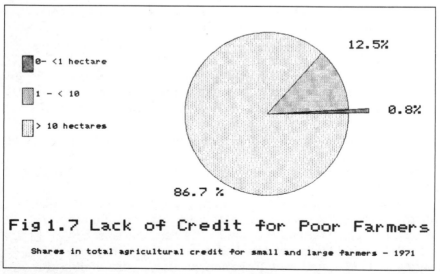

**Fig 1.7 Lack of Credit for Poor Farmers**

Shares in total agricultural credit for small and large farmers – 1971

Source: ILO-PREALC, 1977, Vol I, table 143, in Deere & Diskin 1984, table 13, p.23

(*Justicia y Paz*, 15 September 1973, No. 22)

'*El Salvador is the largest country on earth because they've been carrying out the agrarian reform for ten years and it's still not finished*'

changes which might benefit the poor majority of El Salvador within existing structures of land ownership and power. By way of background, a brief look at the history of government land distribution efforts is necessary.

The 1932 peasant uprising spread deep fears amongst El Salvador's wealthy landowners (see Chapter 3). While peasant unrest had to be firmly repressed to prevent a repeat of the events of 1932 and any talk of a radical land reform quickly suppressed, the need to do something about the appalling level of rural poverty was also recognized. In July 1932 a special fund, the *Fondo de Mejoramiento Social*, was created which would be used partly for housing projects and partly for land redistribution. In November, a government agency responsible for administering the fund was created, the *Junta Nacional de la Defensa Social*. The government bought some run-down *haciendas* at high rates of compensation and then parcelled the land out. The land was given to peasants who had proved their good behaviour and correct credentials through affiliation to the official 'pro-fatherland' party which unconditionally supported the government.[43] The handover of lands never reached, in any one year, even 0.2 per cent of peasant families. The failure of the *Junta* led in January 1943 to the creation of a new body, the *Instituto de Mejoramiento Social*, which was also charged with land distribution and the provision of cheap housing and financial and technical assistance.

The government already owned some land in 1932 and between that year and 1950, it bought a total of 26 *haciendas* consisting of 35,124 hectares (two per cent of the country's land area), and distributed 29,820 of these to peasant farmers.[44] Most of the peasants who received land already worked it as *colonos* or squatters. They were given a maximum of six hectares and had to pay rent for ten years after which they would be given a legal title but not allowed to sell, mortgage or rent the land for 25 years. The peasants themselves defrayed the cost of the programme's extension through the fund created by their rent

'*You've no more appointments now, Minister . . . there's only this peasant left who is waiting for the implementation of the agrarian reform.*'
'*Good, let him come in now.*'
'*How ignorant these people are, they've no patience! The agrarian reform requires a lot of consideration.*'

payments.

The promised technical and credit assistance turned out to be minimal and many of the peasants ended up having to sell their plots to larger landowners. Ironically, the existence of a legal title enabled peasants to sell or mortgage their land when times got tough, which made it easier for landowners to evict them or acquire their properties through legal means; others lost them through failure to pay rent or abandoned them after exhausting the soil.

It was apparent by 1950 that the scheme had failed. That year a new land reform agency was created, the ICR (Regional Colonization Institute). The new body was charged with drawing up and implementing a programme of distribution and settlement, again on government lands, but it was also expected to 'study the needs of the peasant farmer, improve his techniques, and encourage the individual cultivator to grow cash crops'. In addition, the ICR was charged with organizing reafforestation schemes, irrigation and drainage works, and community and recreation projects.[45]

The body's low budget and the rising price of land meant that the programmes had mostly to be implemented on the few thousand acres of land still in government hands. The ICR made the decision to suspend new redistribution programmes and purchases of land (only one *hacienda* was bought between 1951 and 1967), and concentrate on programmes within existing government properties. Its work was thus mostly restricted to small-scale experiments. By 1973 it had 45 *haciendas* in three areas of the country, with a total land area of 64,356 hectares on which 8,202 families were settled.

Most of the ICR projects were paternalistic; the community organization aspect of the work was carried out by 'society ladies engaged in charitable works'.[46] USAID carried out some training and medical assistance programmes and distributed food aid. Different experiments in cooperatives, land use and tenancy arrangements, technical assistance, soil conservation and marketing studies were carried out on the few thousand acres at the ICR's disposal.

The scheme's political rationale was to prevent conflict in the rural areas, assist in improving the technical efficiency of agriculture and convert some of the beneficiaries into peasant smallholders with loyalties to the government. When proposals for radical agrarian reform were put forward, the government was quick to suppress them. In 1967 the Central Electoral Council declared the PAR (Party of Renovative Action) illegal mainly because part of its programme referred to 'the problem of the land and its solution: Agrarian Reform', which contained some modest suggestions for land expropriation.

The ICR helped with the repatriation of peasants forced to leave Honduras after the 1969 war, but by that time it was apparent that more serious efforts were needed to deal with the increasing crisis in the countryside. Pressure was mounting for action, and in 1970 the Legislative Assembly organized the first and only National Congress on Agrarian Reform. The wealthy landowners and industrialists withdrew from the Congress and the only sectors who remained were unions, representatives of the church and the universities and some political parties.

Prospects for any government action were thwarted in 1973-1974 when ministerial changes removed the proponents of reform. Then in

1975, the Salvadorean Institute of Agrarian Transformation (ISTA) was set up and the following year an 'agrarian transformation' bill was presented to the legislature. The term 'agrarian reform' was carefully avoided in favour of 'agrarian transformation', and the rate of implementation of land distribution projects was damped-down by legal prohibition on the initiation of any new project before the previous one was almost completed. ISTA's first and only project, the 1976 proposal to transfer about 59,000 hectares of land belonging to 250 landowners in the cotton-growing areas of Usulután and San Miguel to 12,000 peasant families, was stillborn. Land affected by the law was to be transferred to the peasants who worked the land as *colonos* or wage labourers or to cooperatives and peasant associations (the law still did not sanction peasant unions). But these would still remain dependent on ISTA which would begin the training, promotion and organization of the peasants. Article 24 stated that credit and inputs would be given preferentially to 'peasant associations organized by the state'.[47] The project represented no threat to the interests of the major landowners; it deliberately excluded all coffee lands and would only have affected a small part of the lands of the agro-exporting oligarchy in the area chosen. Nevertheless, they organized an ad hoc association to fight it, the Eastern Region Farmers' Front (FARO), and later the 30 business organizations represented in the National Association of Private Enterprise (ANEP) joined the campaign. The project was viewed as a dangerous precedent. The pressures from the business community and right-wing army officers succeeded in rendering the project ineffective and allowed these sectors to consolidate their political influence in the country. The events surrounding the 'land transformation' were a clear indication of the impossibility of reform within existing social and political structures. Between 1975 and 1980, ISTA purchased and redistributed only 14,000 hectares of land. The Institute found itself in an ambiguous position, charged with solving the agrarian problem but unable to touch the structures which helped create it. Internal power struggles and competition with other bodies working in the same field further weakened its effectiveness.

The kinds of considerations which might have led the landowning elite to consider reform from the point of view of economic self-interest did not exist: 'The usual arguments for a capitalist land reform to stimulate modernization of the economy in general did not apply to El Salvador, since the large landowners were in the main modernized and actively involved in the industrial, financial and service sectors.'[48] Existing forms of land tenure were in fact a positive incentive to the landowning elite not to support reform. They ensured a pool of cheap labour which fed itself on the poorest soils which the landowners could not use for export crops. Thus wages did not even have to take account of the reproduction of the labour force. This structure of domestic salaries may have enabled the coffee oligarchy not only to survive when world prices were adverse, but to increase production and make huge profits as well.[49]

The coffee oligarchy remained the dominant power in the land. Coffee retained its predominant position within the economy with very high levels of output even in world terms. Diversification of production did not lead to a fragmentation of economic or political power in El Salvador. By 1969 three groups had begun to emerge within the oligarchy: first, the planters, who continued to base their wealth primarily on commercial agriculture, diversifying their interests into cotton and sugar cane in the 1950s and 1960s and maintaining strong interests in the banking sector and some 'safe' ventures such as commerce, communications, transport and housing; secondly, a mixed group which kept interests in the land (in the case of the De Solas as exporters rather than producers), but which in the 1960s began to invest in manufacturing industry, frequently in joint ventures with US capital; thirdly, the merchants who were mostly involved in import substitution manufacturing and retailing.[50] Of the top 30 families none were involved only in coffee production; the Regalados and De Solas, for instance, had interests in processing, exporting, finance, manufacture and sugar and cotton production.[51]

Industrialization did not therefore lead to the emergence of an entrepreneurial class capable of challenging the landed oligarchy and pressing for an expansion of the internal market through a redistribution of wealth. Foreign capital dominated the industrial sector with its advanced technology and the scale of its organization and operations. Real economic power in the country remained with the landed oligarchy enabling them to keep control of state policy, mostly through their allies in the military.

However, the system contained a very real contradiction: as it developed it failed to create the means of reforming itself from within when pressures for change became so great as to threaten its very survival. By the 1970s the mass of peasant households were unable to meet their needs from the land and, given the size of the rural labour surplus, many could not make up the difference through wage labour. The system as it was could no longer guarantee survival in any meaningful sense.

In this situation the potential threat to the ruling elite was considerable, given the existence of catalysts capable of mobilizing the peasantry and suggesting alternative survival strategies. But the elite continued to rule through a military apparatus schooled in US anti-communist ideology, confident that the country's geo-political position would ensure US assistance if there was any real threat to the status quo. At moments when the state did attempt some measure of autonomy with minimal changes intended to prolong the life of the system a little longer, it was soon brought back into line. It was, in short, a system incapable of reform.

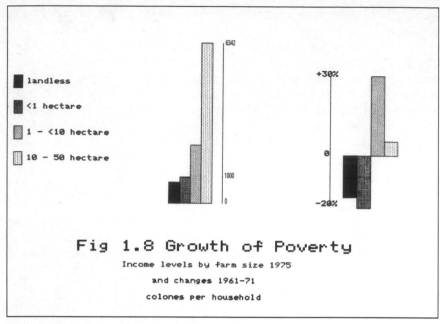

## Fig 1.8 Growth of Poverty

Income levels by farm size 1975

and changes 1961-71

colones per household

Legend:
- landless
- <1 hectare
- 1 - <10 hectare
- 10 - 50 hectare

6342

1000

0

+30%

0

-20%

Source: United Nations Development Programme (UNDP), 1976, Vol.7, page 75, in Deere & Diskin 1984, table 3, page 7

## The Collapse of the Peasant Economy

Colonial exploitation followed by export-led growth and capitalist modernization combined over the centuries to shift the delicate balance which kept the peasant sector precariously alive. In most Third World countries, those in the extended family with a source of income would support the dispossessed of society. But in El Salvador this traditional guarantee of survival has become less and less viable. Sixty per cent of the population live in rural areas, the majority affected by the trends already outlined, while conditions in the urban areas are little better. The effects of this situation are increasing rural poverty and high levels of malnutrition, infant mortality and ill health.

Figure 1.8 above shows that the most disadvantaged sector is the landless and those with less than one hectare of land, comprising some 75 per cent of rural families. Their incomes declined between 1961 and 1975 until they fell below the minimum level of subsistence. An agricultural labourer employed full time at the minimum agricultural wage would earn 1,332 *colones*,[52] sufficient only to meet the minimum food consumption for a family of six. To supply all the family needs, 1,760 *colones* was the minimum required and 90 per cent of rural households received less than this.[53] While the rural poor faced increasing immiseration, the actual income distribution was becoming

Cornell Capa

more unequal. In 1975 4.5 per cent of rural households captured 39 per cent of total agricultural income while the landless proletariat (41 per cent of rural households) obtained only 18 per cent.[54]

C. Deere and M. Diskin draw attention to the political implications of the impoverishment of the rural population of El Salvador and these are examined in the following chapters of this book:

'*Far from the East-West conflict it is sometimes represented to be, the present war seems more accurately portrayed as the open explosion of the class antagonism between agricultural workers and the landowners that has reigned in El Salvador for most of this century. The growth of the agro-export economy has only made these class antagonisms more acute as the majority of the rural population joined the ranks of the landless and suffered increased impoverishment. While growing poverty does not necessarily lead to revolution, nor revolution only result from impoverishment, in El Salvador both are clearly interrelated. What the study of this case points out is that the process of distorted agro-export development which takes place at the expense of the majority of the rural population is ultimately also destructive to the social fabric.*'[55]

# 2
# THE PEASANT CONDITION

## Chalatenango: Forgotten Land

A Salvadorean newspaper once referred to the northern third of El Salvador, of which the department of Chalatenango is a substantial slice, as the *tierra olvidada* ('forgotten land') of the present century. This area was less directly affected by the agricultural transformation which took place in central and southern El Salvador in the nineteenth and twentieth centuries, as it was unsuitable for large-scale coffee production. The social upheaval and population movements which accompanied it did, however, increase the pressure on the region's poor land. Characterized by primitive agriculture, exhausted and eroded soils and little investment, the region is the most backward and neglected of El Salvador. It is here, particularly in Chalatenango and Morazán, that the FMLN established its strongest base areas in the 1980s.

The northern highlands of El Salvador have never been a very hospitable area for human settlement. They were the least densely populated areas in pre-Spanish times, and the Indian villages there declined further in the early colonial period as populations were absorbed into the Spanish *haciendas* in the central highlands.

The area known as Chalatenango began to attract population again towards the end of the eighteenth century as Indian communities collapsed and *ladino* migrants (Indians who left their villages and adopted Spanish language and customs) embarked on the search for land to farm. A significant number made their way north where they often settled on land belonging to private estates. By invoking the right of possession, many were able to claim the land they settled and to establish villages of their own. The department of Chalatenango was created in 1855.

The *ladinos* were mostly small-scale farmers involved in indigo production and some cattle ranching. Indigo production continued in Chalatenango for some time after it had declined everywhere else, and by 1860 it was the most important indigo-growing district in the country. The department began to attract population again at this time; many peasants migrated north as coffee took over their lands in the

45

central highlands. The population of Chalatenango increased between 1770 and 1892 by 50 per cent compared with a national increase of 35 per cent.[1] By 1892, the total population of the area was 54,000.[2]

Small-scale farming persisted into the twentieth century in the northern departments following this early settlement pattern, existing alongside large estates mostly dedicated to cattle ranching. Large landowners had extended their holdings in the region in the 1880s by taking over common lands as happened elsewhere in the country. Prior to that, *ejido* and communal forms of ownership had predominated over private ownership in the departments of Chalatenango, Cabañas and Morazán.

But the value of indigo production declined rapidly in the last decades of the nineteenth century as coffee took over its role as the leading export. In 1864 nationwide indigo exports were worth US$1,130,000 and coffee exports, US$80,000. By 1891 indigo had declined to US$890,000 while coffee sales amounted to US$4,800,000.[3] Indigo had no economic future as the centre of the country's economic life had shifted to the coffee producing areas of the central highlands. Chalatenango sank into impoverishment. Subsistence farming of basic grains, which used primitive technology, and extensive cattle farming became the department's main source of livelihood.

Today the department has a large, unskilled labour force, providing sesonal labour for the coffee, cotton and sugar estates in the centre and south of the country. Increasingly, as the twentieth century progressed, the department has also been a source of permanent migration to the urban areas of El Salvador and to Honduras. Central government has virtually ignored the area, where there are relatively few large landowners and almost no export agriculture. Infrastructure is poor, there are no important local markets, social service provision is very limited and extreme poverty and deprivation of all kinds characterize the lives of the majority of its inhabitants.

## Chalatenango: Profile of the Department

The department of Chalatenango covers an area of 1,857 square kilometres. It borders Honduras to the north and east, the departments of Cabañas, Cuscatlán, San Salvador and La Libertad to the south and Santa Ana to the west. The north of the department is crossed by a rugged mountain chain, the Alotepeque-Metapán range, with elevations between 200 and 2,700 metres. The highest mountain in El Salvador, the Pital (2,730 metres), lies in this range.

The department is divided administratively into three districts, Chalatenango (also the department capital), Tejutla and Dulce Nombre

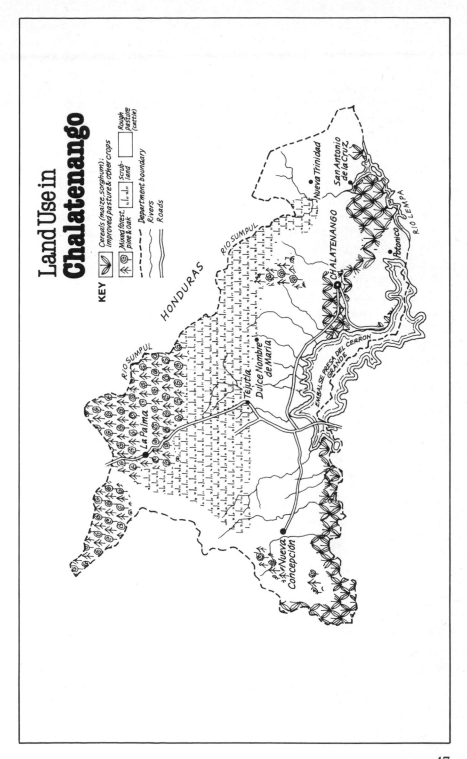

Land Use in
## Chalatenango

KEY

- Cereals (maize, sorghum):
  improved pasture & other crops
- Rough pasture (cattle)
- Mixed forest, pine & oak
- Scrub-land
- Department boundary
- Rivers
- Roads

HONDURAS

RIO SUMPUL

RIO SUMPUL

RIO SUMPUL

La Palma

Tejutla

Dulce Nombre de María

Nueva Concepción

CHALATENANGO

EMBALSE PRESA DEL CERRON GRANDE

Nueva Trinidad

San Antonio de la Cruz

Potonico

RIO LEMPA

de María, and 33 municipalities. A *municipio* in El Salvador is an area which includes an urban centre plus a series of surrounding rural hamlets, known as *cantones* or *caseríos* if they are smaller clusters of houses than a *cantón*. The urban centre can be known as a *ciudad, villa* or *pueblo* according to size, and is more or less equivalent to a village or small town. The people whose stories appear in the text come mostly from the district of Chalatenango and the eastern part of the department.

Chalatenango has some of the poorest soils in the country. The agricultural and ranching ministry, reviewing potential land use in the area, concluded that only 34 per cent of the land is suitable for agriculture, 50 per cent has minimal productive potential except for afforestation, while 13 per cent is totally unsuited for cultivation of any kind.[4] Despite this, the 1971 agricultural census shows that 66 per cent is in fact under cultivation in the department, indicating that even the very worst land is exploited. Chalatenango evidently has no agricultural frontier to sustain a growing population.

The area can be broadly divided into three zones: north, central and south (see map, page 47). The reader will find it useful in subsequent chapters to know broadly which municipalities are covered by these zones. The northern area covers the municipalities of Arcatao, Citalá, Dulce Nombre de María, El Carrizal, La Laguna, Las Vueltas, Nueva Trinidad, San Fernando and San Ignacio. It includes the *cordillera fronteriza*, the mountainous area bordering with Honduras, and an area of very marginal agricultural use immediately to the south and east of the mountain range, geared primarily to subsistence farming and extensive cattle ranching.

The mountainous area is the most underpopulated part of the country and is colder and wetter than the rest of the department. It is a vivid example of how land pressures have contributed to environmental destruction in this tiny country. It was once an area covered with forest, but as population began to increase after 1800, vast tracts of it were cleared for 'shifting agriculture', in which one area was cleared and used for a short time before being abandoned for new, still fertile areas. As population and land pressure intensified in the twentieth century, particularly after 1940, subsistence farmers were forced upland onto marginal highland slopes, and shifting agriculture gave way to permanent agriculture. In permanent or semi-permanent agriculture, land is left uncultivated for less than three years and this prevents the growth of secondary forest. The result has been the destruction of most of the deciduous forest and many of the forest animals, while the unprotected soils have suffered serious erosion in the heavy rain. The topsoil is thin and stony and supports only subsistence agriculture using primitive technology. Its only economic potential lies in a reafforestation programme and the commercial exploitation of the wood.

The southern zone includes the municipalities of Nombre de Jesús, Potonico, San Antonio de la Cruz, San Francisco Lempa, San José Canacasque and San Luis del Carmen. Like the northern area it is poor agricultural land and the main activities are, once again, subsistence farming and extensive cattle ranching.

Unlike the northern and southern zones, the central zone, which includes the valleys of the river Lempa and its tributaries, has economic potential, though considerable capital investment would be needed to unleash it. It covers the municipalities of Agua Caliente, Concepción Quezaltepeque, Chalatenango, El Paraíso, La Reina, Nueva Concepción, San Francisco Morazán, Santa Rita and Tejutla. This area includes some of the large cattle ranches and the major sugar growing areas of the department as well as subsistence agriculture. Much of it is within what is called the *Alta Lempa* zone, an area of considerable productive potential given sufficient investment.[5] Efforts begun in the 1960s were extended during the 1970s to irrigate land and improve the pasture for cattle ranching and dairy farming particularly in the area around Nueva Concepción.

Transportation, communications and infrastructure of all kinds is very poor throughout the department and an obstacle to tapping the little economic potential there is. There is no road system through much of the area, making it inaccessible to motor vehicles. Many of the roads connecting hamlets are dirt tracks and footpaths, often very difficult to use in the rainy season and making some areas, particularly in the north, almost inaccessible at that time of year. The main highway north from San Salvador to the Honduran border runs through the department, and a fork of it runs to the department capital, Chalatenango. But in 1974 there were only 1,040 kilometres of roads in the department,[6] of which 760 were dirt track. In 1970 there were only 177 telephones in the department compared to 2,250 in Santa Ana.[7]

## Population and Migration

The population of the department at the last census (1971) was 172,075, with a population density of 81 inhabitants per square kilometer, the lowest in the country. The majority of the population lives in the rural areas, 73 per cent according to the 1971 census.

The department has lost much of its population through migration – to San Salvador or to neighbouring Honduras – as impoverished soils and lack of land have forced its inhabitants to seek survival elsewhere. From 1950 to 1971 Chalatenango's average annual population growth was 2.3 per cent, the lowest of any department. The table on page 50 shows that in 1961 Chalatenango had the highest rate of internal migration within El Salvador.

## Internal Migration by Departments, 1961

| | | | |
|---|---|---|---|
| Ahuachapán | − 3.7 | La Paz | − 6.3 |
| Santa Ana | − 4.1 | Cabañas | − 15.1 |
| Sonsonate | + 5.9 | San Vicente | − 15.6 |
| **Chalatenango** | − 16.1 | Usulután | − 4.4 |
| La Libertad | + 12.3 | San Miguel | − 4.4 |
| San Salvador | + 25.2 | Morazán | − 8.9 |
| Cuscatlán | − 11.0 | La Unión | + 2.4 |

Source: Monteforte Toledo, 1972[8]

## Social Services

The lack of social service provision in the department, such as health, education, and sanitation, reinforces the image of neglect which it has always held, as Quique, a peasant of Chalatenango, describes:

**When I was little — in the thirties and forties — there were no schools in the *cantones*, only in the *pueblos*; later on they set some up in the *cantones* too, but not in all. In some places the teacher didn't teach though; they were very corrupt, the students were his servants, they had to fetch his cigarettes, buy things for him, so people lost interest in school. At that time the people treated themselves with herbal medicine (my mother was one of those who prepared it). They cured themselves with this — there were no doctors. In Chalate, in the town, yes, but not in the countryside — only midwives.**

Medical facilities in Chalatenango are worse than in any other department. In 1971 only 57 per cent of the population had access to facilities compared to 93 per cent in the coffee growing department of Santa Ana. Chalatenango receives an allocation of a mere two per cent of the Ministry of Health budget compared to twelve per cent for Santa Ana. Figure 2.1 on page 51 compares Chalatenango, Santa Ana and El Salvador as a whole for a range of services.

Chalatenango has one hospital, and that has only existed since 1973. The other health posts and centres are all situated in the municipalities, so that those in the outlying rural areas often have to walk for several hours to visit them. But the figures reveal nothing of the quality of medical care which is notoriously bad in El Salvador:

*'[At a rural hospital] a Salvadorean doctor . . . was paid US$200 a month by the Salvadorean government to care for one hundred thousand* campesinos. *She had no lab, no X-ray, no whole blood, plasma or*

50

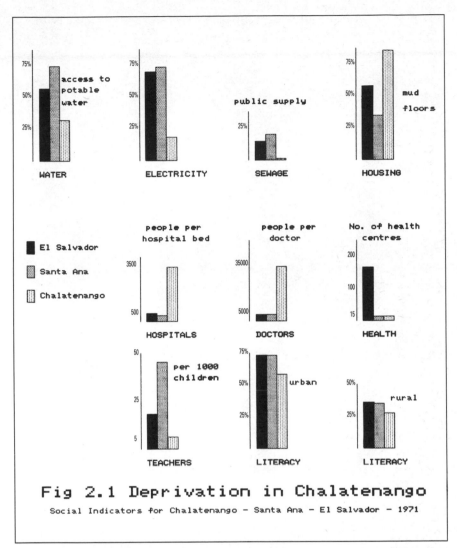

Fig 2.1 Deprivation in Chalatenango

Social Indicators for Chalatenango - Santa Ana - El Salvador - 1971

Sources: World Bank 1979, Valverde 1980, May and McLellen 1972, OAS, 1974. (NB. Literacy figures, 1961 census)

*antibiotics, no anaesthesia or medicines, no autoclave for sterilizing surgical equipment. Her forceps were rusted, the walls of her operating room were studded with flies; beside her hospital a coffee-processing plant's refuse heap incubated maggots, and she paid a campesina to swish the flies away with a newspaper while she delivered the newborn. She was forced to do caesarian sections at times without much local anaesthetic. Without supplies, she worked with only her hands and a cheap opthalmoscope. In her clinic I held children in my arms who died hours later for want of a manual suction device to remove fluid from their lungs."*[9]

51

*Fetching water*

Health is linked to housing conditions, particularly sanitation. In 1961, only 16 per cent of the houses in Chalatenango had electricity and only a third had running water. These are global figures for the department. We can take the example of a typical municipality of Chalatenango, one of the few which has attracted the attention of researchers.

In San Miguel de Mercedes, and the five villages which surround it, there were 3,000 people in 1978, of which 40 per cent lived in the urban area. There were then 428 houses in the area, most of which had rooves of straw, adobe walls and an earthen floor, and three or less rooms. Seventy-six per cent of the houses had on average three persons or more to a room. Half the houses had water from a pipe, usually outside the house but four-fifths of these houses were situated in the urban centre, or municipality. In the outlying areas the most common source of water supply was the river and the well. In 1971, the one-fifth of houses which had electricity were all in the urban area. Ninety per cent of houses used the open fields for sanitation.[10]

Chalatenango also fares poorly with respect to education. In 1961 only 27 per cent of its rural population was literate compared with 56 per cent of urban dwellers (see Figure 2.1). Although schooling is free, uniforms and books are not, and a peasant family would rarely send its children to school for more than two or three years. Eighty per cent of children in El Salvador who enrol in primary school fail to complete the first six grades, which is generally considered to be the minimum schooling necessary to provide the technical and intellectual skills for socio-economic improvement.

In San Miguel de Mercedes absenteeism from school was notorious amongst children from the villages. This can be explained partly by the distance of the village from the town where the school was situated. But it is also related to the considerable differences between the *cantones* and the *pueblo*, and in particular the difference in expectations. The villages are fairly isolated given the poor roads and communications with the outside world. They do not share with the inhabitants of the town the vision that education is an important means of improving the economic opportunities of their children. They prefer their children to help on the land rather than go to school. No-one from the *cantones* went to Chalatenango, the department capital and the only centre for study beyond the primary level of the town school, whereas quite a number went from the town, sometimes even going to San Salvador to study.

## Land and Work in Chalatenango

Chalatenango is little affected by the economic activity of the oligarchy. The economy is dominated by the medium-sized farms between ten and 200 hectares and a few large-scale estates devoted mostly to cattle ranching, the most important economic activity in the department. Despite the absence of the oligarchy (only 0.3 per cent of the country's coffee, 0.6 per cent of cotton and 4.8 per cent of sugar cane is grown in the department), land remains highly unequally distributed.

Figure 2.2 on page 56 shows the distribution of land in Chalatenango. A mere ten per cent of the farms occupy 75 per cent of the land area, while the remaining 90 per cent of farms (those less than ten hectares in size), are squeezed onto 25 per cent of the land.

The overwhelming majority of farmers in the area are *minifundistas* who own or rent a small plot for subsistence agriculture. The *minifundista* of Chalatenango is a poor peasant farmer with access to less than ten hectares of land. At the time of the 1971 census there were 18,989 farms in this category covering a quarter of the cultivated land in the department. Some 8,325 of these were farms of less than one

## The Psychology of Poverty

From the first days of my participation in village life, it was clear that the main quality of life in San Luis for the peasant class was suffering, or as people themselves called it: *tristeza*. Both the villagers and the officials of the Administration expressed their amazement about the fact that I cared to share this kind of life for some time.

The differences between those who had practically enough land to support their family (very modestly) and those who had hardly any or no land at all, disappeared in the face of this general suffering from insecurity. The little security of those better-off was always being threatened by the dangers of sickness and plagues (a year before I came, a chicken plague had killed off all the chickens), indebtedness, government interference, violence, and the growing family which meant the need to split up the small plot of land among the several sons.

It was well known among the villagers that most of the higher officials of the Administration were large landholders themselves or related to them through family ties. The government officials who came to the villages for agricultural extension or community development activities were always armed with a pistol, a factor which did not contribute to winning the people's confidence, and which only emphasized the rigidity and potential instability of the rural power structure. Since the peasants could not openly disagree with or protest against the government officials, they feigned agreement with what was proposed, but expressed their opposition by not showing up to do the voluntary work. An additional factor in this passive refusal to collaborate was found to be the simple fact of undernourishment from which many peasants suffered between the coffee harvest seasons. This resulted in a half-conscious economizing of physical energy, and feelings of insecurity and apathy. (As an experiment, I tried to live for several weeks on the same diet as my neighbours and soon found myself suffering from some of the same phenomena, recalling former experiences of undernourishment during World War II in the Netherlands.)

Some of the psychological factors related to undernourishment, which clearly formed a barrier to cooperation, were the feelings of powerlessness and inferiority that accompanied it. The obsession of a screaming stomach, completely occupied by getting fed, may explain why the villagers said that they live just like animals.

I found that sometimes the dehumanizing effects of malnutrition were even stressed by some of the programs of the Administration. The home economics demonstrators came to the village to tell the people how to improve their diet in order to be healthier, however, without giving them the means to do so. No need to say that such programs often worked against fostering goodwill for the Administration. It was another proof how middle-class people, from an urban environment, trained in rather sophisticated forms of social work, are often out of touch with village life.

It was not only undernourishment that made people feel inferior and incapable of real self-help. The detrimental effect of unemployment on peoples' self-esteem should not be underestimated. The fact that they spent most of the year just idly waiting, in the hope that somehow somebody would give them work, had a considerable impact on their personalities. This was further aggravated by the fact that they had to take whatever came up and that they had no rights at all, since there were so many people available who could take a job if they would not do so. These factors created strong feelings of hostility, towards better-off classes and towards society as a whole. This form of aggression that was turned inward was one of the reasons for much of the drunkenness for which the area was ill-famed. The most distressing fact was that people themselves knew so well the impact of the three above-mentioned factors, and other problems on their lives.

From the intimate reactions of people, it became obvious that under a surface of apathy, indifference and distrust, there was a strong resentment, if not hatred, directed towards the powerful, which created a climate of slumbering explosiveness. Government officials warned often about the dangers of living among the peasants.[11]

**There's a lot of poverty here, because the land doesn't produce or it's very expensive, as are the seeds. So even if you've paid the rent there isn't enough left to buy fertilizer. That's the reason there are poor people here in Chalatenango. The people here all work hard, there's no-one who doesn't work, but there do exist some bad habits, like alcoholism. But it all comes from poverty, not because we are lazy. It's the very system we live in which makes us like that.** (Tomás)

hectare of land. The peasants on these farms are unable to subsist purely on their own production and are dependent on seasonal wage-labour for survival; they are in effect a semi-proletariat. Those with more than one hectare may be able to generate the minimum income for survival but would not produce a surplus and would also depend on seasonal wage labour for many basic necessities.

Those families farming a land area between ten and 50 hectares are the peasantry proper. With that amount of land the peasant can support his family on what he grows and retain a small surplus to sell. Though not rich, he will probably have some animals which will give him access to credit and thus allow him to improve his land. There were 1,951 farms in this category in 1971, covering a third of the cultivated land.

There were 383 larger farms, 57 of them larger than 200 hectares. These medium and rich farmers together occupied 40 per cent of the cultivated land, the same as the 8,300 poorest farmers. While the *minifundistas* cultivate basic grains, these larger-scale farmers concentrate on cattle ranching, which occupies 80 per cent of cultivated land in the department, renting out land they cannot use

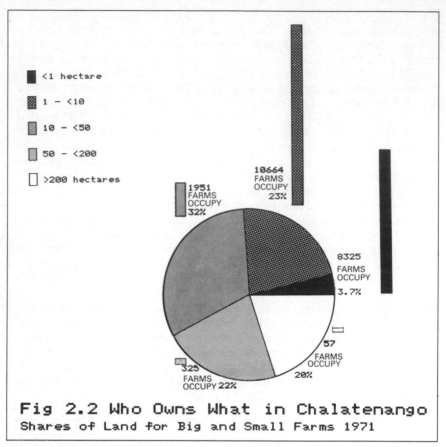

**Fig 2.2 Who Owns What in Chalatenango**
Shares of Land for Big and Small Farms 1971

Legend:
- ■ <1 hectare
- ▨ 1 – <10
- ▦ 10 – <50
- ▨ 50 – <200
- ☐ >200 hectares

10664 FARMS OCCUPY 23%

1951 FARMS OCCUPY 32%

8325 FARMS OCCUPY 3.7%

325 FARMS OCCUPY 22%

57 FARMS OCCUPY 20%

Source: Tercer Censo Nacional Agropecuario (1971) in Flores Valdivieso 1979, Cuadros no. III-4, III-5

profitably to the subsistence farmers (see Figure 2.3 on page 57).

Over the years pressure on the land has, as elsewhere in El Salvador, fallen heavily on the poor peasantry. This is expressed in the growth of the *minifundia* and particularly the *microfincas* (see Figure 2.4 on page 58. In the twenty years between the 1950 and 1971 censuses the total number of farms in Chalatenango increased by a quarter to 21,322. No corresponding increase in land availability took place. All this increase in farms is accounted for by the growing number of *minifundia*. They rose from 14,171 farms in 1950 to 18,989 in 1971. With no new land available to be brought into cultivation this increase implies an ever more bitter struggle for the basics of existence.

The number of large estates or *latifundia* declined from 479 to 381 during the ten years 1961-71, although census data is particularly unreliable for these farms. It has been suggested that the more traditional and inefficient estates have declined while medium-sized

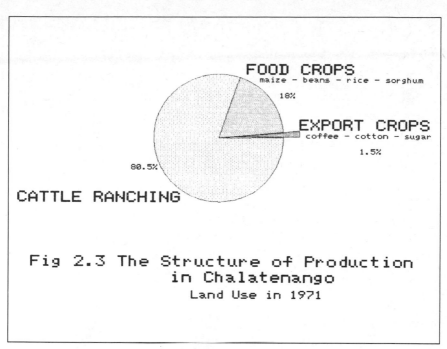

FOOD CROPS
maize - beans - rice - sorghum
18%

EXPORT CROPS
coffee - cotton - sugar
1.5%

80.5%

CATTLE RANCHING

Fig 2.3 The Structure of Production
in Chalatenango
Land Use in 1971

Source: Tercer Censo Nacional Agropecuario (1971) in Flores
Valdivieso 1979, Cuadro no. II-5

commercial farms geared to cattle ranching have enjoyed a relative
expansion, as government policies in the 1960s, influenced by the
Alliance for Progress, sought to strengthen and modernize this
sector.[12] It is worth noting in the light of this argument that improved
pasture *(pasto sembrado)* increased its area by 3.5 per cent during the
intercensal period. It was the only area of land use apart from woodland
to do so and contrasts with the decrease of 12.4 per cent in the total
amount of land under cultivation during this period.

There have also been some significant changes in forms of land
tenure in the department over the years, which also follow national
trends. There are various types of land tenure in El Salvador: those
who own their land *(proprietarios)*; tenant farmers paying money rent
*(arrendatarios simples)*; those who have two or more plots, and perhaps
own one while renting the others *(arrendatarios mixtos)*; sharecroppers
*(aparceros)*; and those who are given land and sometimes a very low
wage in exchange for work *(colonos)*.

The trend has been for a substantial increase in the renting of plots,
(16 per cent between 1961 and 1971). By 1971 half the farms in the
department were rented though they farmed only 19 per cent of the
cultivated land.[13] The increase has been most significant for the smaller
plots or *minifundia*, where 26 per cent of farms were rented in 1950
compared to 59 per cent by 1971. Chalatenango, like other

57

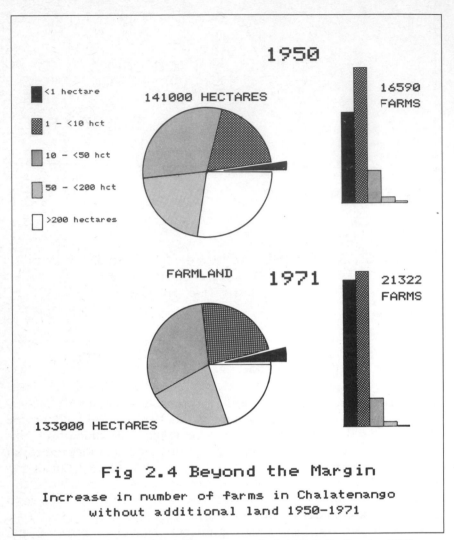

**Fig 2.4 Beyond the Margin**

Increase in number of farms in Chalatenango
without additional land 1950-1971

Source: Primer Censo Nacional Agropecuario (1950) in P. Castro, 1976
Cuadro 'B', Segundo y Tercer Nacional Agropecuario (1961, 1971) in
Flores Valdivieso 1979, Cuadros no.III-1, III-4, III-5

departments poorly endowed with natural resources, has a high
percentage of land rented in both mixed and simple form. Renting has
particular disadvantages for the small tenant farmer:

*'Perhaps the most limiting factor to access to land is the present tendency by
landowners to charge the rent in advance and in money. Formerly, the rent
payment was done through the* censo, *which consisted of payment of an
agreed quantity of the harvest, at the time of the harvest. This kind of
payment is remembered by the peasant as a rather desirable arrangement
which permitted him to obtain land to work on. With the scarce resources he*

*has at present and the trend towards payment of rent in advance, many peasants find it impossible to obtain land to farm the next season ...'[14]*

Sharecropping and the *colonato* are rare now in Chalatenango. The number of *colonos* has declined from 1,800 farms in 1961 to only 500 in 1971, though the workers who farm in this form must rank amongst the poorest of Chalatenango. The department now has the lowest proportion of *colonos* in the country after Cuscatlán.

The poor peasants of Chalatenango are caught in a cycle of poverty from which there is very little escape. Living on very marginal, rocky and infertile land, there is no way they can improve their output without investment, yet they are unable to produce the surplus to enable them to do so. The peasants' dependence on profiteering intermediaries for access to the market, and often for credit, also limits their ability to realize a surplus. In any case, as so many rent their plots — frequently a different plot each year — there is little incentive to invest in improvements to the land. Over the years it has become less possible for the peasants to leave a portion of the land fallow, so the land is overexploited and further exhausted and the cycle of poverty is reinforced.

Between 1961 and 1973 the Administration of Peasant Welfare (ABC) was responsible for channelling credit to peasants from US government assistance programmes. The ABC had an office in Tejutla, but 90 per cent of peasants in Chalatenango in the early 1970s still had no access to official credit because of their low income or lack of collateral.[15] In 1973 the Agricultural Development Bank (BFA) was set up, using funds from USAID and the central government. Its objective, however, still centred on helping the most economically viable peasant farms. Amongst its stated aims was meeting 'basic technical-financial needs . . . strengthening on the one hand the agricultural economic unit and on the other the formation of the peasant middle class'.[16]

Nevertheless, the BFA became an important institution in the lives of the peasants as the principal source of credit, fertilizers and technical assistance. During the 1970s, the main activities of the peasant union centred on trying to get it to reduce prices of fertilizers and give access to credit (see the demands of the Rural Workers' Federation (FTC) on pages 62 and 63, for example).

Without credit to hire oxen, most peasants in Chalatenango (two thirds of *minifundistas*) remain dependent on human energy. Even if a peasant is fortunate enough to have a fairly flat piece of land which could be ploughed, he might not be able to afford the hire of a pair of oxen to do so. If he has a larger plot than average, he might not be able to afford the seed to plant it all or the fertilizer necessary to make it produce.

## The Colono's Life

About the situation of us peasants, well, I know because I worked for 25 years for a man who was pretty rich. I dedicated all my life to working for him, for which I never got anything. I am just as poor as when I started off. When you get sick here, with these landowners, they don't say to you: 'here is some money, go to the hospital and get yourself cured'. What they tell you is: 'go to the hospital', nothing else. I had an accident once at work; I was hurt badly by a horse and broke some bones. When I was feeling very bad, then he did tell me, 'go to the hospital or go and see a doctor'. As I knew I was nearly dying, I had to make the effort to sell an animal in order to get cured. It cost me 500 *colones* to be cured, of which he didn't give me anything, and I had been serving him for such a long time. I had to look after 100 *manzanas*, I looked after it for him, I handled more than 200 cattle. This is the life you lead as a peasant. The *colono* has his house, but it's not his own, nor is the land it's built on. It is up to the landholder to say 'stay here', but when he doesn't like you, then he just tells you to go away, and the house stays there and the land also. I never received a wage during all the 25 years I worked for him. During the week I would work three days for him looking after the animals, and three days were left for me to work on my own plot. This was in winter, when we were in the middle of the harvest. But in the summer we spent six months working for him only. The only benefits we got were because the landholder had a lot of cattle; after the calves had been taken away from the cows, I could take some milk. That was all I got from him. As a *colono* we didn't have to pay any rent for the land nor for the pair of oxen when we needed it. For a family he gave us one *manzana*, with a value of about 35 *colones*. That was all he gave us throughout the whole year.

Because he didn't pay me anything for my work there, I had to go to the *fincas* to work. But he didn't like me going there, because I wasn't looking after his land and animals. But I told him that I had to go and earn money, to buy clothes and fertilizers for my plot, medicines and other essentials, I just had to go and do it. I went to the *fincas* for the first time in 1960; but I only stopped working for the landowner in 1980, because by that time we had already organized ourselves. He thought that we would take the land from him, so he sold it; but he didn't tell me about it, nor ask me to leave but just sold the land and left it to the new owner to throw me out. (Lito)

The situation for the medium and larger farmers could not be more different. They have access to credit and also to markets outside the region. The typical large landowner of Chalatenango has nevertheless shown little interest in investing to improve his land. Chalatenango has a higher percentage of land in natural pasture than any other department. But in the 1960s, the government began to play a more active role in modernizing the backward cattle-ranching sector. In 1963 it set up the *Mejoramiento Ganadero* (MEGA) to promote cattle raising. An office was opened in Nueva Concepción, which was considered the region of greatest potential. It began with a programme to extend the use of fertilizer in order to increase the amount of pasture land. New breeds were also introduced to the region and credit channelled to the ranchers to enable them to build appropriate infrastructure on their farms. In the 1970s, more systematic attention was given to this part of the department. The Aticoyo irrigation project was launched around Nueva Concepción, and the hydroelectric plant at Cerrón Grande was completed. But the benefits of these programmes went to those landowners who could afford to take advantage of them, who had the land and resources to invest, and who could gain from new commercial opportunities. The majority of poor peasant farmers remained locked into strategies for sheer survival.

At one time, there were cottage industries in some Chalatenango villages which enabled the peasants to earn a little extra income. San Miguel de Mercedes was a region devoted to indigo production as well as to basic grains. As indigo production collapsed, the inhabitants searched for an alternative form of income. The weaving of cloth soon became an activity for nearly every family in the area. Each household would have several looms and all the family participated in production. Subsistence farming became for many peasants a secondary activity and often they would buy the food they needed in order to spend more time weaving.

But in the mid-1940s, ruin came to the weavers of San Miguel de Mercedes, when a thread and fabric factory selling cheaper and better cloth was set up with government finance in another department to absorb the increasing production of cotton. The people of San Miguel de Mercedes found it increasingly difficult to sell their cloth profitably. Little by little they abandoned weaving and many were forced to take up seasonal labour:

'*At that time* [the period of the looms] *there was no time to go to the harvests. Now we go because there's no alternative. When the looms collapsed, that was the hard time for us. We had to go to cut sugar cane, we earned two* colones . . . *to earn two colones we had to work all day.*' (Don Esteban, peasant from Chalatenango)[17]

There are few opportunities for paid employment in either the agricultural or the industrial sector of Chalatenango itself. In 1975 there was 40 per cent open unemployment in Chalatenango, the highest of any department.[18] It has by far the lowest national employment rate per unit of land area, the result of the dominance of extensive cattle-ranching.

Few agricultural workers are employed in the department all the year, most are taken on for specific tasks, and any peasant who fails to

61

## Confronting the Agricultural Development Bank

Around here, we have two seasons: the rainy season — which we call the winter; and the dry season — the summer. In winter we cultivate corn, beans and rice; beans are grown twice a year. We sow in May and again in August. At the end of October we dry the bean harvest. To be able to harvest the grains grown in winter we need materials, like fertilizers, insecticides and herbicides. We sell part of our produce to buy the fertilizer. We have to sell at the price set by whoever comes to buy the crop and sell the fertilizer, so that we have to accept the prices imposed by him. But when the small peasant has to sell half his harvest to buy fertilizer, often the other half isn't sufficient to support his family. The next year at harvest time we are already hungry but still have to sell our produce again. So, to be able to pay the rent on the land — to buy essential goods and fertilizers — there is an exodus of people in the first days of November, in the dry season, to work on the plantations of the big landowners in Santa Ana or La Libertad, the coffee and cotton growing areas and sugar plantations. (Manuel)

### LIST OF DEMANDS OF THE POOR AND MEDIUM PEASANTS WITH RESPECT TO THE REPAYMENT OF CREDITS GIVEN BY THE BFA FOR 1979-80

The majority of the poorer peasants are now finding themselves in a desperate situation as the repayment of debts incurred with the Bank of Agricultural Development, BFA, is coming up. The BFA makes us pay high prices for materials — fertilizers, seeds, herbicides and insecticides and high interest rates for credit. We are forced to sell our products cheaply after October, at the same time as they are harvested, in order to pay the BFA, so that when payment has been made we are left without the necessary goods for the needs of our families. This situation forces us to migrate in order to survive and to sell our labour in the rich plantations in the centres of coffee, sugar cane and cotton production.

Given the above, the Christian Federation of Salvadorean Rural Workers (FECCAS) and the Union of Rural Workers (UTC) consider:

1   That the method adopted by the BFA to cancel the credits it gives, is unjust, as it forces all peasants to pay the contracted debts in the months when we are still gathering the harvest.

2   That the prices of fertilizers, seeds and insecticides, on which they base the credits, are very high in relation to our economic possibilities; the proof is that the harvest which we have brought in is not sufficient for us to pay these debts and still less to repay the effort invested.

3   That the majority of those to whom the BFA granted the credits received their credits too late, so that we had to apply the agricultural inputs too late, ie after sowing, and suffered big losses.

**4** That the attitude taken by the BFA is unjust and unfair, as it values the peasant's products at a price below the realistic one, for example with beans.

Therefore we demand of the BFA the following:
**1** That the BFA operate with interest rates of four per cent for short-term credits.
**2** That the BFA from this year onwards eliminate the requirement of guarantees for the concession of credits to the poor and medium peasants, as they cannot fulfil this condition given the economic situation they are in.
**3** That the credits conceded be longer-term, at least for a year, eliminating all short-term credits.
**4** That the BFA should pay the expenses of transport when our products are handed over to the IRA [the Institute for the Regulation of Supplies] and that they are paid out immediately.
**5** That when the peasant repays his debts with the BFA it shall return immediately the guarantees which he had to deposit when signing the contract.
**6** In those cases, where due to factors beyond the influence of the worker, like drought, rain floods and plagues, he cannot repay his debt in time, the BFA is not to retain the guarantees, but to concede him credits for the following three years so that he will be able to pay the contracted debts.

IMMEDIATE AGREEMENT TO OUR DEMANDS!

REDUCE THE PRICES OF AGRICULTURAL MATERIALS AND INTEREST RATES FOR CREDITS!

find a plot of land to rent for a year depends on such work becoming available. Wages are often considerably lower than the minimum wage. In the municipality of Chalatenango in 1973 the daily wage of a migrant labourer was 1.00-2.50 *colones* a day compared with an official minimum wage of 2.75 *colones*. Wages were higher in the department's only agro-industrial plant, the San Esteban sugar refinery in the municipality of El Paraíso.[19]

Figure 2.5 on page 64 shows that there were only 2,750 people employed in industry in Chalatenango in 1971. Most of the industry in the area is small-scale manufacturing of light consumer goods. There were 3,361 people employed in the service sector; but the really significant figure is the 13,752 in the 'informal' sector. This increase, although paralleled by a similar increase in the national figures, is the biggest in El Salvador. The huge rise over the previous census figure is an indication of the number of underemployed or virtually unemployed in the department. Given the lack of both land and work in the department, for many *Chalatecos* the only option has been to leave the department permanently.

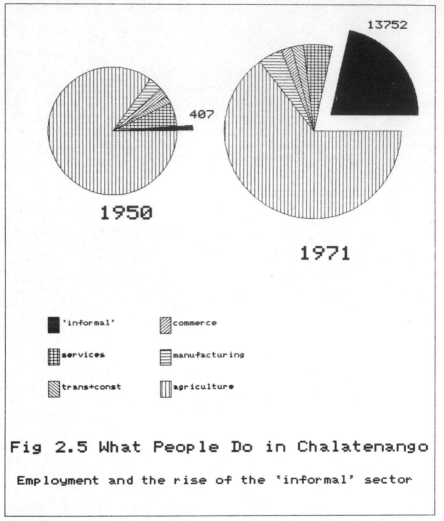

Fig 2.5 What People Do in Chalatenango

Employment and the rise of the 'informal' sector

Source: II, III y IV Censos Nacionales de Póblación, Dirección General de Estadísticas y Censos, M. de Economía, San Salvador, El Salvador 1950-1961-1971, in Castro 1976, Cuadro Estadístico, no.8

## The Peasant Family

The impoverished existence of the Salvadorean peasantry inevitably affects family life, in particular the role of women. Average family size in the rural areas is seven, although it is often larger in the villages and smaller in the town, where there are higher levels of migration and greater use of contraception. According to one study the rules and taboos surrounding female labour do not exist in El Salvador as they did in Somoza's Nicaragua or still do in Guatemala today.[20]

*Village life*

Nevertheless, in practice, a sexual division of labour does exist in the peasant family but it is governed more by custom than rigid taboos.

The father of the family, helped by his sons, is responsible for the land and production. His day may begin at five or six in the morning and he won't return until three in the afternoon. If his plot or *milpa* is far from the house, it may be much later. He will have authority within the household and over his wife.

The mother of the family will be responsible for the home and generally not be involved in production, though she might help out at particularly busy times. Alistair White writes: 'Women generally have very little to do with the cultivation of the basic grain crops: even women without husbands would have to brazen strong local criticism if they were to work on the *milpa*.'[21] She may sew, do some handicraft-work, bake bread or cakes to sell locally to earn a little for the family or take charge of the pig or chickens the family might have. At harvest time she may work alongside the rest of the family on the large plantations. But her main responsibilities are in the home. Of the tasks she has to fulfil, perhaps the most onerous is the preparation of *tortillas* (a flat, maize pancake which, together with a plate of beans make up the staple diet of the Salvadorean peasant), for the three meals. Here is one woman's description of her life, typical of many I heard in Chalatenango, which shows how far it centres around this task:

65

*The peasant family*

*You get up at 4 am. That's the way it is with work in the country. The first thing you do is light the fire, then make the coffee and fetch water from the well. The well I used was quite far away, at least 60 minutes there and back. You have to make several trips every day to fetch water, carrying the bucket on your head and another resting on your hip. The children help with a few of the trips.*

*Then you have to wash, grind and pat, or, as we say, 'tortear' the maize to make the* tortillas. *If you're quick, you spend two hours grinding the maize, but to tell you the truth, I never figured out how much time it took me.*

*Men in the countryside eat a lot and then you have all the children. I would prepare about 60* tortillas. *We would eat* tortillas *and beans because very rarely was there anything else. As we rented a plot of land, I would then have to take the meal out to my husband and the others working the fields. The plot was about an hour and a half away walking. After giving them their meal, I would stay to help them out with the work. We sowed maize, sorghum and beans.*

*At 6 pm we would return home. Then I'd have to prepare the next meal, beans and rice when we had some. I also had to prepare another 60* tortillas. *We would go to bed around 8 pm, because there was nothing else to do except sleep. That's why there are so many children, isn't it? Because there's no television. We didn't have any electricity, only candles and gas.*

*I'd usually leave the washing until Sunday, also the sewing and*

*Winnowing maize*

## The Agricultural Cycle

### Interview with Herman, a small peasant farmer from Chalatenango

*Q* I want to understand the rhythm of life of the peasant, so can you tell me about the yearly cycle on the land?

*A* The preparation for cultivation begins in March. During that month all the peasants look for a landowner to lease them land. Some landowners ask for the rent straight away, others let you have the land on credit, if it's rocky and hilly land. The soil is prepared for cultivation in March so that it's ready in May for sowing. We grow maize, rice, beans and sorghum. The maize harvest is in September and October. The family always helps and other helpers are taken on depending on the size of the harvest. Some cultivate one *manzana*, others a half, or two or three, according to their capacity and family size. When the harvest is done in November, we have time to go to the coffee plantations for the picking, or the sugar fields, or the cotton harvest, so that we can bring back money to pay the landowner his rent. Some pay it out of what they grow.

In the dry season everyone has to go to the *fincas* to pay the landowner, and this has always been the case. We leave the first days of November and return in January to cut sorghum. Then we go back to the *fincas* and come home in March to prepare our own land.

*Q* Is there always land to be rented or is there a shortage sometimes?

*A* In some places there is land to rent, in others not; it also happens that some land is more fertile and produces more than other, harsher terrains which need to be fertilized and better prepared. We often receive land which isn't productive, and on top of that you are asked for the rent before planting; and then the fertilizer is expensive. It is sold by the agricultural bank in Chalate.

*Q* Over the years, has the situation of access to land for renting here in Chalate become worse?

*A* Yes, there have been more problems. Those who haven't any spare money can't cultivate, so that many have become wage labourers, working only for the landowners. Around the 1940s, the rent for one *manzana* was about five *colones*, and then it slowly rose to fifteen. In the 1950s and 1960s it increased to 40-50 *colones*, and the terms got worse. Then you needed two *manzanas* to feed your family and have a little left for sale on the market in Chalate. But there were many people who had only their house and little piece of land, about three-quarters of an acre, some had only their house and some not even that. So, many people left for Honduras, where everyone used to say you could earn a lot more. Some returned and some stayed as life was more comfortable there. But when war between El Salvador and Honduras broke out in 1969, the people came back because they were made homeless. They lost all that they had and returned to Chalate to begin a new life, but with nothing to start off with. The majority here rent land from the medium landowners. Now, the land costs us about 100 *colones* the *manzana*, and the pair of oxen, which we need to cultivate, would cost us the same again. For fertile mountainous and volcanic terrain the rental would be 150 *colones* for one *manzana*; if it is a cornfield that has already been worked for a year, then it might cost 100 *colones*. The next year it might be worth only 50 *colones*, but you can't get anything out of the ground anymore.

*Q*  Do people work the same land every year?
*A*  In some places the same land is worked for two to three years, and then you have to find a different plot because that land is given over to cattle. Some peasants, beside growing maize, have cows, a pair of oxen or a horse, others have no livestock at all.

*Q*  How does a peasant with 100 *manzanas* live in contrast to a poor peasant?
*A*  In my area the life of a medium peasant is different only in the sense that the poorer peasant is always being exploited, 'the bigger fish always eats the little one' as the saying goes. They think, 'if I am exploited, it doesn't matter, because I can exploit someone else myself', so that the poorest feel the exploitation hardest. The medium peasant is exploited because he has to pay higher taxes than the poor peasant, but he can get it back out of the poor peasant.

*mending. They say Sunday's a day of rest, but there's no rest for the poor, every day is a work day.* (Interview with Yolanda, 35 years old, a refugee in San Salvador.)[22]

Women may not be directly involved in production, but they evidently play a key role in the economy of the peasant household. The daughters in the family may play a more direct role. Frequently they will be sent to the urban centres as domestic servants — sometimes even to the capital, San Salvador — earning a very low wage but nevertheless one which may provide some cash input to the household. In the period 1950-1961 a clear majority (58 per cent) of migrants from San Miguel de Mercedes were women; in the period 1961-1971 women were still the majority of migrants from the *pueblo* though they had just been outnumbered by men in the rural area.[23] María, whose story appears on page 141, was a servant in Arcatao before she got married. Other girls have ended up on the streets as prostitutes.

In poor rural societies such as El Salvador, where health and educational provision is so inadequate, women often suffer the consequences more directly and acutely than the men in the community. With children viewed as an economic necessity — to help the father in the fields and support their parents in old age — the strains

*Cleaning sorghum*

of frequent childbearing weigh heavily on the health of the female population. Contraception is still not acceptable to large numbers of the population, most of whom are strong Catholics, though illegal abortions and the accompanying health risks are all too common.

The weight of the traditional teachings of the Catholic Church, with its passive and submissive image of women, together with the cult of the male so typical in Latin societies, have contributed to the low status of women in the community, their subservience to their husbands, and a life centred almost exclusively around domestic tasks. The peasant condition in El Salvador creates a special burden on the women which must be taken into account in any examination of peasant life.

## A Year in the Life . . .

**January**  Many peasants return from the plantations to harvest and thresh the sorghum and take it for storage to the grainstore. Sorghum is an important crop for the peasants as it is more resistant than maize and is a useful supplement to the diet, mixed with maize or used alone to make *tortillas*. It is usually planted in combination with another crop, particularly maize.

**February**  In this month some people go to the sugar cane harvest, others may earn some extra cash from odd jobs such as carpentry or building work. There is also a lot of work to be done around the house, collecting dry wood, for instance, before the winter comes.

**March**  This is the month in which those peasants who rent land begin the search for a plot to be ready to plant in May. This does not depend on the free choice of the peasant. The landowners rent different plots at different prices each year. As a rule, they try to keep some fallow, though with such demand the temptation is to rent as much as possible. The peasant rents as much as he can afford and his family can work. The rent varies according to the quality of the soil, whether it is stony ground or on a slope, for instance. All the peasants I spoke to agreed that an increasing problem over the years is the difficulty in finding decent land to rent, together with the problem of constantly rising rents.

Some peasants prefer to rent always from the same landowner in the hope of gaining some special favour, such as a better piece of land. There is an example of one peasant who always rented two *manzanas* [approximately one hectare] of land from the same landowner. One year he was given some rather stony land about five kilometres from his house and nearer the *municipio* of Chalatenango than his house. But he was allowed to pay for the land partly in kind (the sorghum crop being the most reliable) knowing also that if the harvest was bad the payment would be reduced as the landowner knew him to be a good tenant.[24]

Not everyone has such a good relationship with their landlord. In

*Threshing maize*

the majority of cases, rent is in money not in kind. Many peasants told me that in recent years the landowners had insisted on payment in advance which meant they have to save enough from their work on the plantations in November and December or they have to borrow it. Often they have to sell their harvest in advance or raise a loan.

This month there is very little paid work available in or out of Chalatenango. Activities centre on work around the house.

**April** The land is prepared for planting. First it has to be cleared. Many peasants still burn the land as it is a quicker and cheaper means of clearing it although it also exhausts the soil more rapidly. Very few peasants use herbicides as this involves additional costs. Otherwise a curved machete called a *cuma* is used to cut down the weeds which are then burned.

The first rains usually begin. The peasants hope they will continue so that they can plant the maize, their most important crop. In the past, the May planting would be the first winter planting of the year. There would be another one in the summer, in August or September, and possibly a third in November. But three plantings are only possible when the peasant can let the land rest for a period. With increasing land scarcity most peasants can no longer afford to do this, needing to work every inch of their plot every year to survive and relying on fertilizer to offset declining productivity.

Maize is usually combined with other crops, particularly sorghum and beans. In this way the peasant assures himself a more varied diet and a greater overall volume of basic grains.

**May**  If the winter has set in, the peasant will plant in May and apply the first fertilizer a few weeks later. Fertilizer is essential for grain to grow on most of Chalatenango's poor soils. To pay for the fertilizer, the peasant might get credit from a saving and credit cooperative, a number of which emerged in the 1960s, or from the Agricultural Development Bank (BFA). Bank credit generally requires property as collateral. Many peasants have their own little house and a tiny piece of land in front, perhaps a quarter of a *manzana*. This is not cultivated but the trees are used for firewood and a few animals can be kept there. On the basis of this, the peasant may get some credit which he will pay for by selling a part of his crop or by working on the plantations. Some peasants in San Miguel de Mercedes planted a commercial crop, groundnut, to increase their income.

**June**  The maize field has to be weeded, a very labour intensive task. This is the month for planting groundnut, cucumber, pumpkins, or any other vegetable which can later be sold to supplement the family income.

**July**  The beans are harvested, dried, threshed and cleaned. Those who can afford it apply fertilizer a second time. Though the maize cob can be cut and numerous special dishes made from it, this yields less maize than when it is ripe and to use it now for home consumption means less for the rest of the year. This month, the food is in good supply for the family, with perhaps some cucumber or other vegetable to add to the usual beans and *tortillas*. But it is also a month for hard work on the *milpa*.

**August**  The maize is ripe and has to be kept dry, as rainwater could ruin it.

**September**  At the end of the month the maize is harvested and dried, and taken to the house or to the granary for storage. The peasants may help each other with the harvest, sometimes on an exchange basis and occasionally for wages. One peasant woman, María, told me how the treatment of the peasants by each other differed from that of the plantation owners to their labour force. She would always ensure any helpers had good food and were looked after.

As has already been said, the peasants' priority is to feed themselves and they sell very little of their harvest. The logic is simple:

*Turning coffee beans for drying, privately owned coffee farm, Sonsonate*

'If the peasant sold all he produced, he would have a serious problem: he would sell cheaply to the profiteers of the town of Aguilares, and have to buy back at a later date and at much higher prices what he needed to live on.'[25]

In Chalatenango, the majority of peasants sell through intermediaries. These may be small local traders who buy cheaply and then sell to the lorry drivers, or the lorry drivers may come to the villages themselves specifically to buy grain and later sell it to larger traders. Many of these traders will speculate with the grain. In the northern, unproductive part of Chalatenango, there was a local market and commerce with the Hondurans, but this was severely disrupted by the 1969 war. Here is Alistair White's description of the way the peasants market their products and how this affects their income:

*'Owners of lorries visit rural market places and tour the producing areas, buying the products from the producer; from someone who has bought the crop in advance of the harvest at a very low price; or from a local bulker and transporter who has collected the goods. To give an example of mark-ups at each stage, in January 1971 the price paid for maize at the local market of San Vicente by lorry-owners was 7 colones per 100lb, while that for sorghum was 5.50 colones. The lorry-owner transports the product, very likely to the main market in the capital, and delivers it to a wholesale merchant with premises in the streets around the market place. In January 1971 the wholesale merchants of San Salvador were paying the transporter-*

75

*bulkers 7.75 colones or 8 colones for maize and 6.75 or 7 colones for sorghum. At this stage, maximum bulking has occurred. The wholesaler then sells to market stallholders and shopkeepers, who are often women. The price was 8.25 colones for maize, 7.25 or 7.50 colones for sorghum. The final price for sale to the public was 0.10 colones per lb (or 10 colones per 100lb) for both maize and sorghum.'[26]*

**October**   Some harvest the sorghum this month, otherwise the main tasks centre on preparations for going to the plantations.

**November**   In Chalatenango, there is a mass exodus in November to the coffee, cotton and sugar plantations. The peasant relies on seasonal labour to earn money to buy the rest of his needs: food, medicine, clothing and basic household goods, to pay rent and purchase fertilizer.

**December**   Most people stay on the plantations, returning in January to harvest the sorghum. It is striking how little has changed since the International Labour Office (ILO) first reported in 1954 on the humiliating conditions for workers on the country's commercial plantations, the power base of the ruling elite:

*'How do different categories of agricultural labourers live? Badly, from all points of view. Badly housed, badly fed, badly dressed, without healthy distractions, driven to drink and suffering from numerous illnesses. On top of this, illiteracy and cohabitation rather than legal marriages, contribute to increasing the misery of the peasants, in particular the wage labourers.*

***Food:***   *From the point of view of energy, the Nutrition Institute of Central America and Panama (INCAP), taking into account the racial characteristics of the Salvadorean people, recommends a minimum daily diet of 2,800 calories, but the average ration of the agricultural worker fed by his employer corresponds to 1,926 calories. This is the classic diet, based on maize tortillas, beans and sometimes, rice. In most of the large plantations, the workers receive tortillas, beans cooked in water with a pinch of salt, and from time to time, a cup of coffee or rather a drink which doesn't deserve the name as it's really an infusion made mostly of toasted maize. Such a diet lacks vitamins, and vegetable and animal proteins are totally absent. It should be observed that workers who don't receive food as a complement to their salaries do not get a sufficient diet either, as their scarce resources prevent them from getting better food.*

***Work Conditions:***   *On the whole, none of the permanent or temporary workers have any contract with their employers, except verbally . . . The workers have no chance of negotiating collective contracts for the simple reason that they cannot unite to form unions of any type. There is practically no legislation or regulation of work nor social protection for the rural workers . . . Work conditions are ruled, therefore, by custom and tradition, and vary according to the degree of understanding or goodwill of the employers. The*

*attitude of the latter tends often to be paternalistic, which reduces considerably the freedom of the workers, as can be seen mainly on some large plantations.'*[27]

The story of poverty, exploitation and outright cheating are little different today, as the peasants explained to me:

**When we go to the coffee *fincas* we have to sleep on the ground of the coffee field. Sometimes there are sheds, just with a roof overhead. At 5am we get up to receive the coffee sack, and then to get the *chenga*, the food, and a little water. In all the *fincas* the food is bad, they give us one *chenga* in the morning, at lunch and one in the evening. They are called *chenga* because the *tortillas* are badly made, botched up and they give only a spoonful of beans with them. The foreman gives us each a furrow to work on and we start work. The more determined at cutting earn more than the less determined. At 3pm the whistle sounds and we return to empty the coffee in the big yards; it is cleaned of leaves, the green bits are taken out and it's filled again into sacks.**

Then we go to the weighing and from there to the re-weighing. After that we have to queue up to get some *chenga*. Often this takes us to 10pm and we still haven't eaten, because the queues are long, never-ending. We are paid every two weeks, but never earn enough. But because there isn't any work at home we have to come anyway. The real question is that they don't pay us what we have rightly earned. They cheat us at the weighing; they take the weight with a measuring rod which they put into the sack of coffee, and then say there are so many *arrobas* [one *arroba* = 25lb]; and then, in front of your very eyes, they weigh it again, for the owner's sake, and give the true figure of what has been cut. They pay 65 *centavos* for the *arroba*, but no *séptimo* (payment for the Sunday, which is work-free, spent usually on washing clothes, looking for somewhere to have a bath or going to see a doctor). (Ramón)

The owner has shops on the plantations, and they give credit there, so that one is always under the temptation to take the credit. Then, when we get paid, he's there, charging us, subtracting the debt we ran up from our wages. There was one *compañero* who, when he got the *chenga*, hurried off and went to wrap himself in a blanket so that he wouldn't see how the others were eating other things; he wanted to take all his wages home . . . Another problem is water: the owner fills the water that falls during the winter into big tanks and he measures it out to the workers – one litre a person per day – which is quickly drunk. So you choose a *finca* where they give more water. Or one which is near a place where you can bathe; because this is another thing, you spend all these days without anywhere to wash. (Abel)

The working hours on the *fincas* vary from place to place: in some you begin at 5am and cut until 1pm and then gather the coffee. In some *fincas* you finish at 3pm, in others later. Therefore we decide where to go according to the condition on the *finca*, for example *fincas* where there is more water, where there are sheds for shelter from the storms, or *fincas* where the foreman is not quite as bloodthirsty. But these *fincas* fill very quickly with workers.

And what we earn mostly are illnesses. Seeing how difficult the situation is we tell each other 'I'll spend some time there if only to keep myself alive'. But as the food they give us is so bad, it doesn't help at all. So that many people, instead of bringing home money, bring back illnesses. The little that they have earned they spend on curing themselves again. (Raúl)

After the coffee-cutting, at the end of December, we go home, because then they no longer employ us, and we go to harvest the sorghum here on our plots. And from mid-January onward we go to the sugar plantations. There they exploit us in a different form: they give us piece work to do in the sugar-cutting. For each job they pay 3.50 *colones* but they give us jobs that can't be finished within three days, so that we end up earning one *colón* a day. (Tomás)

# 5
# PEASANTS
# CONTROLLED

In Manlio Argueta's fictional account of life in Chalatenango, the peasants describe the atmosphere following the 1932 peasant uprising:

'That's how Chalatenango has been since I can recall: tranquil, without big problems, only household ones, without robberies or delinquencies. My mother says she always remembers it as having been a peaceful place. The last killing took place about forty years ago, when I was just a child. . . . back then there was so much talk of communism and the authorities were furious. "The Indians have rebelled, and they weren't going to forgive that even if it meant wiping out our entire population here." That's what my mother used to tell me. It was a little after 1932. "You can't imagine how terrible those days were. One couldn't even own a stamp with a saint on it because they believed that the prayers printed on the back were Communist slogans, and we had to burn the Virgin of Refuge, the Holy Child of Atocha, and even the Saviour of the World." And I tell you things were bad. "You even had to be careful how you breathed so they wouldn't think you were grieving for a death and therefore presume that you had a dead Communist relative. More than forty thousand people died in those days." And I tell you that fortunately she saved herself and my father. She explains to me that in Chalate there were no uprisings because there were no coffee plantations, nor were there any workers and no one got rebellious here. They were lucky then, I tell you. "May the lord protect me, you would have been left without a father, because all males were presumed to be Communist." She tells me, "Since there are no large coffee plantations around here, life is more peaceful — one eats when there's something to eat; for us poverty is a blessing."[1]

A doctor who used to visit Chalatenango in the 1960s remembers the peasants as so passive he could never have envisaged a time when they might rebel. They had a reputation for great hard work, warmth and generosity, but no-one saw them as peasant militants.

This chapter is about the legacy of the first great struggle of the Salvadorean peasantry in 1932 and the mechanisms which the state subsequently adopted for political control over the peasantry. Until the 1960s, these mechanisms mostly centred on a highly repressive rural security apparatus which toward the end of that decade included a mass based para-military vigilante organization called ORDEN. The traditional church and government political party also played a role in maintaining subservience and passivity amongst the peasants.

But during the 1960s also, repression became seasoned with reform as the government accepted US advice on the need to pre-empt peasant unrest and allowed the formation, under US tutelage, of a peasant association, the Salvadorean Communal Union (UCS). The church too, tentatively at first, began to confront its social role and worked together with the Christian Democrat party to promote cooperatives, without initially attempting to challenge existing structures. The radicalized peasant movement of the 1970s owes a little to these limited efforts at peasant organization 'from above' and a good deal to their failure to offer any solution to the rural crisis.

The story begins with the peasant uprising of 1932, which was centred mostly on the coffee growing region of the west. But Chalatenango felt its shock waves along with most other rural areas of El Salvador.

## Peasant Revolt

*'From that evil day, all of us are different men and I believe that since then El Salvador is a different country. El Salvador is, above everything, a creature of that barbarity . . . It may be that the style of the rulers has changed but the basic ways of thinking which still govern is that of the massacres of 1932.'*[2]

Tension in the rural areas had persisted for some time since the decrees of the 1880s, sometimes exploding into local disturbances, such as attacks on judges who had handed over communally-owned lands to private owners. The 1907 Agrarian Code banned trade union organization among agricultural workers. In 1912 the National Guard was created, modelled on the Spanish Civil Guard. Its main duty was to control the rural population and protect the coffee plantations.

The miserable conditions of the peasants, particularly the *colonos* or farm labourers on the coffee estates, had deteriorated further with the Great Crash of 1929. The world economic crisis sent coffee prices tumbling; the value of El Salvador's coffee exports fell from £8 million in 1928 to £2.4 million in 1932. The planters tried to shift some of the loss onto their workers, sometimes by cutting food rations or even wages. The results were catastrophic for an already impoverished sector of the population.

The British diplomatic representative in El Salvador at the time, D.J. Rogers, noted that:

*'. . . communist revolution could still be avoided if the planters would*

82

*combine to provide their workers with reasonable healthy and comfortable living conditions together with pay no lower than what they have been accustomed to.'[3]*

The US military attaché in Central America, A.R. Harris, reported:

*'I imagine that the situation in El Salvador today is similar to France before the revolution, Russia before her revolution and Mexico before hers. The situation is ripe for communism and the communists seem to have taken notice of that fact . . . It is possible to retard a socialist or communist revolution in this country for a number of years, let's say ten or twenty, but when it happens it is going to be bloody.'[4]*

The revolt stemmed very clearly from these conditions. But there were other factors as well, including the living memory of the expansion of coffee which had dispossessed the peasants of their communal lands and forced them into wage labour.

A number of areas in which the revolt broke out, notably the Izalco-Nahuizalco area, were still populated by Indians who had retained some of their ethnic identity. In these areas, Indian *caciques* or village headmen, played an important role in the revolt. Some see the uprising as one of Indian against *ladino*, though the ethnic divide corresponded also to class divisions. How far the revolt can really be described in ethnic terms is doubtful, especially as in other areas of revolt nearer to the capital, such as Colón and Santa Tecla, the peasants were predominantly *ladino*. The landowners were, however, to exact their vengeance with particular severity on the Indian population after the uprising.

The other major influence in the revolt was the urban labour movement and the recently organized Salvadorean Communist Party. The first labour union was founded in 1912. From then on a number of small groups of artisans and workers began to organize, and in 1920 and 1921 the first strikes took place amongst railway workers and shoemakers. The Regional Federation of Salvadorean Workers (FRTS) was set up in 1925 and affiliated to the Confederation of Central American Workers based in Guatemala. By 1930 the Federation had some 1,500 members mainly amongst the shoemakers, bakers, carpenters, printers and railway workers. But its influence extended more widely given the discontent and ferment amongst workers and peasants at the time. Intense debates within the Federation between anarcho-syndicalists and Communists had finally been resolved in favour of the latter.

The Salvadorean Communist Party (PCS) was set up in 1925, but did not get off the ground until 1929 when a Mexican Communist, Jorge Fernando Anaya, arrived in the country. Anaya began organizing the farm workers in the western part of the country. A number of other

*Agustín Farabundo Martí (seated right) with Sandino (third from right)*

activists were also at work amongst different sectors, Juan Pablo Wainwright, Modesto Ramírez, Miguel Mármol and Agustín Farabundo Martí. Martí, who became the leader of the PCS, had spent various periods in exile and in prison for his political activities in the 1920s. He had helped set up a left-wing study group at the University which in 1927 became the General Association of Salvadorean University Students (AGEUS), which is still in existence today. The students were encouraged to go into the rural areas and set up 'popular universities'. He also fought alongside Sandino in Nicaragua from 1928 to 1929, breaking with him because his banner was only that of national independence . . . not social revolution'.[5] He was also the key figure in El Salvador in a broad front body established to give aid to persecuted workers, called International Red Aid (SRI), in whose name the Communist Party carried out many of its activities.

The Party remained very small, but in the depression was able to mobilize an increasingly desperate population. Eighty thousand people marched in San Salvador on May Day 1930. The population of the city was only 90,000 at the time. The FRTS for its part had begun to recruit in the rural areas and demand a minimum wage for agricultural workers and guaranteed farm contracts.

In the midst of growing protest, Arturo Araújo was elected president in July 1930 on a programme full of promises for social

84

reform. Sworn in in March 1931, he was overthrown in December and General Hernández Martínez, his vice-president and minister of war came to power. The situation in the countryside was already tense. The Communist Party urged restraint on the peasants who often marched on the local garrison and threatened to provoke retaliation. The Party had decided to participate in municipal and congressional elections and their candidates seemed likely to win resounding victories in the coffee-growing areas. The decision to suspend the second poll in January 1932 led to a wave of unrest. The peasants of Ahuachapán, for instance, launched a general strike in several areas attacking National Guard posts on coffee plantations. A number of peasants were killed in the subsequent repression.

The Communist Party decided on the night of 7th January to organize an armed insurrection on the 16th, a date later postponed to the 22nd. On the 18th the government discovered the plan and arrested many of the organizers, including Martí. The Party decided there was still less to lose in going ahead than in cancelling the uprising. But when it took place, it was virtually leaderless and there had been very little preparation.

The uprising hardly got off the ground in San Salvador, although there was some movement in surrounding areas, notably Colón, Santa Tecla, Soyapango and Ilopango, (the easternmost point of the rebellion). In the west, where it was more successful, it was put down in three days. The peasants achieved most in Juayua, Izalco and Nahuizalco, in the departments of Sonsonate and Ahuachapán. Here Indian *caciques* led the revolt, mobilizing their traditional following. But except in a few cases where the peasants captured weapons from guards, it was machetes against machine-guns. Thomas Anderson in his book *Matanza* carefully examined the evidence of killings by the peasants, and concluded that they could not have killed more than 100 people of whom perhaps 35 were civilians.[6]

The revenge of the landowners and armed forces seems particularly grotesque in the light of this information. At the very lowest estimate 10,000 peasants died in government massacres. Most people put the figure nearer to 30,000, and some to 40,000, out of a population of only one million at the time. Indians were hunted down with particular hatred:

'. . . *all those of a strongly Indian cast of features or who dressed in a scruffy* campesino *costume, were considered guilty . . . Tied by the thumbs to those before and behind them, in the customary Salvadorean manner, groups of fifty were led to the back wall of the church of Asunción in Izalco and against that massive wall were cut down by firing squads.*'[7]

Even the government-sanctioned account of the event which appeared in Gregorio Bustamente Maceo's *Historia Militar de El Salvador* describes the atrocities:

'. . . the machine-guns began to sow panic and death in the regions of Juayúa, Izalco, Nahuizalco, Colón, Santa Tecla, the volcanoes of Santa Ana, and all of the towns on the river from Jiquilisco to Acajutla, there were towns that were wiped from the face of the earth.'[8]

# Fifty Years of Stability

1932 is remembered nostalgically by the right in El Salvador today for its success in dealing with unrest, and many think of repeating its methods. A representative of the Coffee Growers Association said in 1980: 'We *cafetaleros* shouldn't get scared by the present situation in El Salvador; 1932 was similar, and if it could be dealt with then, it can be dealt with now'.[9] The truth is that in 1932 the Salvadorean ruling class did win itself some 50 years of stability.

Having restored order in the immediate aftermath of the 1932 rebellion, the ruling class set about institutionalizing repression in the rural areas. The idea of permanent armed civilian vigilante squads was floated. 'Civil guards' had in fact emerged to help crush the rebellion in the west. El Salvador's leading daily, *La Prensa Gráfica*, had urged the 'honourable' men of each community to organize '. . . *into militias patterned after the Italian* Fascio, *the Spanish armed corps* 'somatenes', *or the patriotic groups of* Action Français *for the defence at any time of our families and homes against the deadly and ferocious attacks of the gangs of villains filling the ranks of the Red Army which hopes to drown in blood the free and generous nation left to us by our ancestors.'[10]

The Salvadorean Civil Association with units of the civil guard attached to each local committee was set up for this purpose. However, it proved a fairly short-lived organization. Once the uprising had been well and truly defeated, the wealthy did not feel so motivated to give their own time to the task of security, preferring to leave it to the army and security forces.

The National Guard and the National Police became the backbone of the post-1932 security system. Identity cards were now issued for all those over 18. Those who donated more than 100 *colones* to a 'Patriotic Subscription of National Cooperation' fund could, however, buy exemption and receive a 'Patriotic Social Defence Certificate' instead.[11] New measures were announced to control travel within the country, and *cantón* patrols were reactivated in the rural areas, usually made up of army reservists working in cooperation with the National Guard to assist in surveillance. In addition to these specific measures, the Agrarian Code of 1907 provided a framework for control in the rural areas, and although revised in 1941, it remained in essence the 'legal' basis on which the government controlled the peasants until the 1980s. Peasant unions were never legalized in El Salvador, for instance. The Code is extraordinarily explicit on the role of the security forces with respect to the peasants:

*'In the Code's explicit instructions to the National Guard, peasants (therein generally termed* jornaleros *meaning agricultural workers paid by the day or* jornada) *are described as virtually synonymous with criminals:* jornalero *becomes almost interchangeable with* reo *or criminal. Guardsmen are instructed to capture any person "on the first request of any* hacienda *or farm owner". On the* haciendas *they were to "gather all information, news and instructions convenient for the efficient persecution of agricultural and other workers and* evil-doers *in general". They had jurisdiction throughout the country for "the efficient persecution of day labourers or workers who have broken the agreements with the farm owners, and in the persecution of evil-doers of all kinds". Guardsmen were to "keep a notebook that will contain the name and employment of the day labourers, workers and criminals they capture . . .".'[12]*

The National Police was the urban equivalent of the National Guard. Another force, the Treasury Police *(policía de hacienda)*, was created to collect taxes and was responsible for border work, such as tracking down smugglers. But they were also in charge of suppressing illegal alcohol production and this often brought them into conflict with peasant communities where alcohol brewed from local corn was, as is common throughout the world, a favoured means of forgetting present troubles.

Until the 1960s, drunkenness amongst peasant men was probably the most serious problem the security forces had to deal with in Chalatenango. There was sometimes considerable resistance to the authorities' attempts to end the illegal production of alcohol (see testimony). But in general law and order and even forced labour for public works was maintained without great difficulty. This situation prevailed into the 1960s.

The system of control changed after the October 1960 coup which overthrew the government of Lieutenant-Colonel José María Lemus. A wave of street demonstrations and protest brought to power a government which seemed, to the military establishment, dangerously reform-oriented. They restored their supremacy with a counter-coup in January 1961. The army then moved to institutionalize its rule and give it an appearance of democracy and popular support through the creation of a new 'official' party, the National Conciliation Party (PCN). The box on page 89 gives a picture of how the party was able to ensure that the peasants of Chalatenango voted for it in each municipal and national election through a combination of intimidation and bribery (promises of improvements in local services and jobs to party activists). The party controlled the state and could use the state to support its campaign. These practices were common in all the rural areas. 'A party activist', writes Alistair White:

### Before the Revolution

Before the revolution, the peasant lived a life of continuous work. The government or the great landlords pressed us into forced work and military service. We were persecuted and forced against our will to serve for one year or even 18 months in the army. Also, we had to pay taxes. In those days the *colono* needed to have a document that stated that he had paid his tax, anything up to 50 *colones*. If he didn't have this card then he was forced into work. Forced labour also included work for the town halls. Everyone had to spend a week at the town hall, doing whatever work the judge or the mayor asked them to do. And when someone in the family died and you didn't have the one and a half *colones* for the burial, then the mayor demanded that you cleaned the cemetery for two days. It was the mayor and the judge who forced the peasant to work at the cemetery or to clean the streets. The local *comandante* was in charge of 'recruitment' into the military service.

In Chalate there were the *Guardia Nacional, Policía de Hacienda* and Municipal Police. They used to pick up the drunks, check disorders in the markets, and if they arrested people they kept them for 8 to 15 days. The *Policía de Hacienda's* job was to go to the hamlets to see who's making spirit illegally, and even if they weren't people were often beaten and taken away. The *Guardia Nacional* were involved when it came to criminals, robberies and murders, though they also attended the traditional fiestas. The *Policía Nacional* controlled the towns, the bars, and buses. Each had their own prison where they took the people and tortured them. But in the *Guardia* prisons they were very cruel, because the more cruel they were, the higher they would rank. (Quique)

*'not paid but hoping for a job through* oficialista *connections, is instructed to visit each dwelling in his area and enter its adult inhabitants as members of the party in a little book, telling them when they have to go and vote, and giving them a ticket for a free meal afterwards . . . When the* campesino *arrives at the polling booth, he finds a person of authority there, and very likely soldiers or* guardias *standing around . . . the ballot boxes are made of transparent plastic. As the ballot papers are thin and the voter marks the party symbol with a thick black cross, another person can stand on the opposite side of the box from the voter, watch his ballot paper come down through the slit into the transparent box, and see through the thin, once-folded paper which party he has voted for'.*[13]

It was also at the time of the unrest of 1960 that the US, increasingly nervous at the course of the Cuban revolution, became concerned with the efficiency of El Salvador's security forces. The US had been providing money and personnel to train the security forces since 1957 through USAID; now it dispatched a two-man team to investigate their effectiveness. Its report, the Hardin Report produced on 24 August

## Voting in Chalate

In those years the women didn't go to vote, because it would have meant leaving the house and the children alone. But the men went. The authorities checked their documents, and hassled those who didn't go to vote; so they had to invent some tale, saying that they were ill. But those who went did so either because they might enjoy the ride to the voting station, or because they might get a drink, something to eat and, of course, in order to get their attendance papers signed. The elections weren't free, it had already been decided who was going to be the president, you only marked the paper, folded it and put it into the box. But the electoral commission could change the result when they saw that they needed more votes and simply filled in more papers, even for those who were dead.

The Christian Democrat Party (PDC) had considerable impact in Chalate when it emerged, because the very name seemed to signify democracy, freedom of expression, of organization; but all this was a lie. It was just their policy to say that there was democracy. The people hoped to get their rights, but the military was still in power really. In practice the PDC and the official party said the same, the same demagogy.

In 1972 many people still participated in the elections, when Duarte stood as candidate, an election that was clearly fraudulent. But for this country the electoral method was not the salvation for the people, here there needed to be an organization of the people which would take us forward, out of the misery into which we had sunk. (María)

---

1960, praised the National Guard for maintaining 'stability' and recommended an urgent programme of security assistance to combat subversion. As a result, assistance to the security forces under the US Public Safety programme was stepped up, including both equipment and training (some 450 Salvadorean 'police' were trained under the programme). By 1974, USAID concluded that the National Police had become a 'well-disciplined, well-trained, and respected uniformed corps', and the National Guard was described in the same terms.[14]

At the same time the US began to build up an intelligence apparatus in the country. General Medrano, then a senior officer of the National Guard and the army general staff, was given a leading role in this process. 'ORDEN and ANSESAL – the Salvadorean National Security Agency – grew out of the State Department, the CIA and the Green Berets during the time of Kennedy', Medrano told an American journalist, Allan Nairn. 'We created these specialized agencies to fight the plans and actions of international communism. We organized ORDEN, ANSESAL and counter-insurgency courses, and we bought special arms – G-3 automatic rifles – to detain the communist movement. We were preparing the team to stop communism'.[15] Allan Nairn takes up the story:

'Medrano gave Washington ample return on its investment. In El Salvador, he organized an intricate, many-tiered intelligence and paramilitary network that extended from the remotest mountain hamlets to the presidential palace. The rural component of this network was ORDEN (Spanish for "Order"), a group founded, in Medrano's words, to "indoctrinate" the peasants regarding the advantages of the democratic system and the disadvantages of the communist system. Green Beret Colonel Arthur Simons was instrumental in the development of ORDEN, says Medrano . . . "Colonel Simons sent me ten men to begin training us". After "talking among ourselves and with Simons, the idea occurred to us to catechize the people. We talked about how we had to indoctrinate the people, because he who has the population wins the war.

"The army can easily annihilate guerillas in the urban zone", says Medrano, "but the peasants are tough. They are good in the mountains. They can walk at night, see in the dark, see among the trees. We couldn't let them be deceived by the guerillas".

Medrano says the Green Berets helped him plan the structure and ideology of ORDEN and then stayed on to train a team of Salvadorean soldiers – among them Colonel Carranza . . . and Colonel Domingo Monterrosa . . . [who] went to the countryside to instruct civilian ORDEN leaders, who in turn established the organization's local chapters. At its peak ORDEN membership reached an estimated 100,000. "It was almost like a religion", Medrano recalls.'[16]

ORDEN was established at a time when there was no guerilla movement, and the only 'opposition' to the existing order was from a weak Communist Party and the rather mild proposals for reform emanating from the recently founded Christian Democrat Party. Counter-insurgency, in other words, was implemented in El Salvador prior to any insurgency. ORDEN eventually became a powerful instrument of rural control and intelligence-gathering, though it did not prevent the growth of an independent and radical peasant union movement. Not even sophisticated and increasingly repressive US techniques of rural control could ultimately prevent a peasant rebellion.

Originally, recruits to ORDEN were from the military reserves, young Salvadoreans who at the age of 18 could be called for active military service followed by a year of army reserve service in their communities. Local army commanders working closely with local National Guard commanders – themselves usually army officers – acted as the link between Medrano and the local ORDEN recruits.[17] By 1967, ORDEN was in the process of evolution from an information-gathering network into a political organization in its own right, with its own ideology. Its role was expanding to include cooperation with the army and National Guard on 'civic action', which included community development projects such as school building and road repairs. That year, the new President, Fidel Sánchez Hernández became its Supreme Chief, although Medrano, now Director of the National Guard, ran the organization. ORDEN had played a useful role in the elections of that year, disrupting opposition party meetings. 'ORDEN', said the new president, 'puts at the disposal of the Salvadorean state and the most responsible sectors of the country a civilian army that can be armed in 24 hours, that will defend the democratic system and that could easily reach 150,000 men.'

In January 1970 Medrano was removed from his post as head of the National Guard and executive director of ORDEN. But a number of proteges who had served with him in the National Guard, including Lieutenant Roberto D'Aubuisson, remained key figures in the intelligence system. By the early 1970s this was already fairly sophisticated. The National Intelligence Service (SNI), which had been set up on the advice of US personnel following the 1961 coup, linked the special investigations sections of each security service and gathered in the information provided by ORDEN members. It was at the centre of the security system and operated out of the presidential palace. President Molina came to power in 1972; during his presidency the SNI was renamed ANSESAL. The US continued to have a close relationship with ANSESAL and the Salvadorean security forces throughout these years, supplying ANSESAL with the names, photographs and whereabouts of suspected dissidents and dossiers on Salvadoreans working abroad.[18]

*'ANSESAL was formed of the heads of the military services and internal security forces and answered directly to the President. From its offices in the presidential palace, it functioned as the brain of a vast state security apparatus that reached into every town and neighbourhood in the country. By conservative estimate, at least one Salvadoran out of every 50 was an informant for the agency. In addition to gathering intelligence, ANSESAL was used to carry out death-squad activities before the [1979] coup, according to Salvadoran and US officials.'[19]*

The apparatus of social control in the rural areas which had been established after the 1932 uprising was therefore updated and modernized long before there was any threat to the existing social order. Following the Cuban revolution, the US was not taking any chances; it invoked all the means at its disposal to both pre-empt and control peasant unrest. The repressive side of this strategy was warmly welcomed by the military establishment and landed elite of El Salvador but the 'reform' component was more controversial. It was this which resulted in the first social organization of any kind in rural El Salvador.

# Cooperatives, Communal Associations and Peasant Leagues

Political opposition of any kind was carefully controlled in El Salvador. But in the early 1960s some expression of opposition was permitted in the urban areas, though channelled into electoral activity and a virtually powerless Legislative Assembly. New parties reflecting the rise of a professional middle class emerged at this time. The most significant was the Christian Democrat Party which was founded in 1960. But even this party found it difficult to organize in the rural areas where there was virtually a separate legal code, the *ley agraria*, harshly enforced by the National Guard.

But in the 1960s, state-supported peasant cooperatives and organizations began to appear, aided by US agencies under the 1961 Alliance for Progress scheme. The government aimed to pre-empt any independent organization by trying to solve some of the immediate material problems facing a sector of the peasantry and creating an organized base of political support out of this more privileged group. These efforts included the development of cooperatives and peasant associations led by US-trained peasant leaders.

More or less at the same time, sectors of the Catholic Church began to search out a role for the institution in the social as well as the spiritual realm. The early steps in this direction were by no means radical, but both the state and the church contributed to breaking down, albeit partially, the extreme isolation in which the peasantry had lived since 1932. They brought peasants together for the first time into some kind of social organization and created expectations which in most cases were not fulfilled.

# Cooperatives

The Salvadorean government had in fact considered cooperatives as a possible solution to some rural economic problems in the 1950s, though it had in mind the large landowners as well as small farmers. The idea was attractive: politically, it might generate an organized social base of support for the government, while economically it allowed for collective solutions to certain immediate problems, particularly related to the need for credit. In 1957 the Ministry of Agriculture set up a section to encourage cooperatives which functioned until 1964 when it was transferred to the Administration of Peasant Welfare (ABC). Another government body, the Salvadorean Institute for the Development of Cooperatives (INSAFOCOOP), was founded in 1971 to stimulate further the development of cooperatives.[20]

By 1967 there were 154 state-directed cooperatives officially in existence, of which 111 were active. But 74 of them were in San Salvador and were mostly credit cooperatives, with strong financial support from USAID and the Inter-American Foundation. The majority of the 21 agricultural and ranching cooperatives were amongst cotton growers and mostly involved medium and large landowners. Only a very small proportion were made up of agricultural cooperatives which included poor peasant farmers. The state-directed cooperatives never advanced very far beyond credit assistance and the government's main concern was promoting efficient economic enterprises.[21]

There was another cooperative movement developing at the same time but originating from within the church, which put much more emphasis on the social aspects of cooperatives and on their role in helping to solve some of the immediate problems of the poor peasantry. Archbishop Chávez y González was very open to the renewal movement in the Catholic Church of the 1950s and 1960s, and the idea of social action inspired by it. The Second Vatican Council (1962-65) gave further impetus to this movement. In the 1950s a group of priests in La Libertad had begun encouraging cooperatives amongst the *minifundistas*, and the inter-diocesan social secretariat was given the task of further developing such initiatives. It concerned itself with increasing the use of fertilizers, insecticides and ways of improving productivity. At first, credits were negotiated with commercial companies but later given directly through funds from a German Catholic agency, Misereor. The number of cooperatives grew from just two in 1963 to 14 in 1965, and leapt to 54 in 1971 following the establishment in 1967 of the Foundation for the Promotion of Cooperatives (FUNPROCOOP). In 1967 there were 7,493 peasant members of FUNPROCOOP cooperatives, all of them *minifundistas*.

FUNPROCOOP began to develop educational programmes for cooperative members, and in 1970 a training school for cooperative leaders was set up in Chalatenango. Chalatenango was a major focus of the organization's work, and in 1969 one third of FUNPROCOOP's 37 cooperatives were located in the department. The others were in La Libertad, San Salvador and Cuscatlán.

The cooperatives were initially welcomed by the peasants of Chalatenango. They offered some concrete solutions to the problems of access to credit and agricultural inputs, and brought peasants together to solve their problems for the first time, though in a rather paternalistic manner. On page 143, one peasant leader describes how the cooperatives acted as a first tentative step in community organization, helping to pave the way for the subsequent development of the peasants' own union movement. But their impact was limited both by the nature of the movement itself, which offered only small improvements and not solutions to fundamental problems, and by the movements' own economic constraints which made it difficult to sustain even minor improvements. In 1970 the movement entered a period of decline, mostly through lack of economic resources.

## The Unión Comunal Salvadoreña (UCS)

The US gave considerable support to the state-directed cooperatives, channelling credit at favourable rates through USAID, the Credit Union National Association and the Inter-American Foundation. But its most direct involvement was in the setting up of a peasant association, the UCS (Salvadorean Communal Union).

In 1962 USAID signed a contract with the American Institute for Free Labor Development (AIFLD) to train peasant leaders as part of the programme of the Alliance for Progress. AIFLD was created by the US national trade union federation AFL-CIO, officially 'to buttress democracy in Latin America through free and strong labor unions'. It is very much a creature of the Cold War and its political role in counteracting 'communist' organization amongst workers and peasants has been well documented.[22]

AIFLD began its work in El Salvador by organizing courses at Georgetown University, Washington, in agrarian reform and peasant problems for selected urban labour leaders from the Union of Construction Workers (STUC) and the General Confederation of Trade Unions (CGS). AIFLD also held training seminars for 'peasant leaders' (the first, in November 1965, involved 18 people), and implemented social projects, such as the building of schools, bridges and roads which were the culmination of the seminars.

AIFLD had to operate fairly cautiously in the rural areas, where no form of unionization was legal. It made contact with rural communities through parish clubs run by the aid agency, Caritas, and the Agricultural Extension Programme of the Inter-diocesan Secretariat and the Christian Democrat Party. The peasants received a daily wage while they attended the courses, but committed themselves to go back and work in their communities in accordance with the instructions given, setting up cooperatives, health centres and schools. In 1967 AIFLD carried out five more seminars in conjunction with the Christian Democrat Party which hoped that the graduates (150 that year) would go on to build up its electoral support in the countryside.

AIFLD then decided to promote the organization of peasant unions, though they were given the less provocative name of 'communal unions'. Between February and March 1968 the first of these were set up in the departments of La Paz and Usulatán and more in the same year in other departments. AIFLD also established the first cooperative in the *cantón* of Platanares in La Paz with help from the Salvadorean government and USAID. Thirty-two peasants, mostly

94

## Change through Dialogue — the UCS

It's the first peasant organization in El Salvador, the one recognized by the government. It has had legal status since October 1971 because the government finds nothing bad in it. We met in Zacatecoluca in 1967; there the movement began. We formed the directorate and the national executive and continued meeting in San Salvador. We took courses in the American Institute of Central American Union Studies (IESCA), where they helped educate us about how to work in our communities and how to help the government; the government can't do anything without the people. We came together to defend the interests of the peasants, it was our last resort. We formed cooperatives so that the peasants could save with the help of the Agricultural Development Bank (BFA). Departmental directorates were formed and after the courses we went into the villages.

. . . To be a member you have to go into the villages; we meet the peasants, we show them the statutes, and when they become aware (*concientes*) they can join our organization, paying 3.75 *colones* . . . Then they can become members of the cooperative and also get the nightly distribution of milk, flour and oil for the children (donations from Caritas), and sewing and dressmaking courses for the daughters of the family. In the town the academies charge 15-20 *colones*.

We serve as a bridge for any help from the government. For instance, we had problems with the price of fertilizer so we complained about it. The commercial agencies dropped their prices and we met to implore the government to lower the official prices to the same level, to the market price. They told us that they would lower the price for the cooperatives. We received the fertilizer from the BFA and the reduction was only for the members of the cooperatives.

The objective of the UCS is for change, but not achieved through destructive means. We don't think that violence achieves change; violence brings violence. We agree with dialogue, including demonstrations. We analyse the problems of the communities and we ask that they solve them for us, that they give support for renting land, in the renting law. The last demonstration we made was for cheaper fertilizers. We have always felt that the representative is the father of the family, that the government must have the good will to smooth out the difficulties of the people, but if the government doesn't realize this then we organize the demonstration so that it does . . . We suffer most from social injustice. This is the strength of the organization. As there are groups in each place, we communicate the problem . . . the government is always willing to help.
(Interview with UCS member.)[23]

labourers on the cotton plantation, rented 31 hectares with a loan of US$3,000 from USAID. Food was provided by Caritas. Local landowners denounced it as 'communist'. In 1969 another cooperative was set up in La Palma in Chalatenango with 472 *manzanas*.

That same year some 20 of the local communal unions representing

4,000 members were brought together to form the UCS. There were 68 peasants present, all graduates of AIFLD's courses, from the departments of San Miguel, Usulután, La Paz, Sonsonate and La Libertad. The cooperatives in particular had attracted peasants to the UCS as they seemed to offer a genuine opportunity to improve their lives.

The Honduran-Salvadorean war in 1969, which forced thousands of Salvadorean peasants to leave Honduras, helped convince the military and hence the Salvadorean government that it should support AIFLD's training programmes as a way of preventing rural social unrest. In March 1970 AIFLD signed a contract with USAID which gave a grant of US$136,000 to train peasant leaders. A number of other grants were received over the next two years which were also used to expand the UCS cooperatives. According to the list of UCS pre-cooperatives (those without legal status but functioning as cooperatives), the organization was establishing a considerable base in the western departments of Santa Ana and Ahuachapán, followed by Usulután, San Miguel, La Unión, Sonsonate and Morazán.[24] The list more or less coincides with the areas where the radical unions of the 1970s were weakest.

The UCS remained dependent on AIFLD and external funding, but it established quite a powerful grouping, at least in numerical strength, which evoked some suspicion from the Salvadorean military and landowners, who feared any form of peasant organization. In 1973 the Salvadorean government expelled AIFLD, though the immediate cause of this appears to have had more to do with a dispute over the appointment of a UCS director by AIFLD than with the organization as such.[25]

As a result, USAID funding for the AIFLD programme was cut off for 1974 and 1975, but replaced by large grants from the Inter-American Foundation (IAF), a semi-governmental private organization. Some 22 new peasant groups joined the UCS in this period, involving an estimated 545 members. The IAF hoped to increase the independence of the UCS from AIFLD,[26] but AIFLD had appointed a technical adviser, Tito Castro, a school teacher and former employee of Caritas, and an administrator, Jorge Camacho, who virtually controlled the central office. Camacho was also an agent for ORDEN and used his leadership role in the organization to control the cooperatives and their peasant members. When USAID resumed funding of AIFLD projects in El Salvador in 1975, the IAF also continued funding UCS with grants amounting to US$700,000.

With such funds flowing into the UCS there was plenty of scope for growth in its membership, which between 1973 and 1975 had increased from 30,000 to 70,000. But strict accounting was not required by the funding agencies, and there was considerable opportunity for corruption. AIFLD nurtured dissent within the organization, and

96

created suspicions between staff members by which it hoped to regain direct control over it in the resulting crisis. Suddenly in 1977 it cut off all funds to the UCS and asked the IAF to audit its finances. As a result, the UCS's 13 cooperatives almost went bankrupt. The report of the IAF auditor-investigator found widespread misappropriation of funds which it blamed on Tito Castro.

Michael Hammer, AIFLD's regional director for Central America, openly supported Castro and levelled countercharges against Rodolfo Viera and other UCS leaders. In late 1977 and early 1978 a struggle took place within the UCS over its future leadership. By this time, some politicization had taken place at the base of the movement, particularly during the Agrarian Transformation project of 1976, and partly as a result of growing repression. The UCS membership supported Viera in the struggle and Camacho was forced to leave. Subsequently the IAF and USAID cut off funding to the UCS and the membership of the organization began to decline. The activities of the radical organizations seem to have attracted some of its members, as a faction split from it in August 1978 to ally itself with one of these, FAPU (United Popular Action Front).[27] But the ideology on which the organization was founded, in particular the avoidance of any conflict with the authorities and the search for peaceful solutions to particular problems, retained its hold over many of the peasants. One estimate put its membership at 120,000 by 1980.

The organization had a brief period of relative independence, but in 1980 AIFLD once again became involved in the UCS, using it to implement the Agrarian Reform of March that year (see concluding chapter). From then on the UCS became in the words of journalist Ray Bonner, 'little more than an alter ego for AIFLD and US policy'.[28] The organization's history – its dependence on external funding, the weight of its bureaucratized central office and the careful selection and limited training of peasant leaders around certain objectives chosen for them by outsiders – had left it prey to the manipulation of those able to offer sufficient material incentives.

## The Christian Federation of Salvadorean Peasants – FECCAS

The background to the other peasant organization which emerged in the 1960s, initially as a federation of peasant leagues, lies in the Social Christian movement whose political expression was the Salvadorean Christian Democrat Party (PDC).

Christian Democracy in Latin America is a relatively recent movement. Most of the parties were founded after World War II, inspired by the role of European Christian Democrat parties in the reconstruction of West Germany, Italy and France. The movement's ideological roots lie in the social doctrine of the Catholic Church, in particular the encyclical of Pope Leo XIII, *Rerum Novarum*, in 1891. The Pope criticized both liberal capitalism and Marxist socialist theory, defending private property as a natural right but asserting that it should be used in a socially just manner. He called for state intervention to defend workers against the abuses of capitalism and supported trade unions, collective bargaining and agricultural cooperatives as a means of promoting collaboration between classes, which he denied were in conflict with each other. These ideas were developed further over the years.

In El Salvador a group of men, mostly lawyers, formed a study group to examine some of these ideas, and the Christian Democrat Party was founded in 1960. The party's first national convention was held in San Salvador in 1961; it condemned the Cuban revolution as a betrayal of the Cuban people's struggle for liberation and warned of the danger of Soviet domination of the Caribbean region. But the party was also prepared to condemn the US for its interventions in Latin America. Christian Democracy was intended as a third way in the struggle between capitalism and communism, with a spiritual element which transcended the materialism of these ideologies.

The party considered that structural reform was the key to social justice in the country but were rather vague as to how it would be brought about. Party leaders talked a great deal about economic planning through the state and the promotion of industry. But unlike a communist system where the means of production would be in the hands of the state, or a liberal system where they were in the hands of private capital, production in the ideal Christian Democrat society would be 'a free and dignified collaboration of capital and labour' with what they termed 'communitarian' ownership of the means of production:[29]

*'In spite of the protestations and denials of Christian Democratic leaders, not only in El Salvador but all over Latin America, it is hard to avoid the judgement of one North American scholar that Christian Democratic social theory is "essentially traditional, Catholic corporatism". Christian Democracy is not forward-looking; it is backward-looking: back past the dehumanizing rise of liberalism and nationalism, past the centralizing age of political absolutism, past the secularizing world of the Renaissance, back to the medieval ideal of unity and order, to a world where all Christendom was theoretically a community and where the moral laws that guided man's spiritual and personal life supposedly guided his political and economic activities as well. The applicability of this charming vision to modern industrial society is, of course, highly questionable.'[30]*

During the 1960s, the party established itself as the 'opposition' party, and in the 1968 municipal and assembly elections made sweeping gains in the major cities, including the capital. The party's strength lay in

San Salvador department, but it was increasing its support in nearby areas such as Cuscatlán, La Paz, La Libertad and to a much lesser extent, Chalatenango. In Chalatenango, some peasants, especially those involved in the church-organized cooperatives, had begun to see the PDC as a possible vehicle for change and identified with it until the fraudulent elections of 1972 and 1977 convinced many that elections and the parties associated with them were incapable of changing anything.

Agrarian reform as such was not put high on the PDC's list of priorities in the early years, though much emphasis was given to increasing productivity in the rural areas. In 1961 land redistribution was placed fifth on a list of seven proposals to improve the situation of the rural workers. Job security, an attack on rural cultural isolation, profit sharing, and the regularization of the landlord-tenant relationship came first. Throughout the first part of the 1960s, as we have seen, the party was collaborating with the peasant training schemes of AIFLD. The 1967 programme gave higher prominence to proposals to 'strengthen the family' than it did to agrarian policy. The party's proposals for agrarian reform were very moderate and not that different from government proposals of the time. It was not until the National Agrarian Reform Congress of 1970 that the party, along with other delegates to the Congress, countenanced some form of direct expropriation of property as one instrument in the redistribution of land. By then there was some shift in the climate of opinion within El Salvador as opposition forces grew a little more confident, and also as the Catholic Church entered a period of intense debate about its social role, a process which is examined in the final part of this chapter.

The party had always supported the rights of rural workers to organize in accordance with the general philosophy of the Social Christian movement. In 1954, the Latin American Confederation of Christian Trade Unionists (CLASC) had been founded to coordinate and strengthen those trade unions with Christian inspiration which had emerged in the region over the decades. In 1960 the Union of Christian Workers (UNOC) was set up in San Salvador, based on the principles of CLASC. From 1963-1964, UNOC began to establish links with peasants with the aim of promoting peasant organization, and by 1964 the first sympathetic peasant groups had appeared in the departments of San Salvador, La Libertad and Cabañas. They were called unions, associations, leagues or committees and were to be the first bases of the Christian Federation of Salvadorean Peasants (FECCAS). The movement was encouraged by a number of priests and the Christian Democrat Party.

The first Peasant Congress took place from 22 to 26 July 1965 in Cabañas. It defined some of the principles of the Federation which took their inspiration from Social Christian doctrine. The second National Council of Christian Peasants took place in December 1967 with

## FECCAS

At first the peasant movement was too much influenced by different political tendencies, especially certain 'reformist' parties. Many of us participated in the Christian Democrat Party at the time. The situation under which the peasantry was being exploited was intolerable, in no way could it be suffered any longer. The first peasant union of the Christian Democrats, the Christian Federation of Salvadorean Peasants, FECCAS, emerged in the mid-sixties and really didn't last much longer than nine years. It evolved solely around demands for economic improvement. This in turn gave the peasants a certain political confidence. But as there were no other activities taking place, and as there was not too much political clarity amongst the agricultural workers, the different tendencies were able to manipulate the union.

What soon became clear to a number of us was the need for an organization solely representing our interests, which would be independent; an organization that would involve the workers and peasants in the economic struggle and extend it to the political struggle. But from 1974 onwards, FECCAS changed, as people lost faith in its politics and style of organization. It began to change its passive Christian methods towards more combative methods. The UTC also emerged at this time in Chalate, through a few Christian communities which had become aware and politicized. (Ramón)

representation from 16 agrarian associations, with about 30 members each, a total of some 480 affiliates.[31] The second Peasant Congress was held in August 1968 and this defined the organization's objectives more fully and included agrarian reform. The organization began to stress in its publications not only agrarian reform and the need for peasant organization, but also the need to seek changes in the existing social order.

On 1 May 1968, FECCAS in conjunction with UNOC organized its first public meeting in Suchitoto for all the peasants in the area. But the organization was not growing very rapidly and was soon weakened by the collapse of UNOC in 1969 which had helped hold the organization together. By 1969, according to the report of the General Secretary to the VIth Latin American Seminar of Peasant Leaders, FECCAS had increased its total membership to only 500 with 20 affiliated peasant leagues. It probably had no more than 1,000 to 1,500 members by the early 1970s.

FECCAS now tried to link itself with different union federations which emerged after UNOC and with the Latin American Workers' Congress (CLAT). But it never achieved any real coherence or clarity of purpose, nor did it attempt to organize a peasant movement as such around its stated objectives. There is little evidence, even, that at this time it attracted much attention from the authorities. It seems to have kept mostly within legal bounds, though undoubtedly it was watched by the repressive forces. The Third Congress of the organization in 1970 stressed again its commitment to structural economic, social, cultural and political change: 'We don't want to create exploiters or exploited, we want the liberation of the peasant from the system which hurts his dignity as a human being', (FECCAS, *III Congreso Nacional de Campesinos Salvadoreños*).[32] But from then until 1974 when new life was breathed into the organization through the work of a radicalized church, it remained a weak and ineffective organization. The Christian Democrat Party used it to rally electoral support, and as a result of the party's alliance with the Communist Party in the 1972 elections, FECCAS allied itself briefly with that party's peasant association, ATACES (Association of Salvadorean Farmworkers), which was set up in 1971.

## The Church and Change

The 1960s had seen important debates open up in the heart of the Catholic Church and many new experiences to feed into them. The second Vatican Council of 1964 had launched the church into a new realm of social responsibility which was clearly welcomed by Archbishop Chávez. In August 1966 he had issued a pastoral letter, 'The Responsibility of the Laity in the Ordering of Temporal Life', which publicly distanced the church from the military government who saw it as supporting the Christian Democrat Party. That same year a number of peasants had been imprisoned for possessing 'subversive literature' which turned out to be copies of Pope John XXIII's encyclical, *Pacem in Terris*, which the Christian Democrats had distributed.

Through the cooperative movement, some priests had become more directly involved in peasant life and a few began to help members of FECCAS. In 1967 the Centre of Social Studies and Popular Promotion (CESPROP) was set up under the direction of the youth wing of the Christian Democrat Party, but sponsored by the Archdiocese. It offered advice to FECCAS and prepared papers on the country's situation; a number of its members would later join the revolutionary movement. Another group inspired by the Social Christian doctrines which were also behind the Christian Democrat Party had emerged in the University in 1964. By 1967 it was questioning the party's conservatism, its community action projects in some of the towns it controlled, and ultimately its electoralism as such. In 1968 the Salvadorean bishops attended the conference of Latin American bishops in Medellín where the 'option for the poor' was adopted, resulting in a deeper commitment amongst greater numbers

## The First Base Communities

In December 1968 I was asked to take Suchitoto parish for a while. The message of Medellín was very familiar to me. We studied it in the Institute in Ecuador with many of the most important Latin American scholars at that time. So when I came to my parish, I immediately started to try to inform my people about the message from Medellín, and to think about the possibilities of organizing Christian 'base communities'. In February 1969 I visited each village in the parish and I gave a speech on the need for change following Medellín and tried to make them understand that the change was not coming from the outside but from the inside, from their own communities, about the need to have leaders, native leaders and also to prepare them in a better way. I had 24 villages in my parish of 45,000 people. After every meeting people were divided into different groups. They chose one person to come to Suchitoto and I gave the first course which lasted two months. They lived in my house, sleeping and eating there, and began the formation of the community with the teachings of the Holy Bible. One week before the end of the course I asked them which main themes they wanted to transmit to the people and we developed a scheme summarizing all the topics they wanted to teach their *compañeros* in the countryside and the villages, and that was the programme for a year.

For example, there was one case when we discussed the reading of Chapter 4 of the Apostles which talks of the first Christians who owned everything together and there was no poverty amongst them; so our work was to read the Bible text and to give a short introduction. The people split up into groups to comment on the text; they elected a secretary, who celebrated the Eucharist, instead of me. And then everyone came to give their reaction, and finally I summarized the message which the peasants had given in order to provide a common representation of the different groups' views. On that occasion, I remember it well, the children, who were always present, came and said to me, 'We have also studied the text of the Bible, and we think that here in our village it's not like it was in the first Christian communities, but we would like it to be that way.' I asked them why: 'Because our parents continue fighting over their things, my mother says the chickens are hers, and my father says the cows are his; all this means that they are not working together, that they don't own things collectively. We would like our parents to put their things together, own them collectively, and we would help them with it, too.'

As a result of a direct confrontation in 1969 between the authorities, the *Guardias* and the peasants, we started a peasants' organization. FECCAS was already there, following a Christian Democrat line at the time, being more a tool of the PDC than anything else, yet they gave a lot of support. We also discussed the new relationship between the state and the individual, another lesson from Medellín. In 1970 we looked at baptism, the role of prophets and priests, and applied our study to the socio-economic realities of El Salvador. The peasants discovered they were not kings, they were slaves. So we discussed how to have domain of the land in order to be lords not slaves, and we discovered that the way was through land reform. The peasants participated in all this, and we had many, many courses. So I would say that that was the beginning of a new way of thinking in our peasantry. At the end I had 33 people, they called themselves *'responsables de comunidad'* (those responsible for the community), and they organized Christian base communities in their own villages.

We organized the peasants to defend themselves. If they heard the bells ringing in a certain way they were meant to come to Suchitoto immediately. During the second teachers' strike, 37 teachers were arrested in Suchitoto; when I arrived at 1.30pm I talked to the teachers in prison through a loudspeaker and told them that we needed to involve the peasants, so I went to the agrarian school which teaches peasants how to cultivate the land. I put 12 people in my jeep and I said we should take the horses and go to the villages. We started ringing the bells at 4pm, and by 7pm we had 10,000 people in Suchitoto — that was the organization we had created in a year and a half. The day after, the judge released the teachers.

I used a number of methods in my pastoral work: one was cultural anthropology, the analysis we made with the peasants about the value of land, of work, of health or death, the concept of religious celebration, of sacramental celebration, all these were values which I tried to help them to discuss, so that they might acquire a new evaluation of life. For example, in the case of the death of a child, we had to ask ourselves why that child had died, whether it was because God had wished it to, or because in a society where there are no hospitals, no health programmes and where the doctors are concentrated in the capital, whether all these factors caused the death. When later the people from the city came to work with the peasants, they brought with them the ideological paternalism which created certain difficulties. But the peasants could still respond with their own answers. You see, we had to deal with another element, which belongs to both culture and history, and which is one of the most important instruments of oppressing the people: to deny it the right to express itself. And in this the Church has been one of the principal instruments of oppression. The priest knows what he is saying in his prayers, no-one else knows how to articulate, and it is he who can interpret the Bible. The others don't know what to say, so that concern was to give the Word back to the people, and one of the ways of doing that was through the celebration of the Word. (José Alas)

of the Salvadorean clergy to work for change.

One of the first priests to try and implement some of the new ideas of 'conscientization' emerging at the time was José Alas. He came to the parish of Suchitoto in December 1968, having spent some time studying in Quito with the Bishop of Riobamba. He established the

*The changing role of the church; lay preacher*

first Christian Base Communities in El Salvador in 1969, and began short Bible study courses for peasants at the end of which they elected Delegates of the Word. He describes his work in the box on pages 102-3.

Alas' work soon involved him directly in the peasants' problems. Resentment had developed amongst the peasants of the area at the way two of the local landowners, Roberto Hill and Miguel Salaverría, were speculating with land in the area. Some 3,000 peasants marched to one of the *haciendas* that Hill had purchased for subdivision into plots and resale. Four hundred then went to San Salvador to demonstrate, the first such event since 1932. José Alas went with them and managed to get the support of the Archbishop. Subsequently the National Assembly voted to force Hill to sell the plots at a lower price. It was, however, a sign of things to come when the following year, Alas was chosen to present the church's position on the question of agrarian reform to the Agrarian Reform Congress convened by the National Assembly. Hours after his presentation he was abducted by men in civilian clothes, beaten, drugged and left naked on the edge of a cliff just outside San Salvador.

Cornell Capa

*A Delegate of the Word taking church service*

# 4
# PEASANTS AND CATALYSTS

## Catalysts

What makes peasants rebel? It is one of the great questions of twentieth century world history. Contrary to expectations, most of the revolutions that have taken place have been in predominantly peasant societies. 'The process of modernization begins with peasant revolutions that fail', writes Barrington Moore: 'It culminates during the twentieth century with peasant revolutions that succeed. No longer is it possible to take seriously the view that the peasant is an "object of history", a form of social life over which historical changes pass but which contributes nothing to the impetus of these changes'.[1]

Violence simmers below the surface of peasant societies where inequalities are as evident as in El Salvador. This may lead to localized, spontaneous and bloody uprisings. They are usually incapable, however, of becoming a sustained threat to the existing social order. Such outbursts are numerous in history, sometimes provoked by frustrated expectations of a better life. More often the lid is kept firmly on the rural communities by the threat or practice of violence, what Gerrit Huizer calls the 'culture of repression', and this is certainly one major way control has been exercised in El Salvador. Often there are other more subtle ways of ensuring passivity as well; the traditional teachings of the church being an example.

The weight of repression, together with the peasant's preoccupation with everyday survival, his parochialism and his attachment to his own plot of land, are often used to suggest that peasants are unable to act cohesively as a class, work out their own ideology and objectives or produce their own leaders and organization. The conclusion usually drawn is that they are not a revolutionary force capable of overthrowing the existing social order on their own. Eric Wolf poses the problem:

*'But what of the transition from peasant rebellion to revolution, from a movement aimed at the redress of the wrongs, to the attempted overthrow of society itself? Marxists in general have long argued that peasants without outside leadership cannot make a revolution; and our case material would*

*bear them out. Where peasantry had successfully rebelled against the established order – under its own banner and with its own leaders – it was sometimes able to reshape the social structure of the countryside closer to its heart's desires; but it did not lay hold of the state, of the cities which house the centers of control, of the strategic agricultural resources of the society. Zapata stayed in his Morelos; the "folk migration" of Pancho Villa simply receded after the defeat at Torreón . . ."[2]*

More than this, Wolf asserts, the peasantry are 'natural anarchists'; they reject the state as an evil intrusion which must be replaced by their peasant Utopia, the free village, and a social order organized without a state.

The element which turns peasant anarchism into peasant revolution comes, it seems, from outside the peasantry. Gerrit Huizer writes: 'Whether the increasingly favourable climate for militant peasant movements will be utilized depends to a large extent on the willingness of urban allies to support and guide the peasant organizations. Practically all cases of peasant movements known to be strong have had such allies.'[3] The 1932 uprising in El Salvador certainly illustrates the crucial role of urban workers and intellectuals in organizing the peasant movement.

Having said that outside 'agents' have a critical role to play, how does the relationship develop in practice? Do the peasants become a tool of these 'agents' or is a genuine alliance forged, with the peasants producing their own leadership? This chapter attempts to illuminate these issues in the case of El Salvador.

In Chalatenango, as elsewhere in El Salvador, there were two clear stages in the political awakening of the peasantry involving external elements. The first was the 'conscientizing' process itself, in which the peasant came to understand the forces which exploit and oppress him, and for the first time was encouraged to see organizing against those forces as a possible response. This process came as a result of dramatic changes within the very institution which had previously controlled the peasant's view of himself and his universe: the Catholic Church. The second phase of the process was the emergence of organizations which could turn a newly-awakened peasantry into an organized and disciplined revolutionary force, and forge the alliances needed to guarantee a sustained challenge to the ruling order. This role was played by the revolutionary movements which emerged in El Salvador in the early 1970s.

What some have called 'agents', I prefer to call catalysts, as does Carlos Cabarrús in his study of the peasant movement in Aguilares. The peasants were not passive recipients of a revolutionary message from outside. Peasants are cautious and distrustful of outside attempts to mobilize them unless these relate to aspirations they already possess.

The efforts to organize cooperatives and peasant associations in the 1960s had created expectations of improvements in the peasants' lives. These, though they were in most cases quickly frustrated, did begin the process of breaking the ruling party's monopoly over political life. At this point the first catalyst emerged: the radicalized sector of the Catholic Church, whose objective was to implement new pastoral methods in accordance with the teachings of Vatican II and Medellín. The significance of this work was not that it presented the peasants with ready-made answers for them to act upon. The church's new pastoral methods brought the peasants together in a structured form through the Christian base communities. They were encouraged, with the guidance of the priest, to participate in a process of awareness-building aimed at putting them in control of their own lives. In the past, parishioners had been passive recipients of the 'Word' from an unapproachable priesthood. Now, lay people, elected by their fellow parishioners, were given active roles as teachers and preachers in the church, with a dramatic and ultimately political effect which no-one could have entirely predicted.

The second catalyst, the revolutionary organizations – in Chalatenango the FPL (Popular Liberation Forces) – did not then turn the peasants into revolutionaries overnight. The peasants gained experience of organization through the peasant union, the UTC (Union of Rural Workers). They ran the union themselves, fighting over issues of concern to them and collaborating with their allies: the students and workers in San Salvador. This experience proved far more powerful than anything they could be told by the revolutionary organization. Through it, the peasants were forced to confront the state. What began as an organized effort to gain cheaper fertilizer, access to credit, better wages on the plantations, was turned by the immediately repressive response of the government into a political movement. It was at this moment that most peasants chose to look to the revolutionary organization for guidance and support (though many of their own leaders were already collaborating with the FPL), and a genuinely popular revolutionary movement was born.

# Catalyst One: The Church

By 1970, the Salvadorean church was no longer the monolithic pillar of the establishment it had once been. Fissures had begun to appear when Vatican II and Medellín challenged its traditional relationship to politics and society. Archbishop Chávez and his auxiliary, Bishop Rivera, played an important part in the subsequent reassessment of the church's role and actively promoted new pastoral methods. The adoption of these new pastoral methods was reinforced by the great

109

difficulties the church faced in fulfilling its pastoral role. The Church in Latin America in general suffers from a shortage of priests. In El Salvador the proportion of parishioners to clergy is 10,000 to one.

The Archdiocese of San Salvador (which includes the departments of San Salvador, Chalatenango, La Libertad and Cuscatlán) was at the centre of debates on how to implement the new social doctrines which came out of Vatican II and Medellín. In other dioceses the Bishops were mostly reluctant to consider the changes under discussion, but they could not shelter all the priests and nuns working in their diocese from the influence of the new ideas.

In any case, the largest number of priests and nuns were in the Archdiocese. There were 106 priests in the Archdiocese in 1965, compared with 30 in the dioceses of Santa Ana and San Vicente, and 29 in San Miguel. The priests were predominantly Salvadorean nationals of peasant origin, though usually not from the very poorest families. There were also 1,125 members of religious orders (775 women and 350 men) concentrated mostly in the Archdiocese, three-quarters of whom were foreign. Most of the non-Salvadoreans were Spanish and Italian, but there were some North American missionaries and a small community of Irish Franciscans and Saint Clare nuns working in the Gotera area.[4] But with many of the religious orders involved in education and with the small number of priests, pastoral work was neglected, particularly in the rural areas. The diocese of San Miguel for instance, had over 30,000 parishioners to every priest, and much of the area was remote and difficult to reach. One of the major changes which came in the 1970s was that many of the religious orders went into the rural areas and played an important role in the spread of the new pastoral methods.

By 1970, the church was debating its role intensely: ferment which would intensify in the ensuing years as the church's work brought it into confrontation with the state. Archbishop Chávez reflected a position within liberation theology which did not countenance the priests taking their own political stance, though they could 'accompany' the people. Many priests began to move more directly into the political realm; some, in their search for a method for understanding society, turning to Marxism though rejecting its materialist base. They began to put forward the view that the church should not just defend the right of the people to organize but should become actively involved in the organizations which emerge from the people.

Others, such as Oscar Romero (appointed in 1970 as auxiliary Bishop to Archbishop Chávez), wanted to keep pace with the changes within the church but were more cautious in their interpretation of Vatican II and Medellín. Romero was worried that the new theology would threaten the authentic teachings of the church and the divinity of Christ, and that liberation would be interpreted in too temporal and

110

material a manner.

In the midst of the debates, the Salvadorean Episcopal Conference (CEDES) agreed to the convocation of a national pastoral week in July 1970. The Archdiocese of San Salvador played the dominant role in organizing the week. First there was to be a study of the socio-economic situation of the country, followed by theological reflection from which some conclusions would be drawn.

In the end only Archbishop Chávez and Bishop Rivera from the hierarchy participated for all five days of the event, together with 123 priests, clerical and lay workers from all over the country. Oscar Romero participated for some of the time, while of the other four Bishops, only Bishop Barrera of Santa Ana responded to a telegram from the assembly asking him to attend for the last two days.

The final document caused great controversy with the Bishops who had not attended. The document was very critical of the existing work in the church. 'There is no proper evangelization', it stated and criticized the church for not working to advance liberation, partly out of 'fear of losing privileges or suffering persecutions'.[5] The document included a list of decisions: to establish base communities, to end clericalism and 'to form leaders who will be not only catechists but responsible individuals dedicated to the integral development of the human person and the formation of communities'. Lay pastoral agents were seen as an indispensable means of bringing the Gospel to the peasant masses, but the Bishops objected very strongly.

The Bishops then modified the document, diluting the first part which was an analysis of the structural injustices and institutionalized violence in the country. The amendment drew strong criticisms from many participants, among them the Jesuit, Rutilio Grande, who had been on the drafting committee of the original document. He argued that a good analysis of national reality was a prerequisite for the clergy. He denounced the Bishops' deletion of the references to Vatican II and Medellín in the second part and their stress on individualism to the detriment of 'the dimension of community between man, society and the church.'[6]

But the Bishops could not prevent the impact the week was to have on the church's future pastoral work. The document was seen by many as a break with the 'new Christianity' which had dominated debate until then, and the beginning of a 'new model of the church':

*'Firstly, because it meant the break with the elitist pastoralism of the new Christianity, giving way to a new pastoralism of the Christian base communities. Secondly, because it represented the official recognition of the active participation of lay people in the spiritual work of the Salvadorean church. Thirdly, for the importance which it gave to the word of God, to the Bible, in the work of the communities. And finally, for the great impulse which the prophetic pastoral received from the support of the information*

111

*media of the church.'*[7]

Christian base communities were now organized in many parts of the country in a wave of new pastoral activity, particularly in the rural areas, but also in the marginal zones of the capital. The experience of the Jesuits which began in September 1972 in Aguilares, San Salvador department, is probably the best known and documented of this work, but it was by no means the only one. There was already a group of priests whose work was greatly stimulated by the pastoral week. They were mostly Salvadorean (the Alas brothers, David Rodríguez and Rutilio Sánchez), but included some foreigners. They worked in San Salvador, Chalatenango, San Vicente and Morazán and began coordinating their efforts more closely. They were joined by a number of sisters whose religious orders now sent them into the countryside encouraged by Archbishop Chávez. According to the assessment of Bishop Rivera, the most significant areas of work were Aguilares, Guazapa, Ilopango, San Sebastián-Ciudad Delgado, the zone of Zacamil, San Antonio Abad, Ayutuxtepeque as well as Suchitoto, Opico, Quezaltepeque, Ciudad Arce, Chalatenango town, Dulce Nombre de María, La Palma and Cojutepeque.[8] Father Benito Tobar who played an important role in Chalatenango at this time described the work which rose out of the Pastoral week:

*'From that moment pastoral agents began widespread Bible distribution, not just for people to get to know it but to have it in their communities and to use it like a machete as the working tool every Christian ought to have . . . It was during the first half of the 1970s that lay people took charge of the work of the church . . . bringing people together . . . planning courses . . . meeting to study and see how to solve community problems. It is interesting to see the changes brought about . . . There are* cantones *in Chalatenango, San Vicente, Morazán, Cuscatlán . . . where . . . peasants just got together to get drunk, celebrating the weekend, getting 'happy'. Starting with the Word of God . . . with the work of catechists and communities, everything changes . . . They feel that they are not just the catechist . . . but the priest in the community, they bring the community together, prepare an agenda, celebrate the liturgy in their own way, starting with God's Word, asking questions about what the reading says, then discussing the commitment they are going to make.*

*We would see how they would go out of the celebration of the Word to destroy a clandestine liquor-still that someone might have that was doing damage to the community. Or they would go to help Don Pedro who was sick, giving him a little gift, some money, a pound of corn or beans, whatever they could. Or they would go to help Doña María, whose house was sagging because she was a widow and had no one to help her.'*[9]

The Christian base communities were seen as a means of implementing

112

the teachings of Vatican II through the participation of the laity in church life. One of the key elements of the grassroots communities was the way they sought to involve lay people in church functions previously closed to them. This was also a way of extending the church's reach; given the small number of priests in relation to the population, this reach was very limited. For many poor peasants Catholicism had been reduced to a few rituals to ensure protection against an uncertain future.

Each base community would be quite small, about 30 people, and would concentrate on Bible study and a community approach to the sacraments. Instruction in the faith was seen as essential, not only to prepare for first communion, but also for confirmation, marriage and baptism. A priest would direct the work of the group, but they would be encouraged to elect their own leaders – those who showed most willingness to serve the community. Catechists, or lay teachers, would be elected to teach Christian doctrine and take responsibility for the Christian education of the community. Delegates of the Word – men or women – were lay preachers who could do most of the tasks of the priest, including the weekly celebration of the Word of God, though not the sacramental functions.

Often the lay leaders would receive additional training. Between 1970 and 1976, seven centres were set up in El Salvador for training catechists and delegates, and some 15,000 leaders were trained over the decade.[10] They received a broad training not only in Bible study but also in agriculture, cooperativism, leadership and health, 'because', said Walter Guerra, a Salvadorean priest involved in the training centres, 'the catechist, among us, is a man who works not only as a religious person, but assumes leadership that is also social, including, at times, political in our rural communities'.[11]

## The Results of the New Pastoralism

Although the emphasis of the base communities was pastoral, the political implications of the work are inescapable. The first of these is the content of the new pastoral message itself. The Bible was used to reveal to the people a just God who cares for the poor and oppressed, who had made the land so that all could enjoy its fruits and who certainly did not will any of His children to be poor. Gone was the traditional church's message of passivity and submission, with its stress on heavenly rewards to relieve present pain. The message, drawn from the Bible, was that the poor had the right to seek justice here and now through their own organizations.

A second political implication was the promotion of community organization. The base communities were intended to strengthen the community, but they also helped forge links between communities, providing a structured network of the most oppressed, but increasingly the most politically conscious, sector of society. It was a network out of the reach of the existing political parties and therefore the seed of a genuinely independent peasant movement. Many of the lay leaders who emerged from the base communities were to take the work of the priests a stage further when they saw the need for a broader organization of all the peasants; a development, as we shall see, not without certain dilemmas for the priests.

The diffusion of the new work of the church was greatly facilitated by its communication media. Particularly important among these were the archdiocesan radio, YSAX, and *Justicia y Paz*, the bulletin of the rural Christian communities, edited by a priest of the Archdiocese with the moral backing of Bishop Rivera. In a country where the media is firmly in the control of the right such alternative sources of information had quite an impact.

One of the most significant experiences of the new pastoral work was that of the Jesuits in Aguilares. Although much has been written about their work it is worth recalling the major elements here as a concrete example of how the church's activities affected the emergence of the peasant movement in El Salvador.

There were some 59 Jesuits, 44 of them priests, living, working and studying in El Salvador in the early 1970s.[12] They operated the Central American University (UCA) and a large high school, the Externado San José. They also ran the seminary of San José de la Montaña until 1972 when the Bishops grew concerned at the 'liberating education' the seminarians were receiving. Their work was chiefly in the capital and mostly concerned with education. Rutilio Grande was one of those who saw the need to work amongst the poor in the countryside. A fellow Jesuit, Angel Chus, had spent a little time with José Alas in Suchitoto getting to know his methods of work with the peasants, and saw the impact Alas had had in the area.

Rutilio Grande was the Jesuit who led the team into a new area of work in Aguilares. He had spent some months in the Latin American Pastoral Institute in Ecuador in 1972 where his contact with the work of Monseñor Leonidas Proano, Bishop of Riobamba, helped him to formulate his ideas more clearly. The choice of parish was not his own as he had been born in El Paisnal and was not anxious to return to the same area. But encouraged by Archbishop Chávez, this is where he began to work in September 1972.

It was a highly populated parish of 33,000 people: 10,000 in Aguilares itself, 2,000 in El Paisnal and the rest scattered in various *cantones*. The area was dominated by 35 large estates mostly dedicated to sugar cane. There were three large sugar mills in the area, La Cabaña, San Francisco and Colima, which employed temporary labour. The sugar harvest absorbed more labour and drew it from other

114

regions, notably Chalatenango. Land use differs from Chalatenango as it is quite a fertile region and an important part of the agro-exporting economy. But in practice the situation of the peasantry is very similar. They live on the poorest soils that the landowners cannot use. The majority of the peasants form a semi-proletariat, renting or owning tiny plots which cannot sustain the family all year round.

The region thus manifested all the problems of Salvadorean rural society as a whole. From the pastoral point of view there was a concern that the neglect of the area contributed to a semi-magical form of peasant religiosity: a great worship of the saints, an almost reverential acceptance of the present order of things, and fatalism – a belief that only a holy miracle could change the peasants' lives. The new team aimed to 'bring the Gospel down to earth'.[13] Rutilio's message was 'God is not in the clouds lying in a hammock, God acts and wants you to build his Kingdom here on earth'. There were three dimensions to the mission of the team: evangelization, community and leadership. The first was the responsibility of the priest, Rutilio maintained. But once there was a movement, pastoral agents (who would serve as a link between the community and the parish) and the communities themselves must continue it; for the objective was that the people take control of their own lives.

The team was made up of four Jesuit priests and a number of students preparing to be Jesuits, together with other students who came to help on particular tasks. The Jesuits brought with them a strong organization and structure and a very methodical approach to the task they had set themselves. The first phase of their work, between September 1972 and June 1973, was one of evangelization and getting to know the area. The parish was divided up and there were two-week missions to each part during which the team lived and ate with the peasants and gathered data on the area. The whole community were invited to an evening session, when the scriptures were read, with periods for questions and comment. This was followed by smaller group discussions. The community elected their Delegates of the Word at the end of the two weeks, but the emphasis was on everyone's involvement in the life of the community. The leadership was as collective as possible, with the stress on service to the community rather than domination in it. There was a Delegate in fact for every four or five people with sometimes 15 or 20 in each community. The biography of Rutilio Grande published by the UCA points out the difference between the approach of the Aguilares team and that in other areas of Latin America:

'The method used in Aguilares was different in certain characteristics from other base communities in Latin America. At times the base communities emphasized the establishment of a small community counterposed to the great church community; communities with a human dimension, able to *question and rise above cultural Catholicism. The leaders of these communities were sometimes called Delegates of the Word, although other lay ministries had been developed in the communities . . . (in these cases) the permanent training has been monopolized by the priest, the religious or the lay person. The work in Aguilares took another direction towards the base. No clear definition of the Christian community was given; the leadership was more collective and varied. The people were prepared to use the Bible spontaneously in response to daily events. If the focus of the experience was evangelization, it had political repercussions. It was not necessary to tell the peasants that they were oppressed or who were the oppressors. Both things were clear to be seen. They came to understand perfectly that such situations were anti-Christian and the Gospel, far from exhorting resignation, asked them to fight against it.'[14]*

By the end of the end of the first phase of the mission there were ten communities in the urban areas and 27 in the rural areas, with one priest in charge of the urban and one in charge of the rural work, maintaining close contact with each community.

The political repercussions of the work were soon apparent. Attitudes were changing in the wake of the fraudulent 1972 presidential election. Many were disillusioned with the electoral system, and with all parties participating in it, including the three opposition parties (the Christian Democrats, the Communist Party, and the Social Democrat Party) which had contested the election with a unified slate. With the arrival of the Jesuits, the Christian Democrat Party and the Communist Party found it much more difficult to work in the parish. On 25 May 1973, only eight months after the parish team had arrived, the 1,600 workers of La Cabaña sugar mill went on strike and refused to accept wages which they claimed were lower than they had been promised.

The strike had nothing to do with the parish team. Indeed it was a spontaneous movement, though some members of the peasant union FECCAS, were involved. But, most significantly, a number of the leading participants were Delegates of the Word. The evangelizing work of the priests had had its impact. The Ministry of Labour sent an inspector who upheld the company's position and then the National Guard was called in. This pressure persuaded some workers to accept the pay. Other workers remained firm and the company had to grant a wage rise, although not quite at the level originally promised. It was a first victory and boosted the peasants' confidence, although many strikers were subsequently blacklisted by all the mills in the area.

The second phase of the work of the parish team began in June 1973 and was extended until August 1976. A key element in this period was the preparation of the Delegates of the Word who would take over many of the functions of the priest, thus avoiding dependence on them. There were 326 Delegates by the end of the period and a number of

116

*Preparadores* (literally: 'preparers') elected by the community, who acted as a link between the priests and the base community. The priests organized a series of courses in this period to help the communities and the Delegates to develop. They dealt with social as well as religious issues: such as the Bible, national reality, history and cooperatives. A course was also held on the municipal elections of 1974, which was called a 'political vaccination' against attempts to manipulate the people during the forthcoming campaign.

At the same time, similar work was begun independently in Chalatenango. A number of *municipios* became centres from which the organization of the base communities spread to the outlying rural areas such as: Arcatao, San José Las Flores, Nueva Trinidad, Las Vueltas, Dulce Nombre de María, Tejutla and a number of *cantones* — Portillo de Norte, El Jícaro, Hacienda Vieja, San José Conacaste, San Luis de Carmen and El Terrero. The following are the peasants' own accounts of the impact this had on them:

**At that time, there was no such thing as the popular church, but some priests, who could be called neither political nor revolutionary, began to explain things to the people. That as religious people, it was necessary to think more about the future, to think more about liberation, that man must be free and that this was one of the laws of the Bible and we should read and think about it. Of course, for the peasants this had a lot of political content. But that wasn't the intention of many of the priests who talked in those terms; there was one priest whose family were coffee growers near Santiago de María. But it made the people think when they heard these things. The church gave the people a different interpretation of their lives, one related to the problems in the Bible. When they thought about concrete issues they began to organize themselves. The priests preached the Gospel, but it was us, the peasants, who set up our organization. (Caravina)**

---

**The first thing that motivated me was what I studied in the New Testament; I found one of the texts where it made me think that it was necessary to feel more committed to the people and to find a way of organizing. And when an organization emerged, which was working in defence of the interests of us peasants, when the UTC was born here in Chalatenango, I felt myself committed to the people, and I joined the UTC. I didn't have the opportunity to study with priests, but in my village I got close to some Christians, who brought the Word to the people and I learnt something of the Bible through them. (Enrique)**

With me it was the same: it was through the study of the Bible that I decided to join the UTC; it was there that I realized that a man can't do things alone but that his capacity comes through working with the *compañeros*, and then being able to form an organization. So through the popular church I began to recognize the need for an organization of the people. Because when we are alone on the sugar cane, cotton or coffee plantations, by ourselves, if we demand our just rights there is repression. Under these conditions we saw that we needed an organization to join the people together. In that way we could put forward our demands with more security. (Evaristo)

---

What made me first realize the path of our farmworkers' union was when I compared the conditions we were living in with those that I saw in the Scriptures; the situation of the Israelites for example, . . . where Moses had to struggle to take them out of Egypt to the Promised Land . . . then I compared it with the situation of slavery in which we were living. For example, when we asked for changes in work rates on the plantations, instead of reducing them for us, the following day they increased it, just like the Pharaoh did with the Hebrew people making bricks, right? . . . Our struggle is the same; Moses and his people had to cross the desert, as we are crossing one right now; and for me, I find that we are crossing a desert full of a thousand hardships, of hunger, misery, and of exploitation. (Vidal)

---

The church has undergone a true deepening in understanding of what evangelization and Bible study really means; in a certain way this also allowed us to realize that we are brothers, and that as brothers we ought to unite rather than divide. The UTC had its origins in Chalate and San Vicente, both with a truly popular church. The priests were already stigmatized as agitators.

The need to set up a popular church emerged as the people needed an authentic religion, to be able to understand the reality they lived in. Christian base groups were set up and then Bible study groups where one discussed, read a parable and from there we went to talk to the people about what was happening and what the Bible had to say about it. As *celebrador* I went to Arcatao where we were given talks and later I went on a course in San Salvador, in the Seminary of San José Montaña for 18 days. There we discussed the need for an organization of the peasants. Later I was elected secretary of the local UTC branch, to organize the demonstrations. We organized some entertainment like protest songs and dances, and we talked about how to advance the struggle by peaceful means.

We talked to those who were against the organization, telling them that they too were peasants and could take part in their organization. (Fausto)

---

I first noticed a change . . . because the priests spoke more clearly to us, not deceitfully, telling us that Jesus Christ came to earth to liberate people. There is a difference, because a priest that only prays and prays and doesn't concern himself with what the people are suffering, stops being a priest, however much he might have studied. The priests would charge 10 *colones* for a christening, 15 *colones* for a wedding, or more, but the priests of the popular church wouldn't charge anything. (Tomás)

The political impact of the pastoral work was growing day by day. As consciousness grew amongst the peasants, so did their desire to organize. FECCAS began to increase its numbers considerably in Aguilares: in the first six months of 1974 it founded local groups in the Christian communities of the parish. The increasing cost of living in these years mobilized many peasants, particularly as the rising costs of chemical fertilizer undermined the cooperatives and disillusionment with this option set in. The new, more militant, members of FECCAS proved a major challenge to the traditional influence of the Christian Democrats. In August 1974, FECCAS ended its ties with the Communist Party's peasant organization, ATACES, breaking alliances of the 1972 electoral period. In December, some 200 peasants from FECCAS attended a seminar at the UCA, dividing themselves into fifteen groups each led by one student. The seminar concluded that the capitalist system was the root cause of the peasants' problems.[15] Already, the church's activities in stimulating consciousness at the base through discussion and debate, was producing an increasingly self-confident peasantry. Peasant leaders were now much more capable of making up their own minds on the political options competing for their support.

For Rutilio Grande and some other priests, this growing radicalism produced real personal dilemmas. From the middle of 1973, in the words of the UCA biography of Rutilio, 'he lived with a deep internal conflict between the purity of his ideals and hard reality. On the one hand, he wanted to carry out his work as religious leader amongst his people without committing himself directly to the activities of the peasant organization; but on the other, the very fact of living with his people led him at times to involvement in situations with political repercussions, in the broadest sense of the word.'[16]

In December 1975 FECCAS was organizing its first public

120

demonstration and some Delegates of the Word asked him to celebrate a Mass for the occasion outside the normal hours and exclusively for FECCAS. Grande and his team refused, but agreed instead to celebrate a 'Peasant Christmas' in the church at Mass time and allowed FECCAS to hold its demonstration outside the church afterwards, on condition that there were no banners or slogans shouted in church. Grande's homily summed up his dilemma: 'We cannot marry ourselves with political groups of any kind, but we cannot remain indifferent to the politics of the common good of the great majorities, the people . . . we cannot wash our hands of this today nor ever.'[17]

Priests reacted differently to similar situations in various parts of the country. In parts of Chalatenango there seems to have been less concern with keeping a distance between evangelization and collaboration with the peasant union which emerged in 1974, and a greater openness toward the revolutionary movement itself as it began work in the area.

In Suchitoto, José Alas, who had been joined by his brother Higinio in 1972, became increasingly involved in helping the peasants organize an independent movement. His parishioners had been particularly affected by the flooding of thousands of hectares of land to build the Cerrón Grande dam on the river Lempa below Suchitoto. They had decided not to try and stop the construction of the dam, but to demand better wages and a good relocation of dispossessed peasants. Some of the tenant farmers who were affected had lived on the land for fifty years or more. Often the owners had sold the land to the government and felt no compulsion to help the peasants to relocate. A number of demonstrations were organized in Suchitoto and San Salvador. This experience, together with disillusionment with the electoral process particularly after 1972, led many to the conclusion that the peasants needed their own organization to work at the political and national level. José Alas describes this period:

**Until 1972, we thought that maybe changes could be achieved through an electoral process. That is why, even if we did not want to, we supported Duarte . . . There were priests who genuinely supported the Christian Democrats, and we thought that through them there could be the possibility of an agrarian reform and other reforms in the country. But after the flooding, many of us decided that change was impossible through elections. In 1974, there were elections for mayors and deputies. Few people participated in the elections, and we decided in my parish to prepare our programme and put pressure on the new Assembly. I held meetings in my parish with the peasants' leaders every first Saturday and we decided to invite other people from the university, the unions and some others. We held the first meeting in Suchitoto with all these people, to**

present the programme we had decided to put forward. We asked for their support, their contribution to the programme and to form a group . . . We had three more meetings but then we thought that it could be dangerous for everyone to come to Suchitoto, and we decided to move to San Salvador. We had a big, big meeting in the Basilica of the Sacred Heart, my former parish, with about 300 people, and in that place we started FAPU, the United Popular Action Front.

## Catalyst Two: The Revolutionary Organizations

Present at the formation of FAPU were the organizations which were to carry forward the process of catalyzing the Salvadorean countryside: the revolutionary organizations. These were to set light to a country which was a tinderbox of mass discontent. Since the early 1970s they had been gaining influence within a number of peasant, trade union and student bodies. The rest of this chapter describes the three main revolutionary groups, the issues which separate them from each other and from the traditional Salvadorean left (the Communist Party), and their attitudes to the process of creating change in the countryside. Later chapters deal with the reality of that process in Chalatenango once the peasants themselves took charge.

Chapter three described the system of repression and control erected in El Salvador after the 1932 uprising and refined over the ensuing decades. For much of this period, the Salvadorean Communist Party was the only opposition force of the left. It had, however, been badly defeated in 1932, reduced to perhaps a dozen members, and forced into clandestinity. Henceforth its political positions, like other communist parties, were distorted by the needs of Soviet foreign policy. The two great issues which led to twists and turns in policy, then as now, were how far a workers' revolution was possible in a economically and socially undeveloped country and whether peaceful or violent methods were appropriate. One course led to an alliance with the liberal middle classes (and any other 'progressive' forces which could be detached from the ruling order) and electoral politics; the other to an armed workers' struggle.

The Communist Party maintained a theoretical adherence to armed struggle, while in practice it abandoned this means of achieving change except for a brief period following the Cuban revolution. Its involvement in the 1944 movement which overthrew the dictatorship of Maximiliano Hernández was weak and ineffectual. The few surviving leaders from 1932 had met to reform the party but they were unsure of the appropriate strategy to pursue and nervous of the popular movement. The ruling order was able to re-establish itself and the

122

communists were once again forced underground. As Alastair White writes, 'even after May 1944 the members maintained such complete discretion that it had no noticeable effect on political life'.[18] The party adopted the view that socialist revolution was not a viable option in El Salvador in the short term. The party should direct its efforts first towards the overthrow of feudalism by building a 'popular front' – a broad alliance of anti-feudal and anti-imperialist forces aimed at achieving a 'bourgeois democratic' revolution – and its methods were peaceful.

The Party's influence grew in the 1950s, peaking at the end of the decade when students and other members of the urban middle class moved to bring down the government of President Lemus. This also coincided with the Cuban revolution. Between 1961 and 1963 the Party briefly reconsidered the question of armed struggle and made some military preparations but these limited efforts were soon abandoned. El Salvador was then embarking on a process of industrialization and economic change. The Party leadership argued that peaceful and legal agitation would be more appropriate in a period of economic upturn. From 1966-1977, Party activities centred on elections. Through its legal arm – the Democratic Nationalist Union (UDN) founded in 1969 – the Party entered a coalition with the Christian Democrat Party and the social democratic National Revolutionary Movement (MNR).

Throughout the 1960s the Party's official position was challenged, both from within and from outside. Socio-economic change, the influence of Social-Christian thought, and the political impact of the Cuban revolution all contributed to significant political developments in El Salvador. An increasing variety of options for change emerged. The Christian Democrat Party grew into the most influential and popularly-based party of moderate reform. Another reforming party, the MNR, was formed in 1964, and in 1965 there was a split in the Party of Renovative Action (PAR), a twenty-one-year old party which had claimed to offer a 'liberal' alternative to the official party. A more radical section led by the rector of the National University, Fabio Castillo, won control of the party for their 'new line', a significant move to the left. The party fought the 1967 presidential election around the demand for agrarian reform, to be completed in two years. In the face of increasing police harassment the party gained 14.4 per cent of the national vote, compared with eight per cent only a year earlier. This increase appears to have been largely at the expense of the Christian Democrats. In San Salvador PAR gained 29 per cent of the vote while the PDC received 25 per cent. The PAR was promptly banned. The experience further radicalized those whose faith in electoral politics was already waning. It reinforced the argument for armed action now reaching the Salvadorean student movement from Europe and elsewhere. The 1967 general strike and 1968 teachers' strike reflected the emergence of a more combative workers' movement responsive to militant leadership which the Communist Party had traditionally been unwilling to provide.

Within the Party, dissidents were voicing their frustrations with the Party's cautious politics and the strategic position which underlay it. In 1969 the Party supported the war with Honduras on the grounds that it would be led by a national bourgeoisie in the interests of national independence, strengthening it against the pro-imperialist oligarchy. This brought the latent rebellion to a head. Dissidents rejected the thesis that a 'national bourgeoisie' existed in El Salvador, and pointed out that it was in fact the most reactionary landowners who backed the war most fervently. They rejected the Party's electoral bias and advocated a combination of armed struggle and political mobilization.

These are the roots from which the revolutionary movement grew. The strategic debates which accompanied the growing disenchantment with the Communist Party were, however, to resurface again and again in the ensuing years. Even after the Party had opted to join the armed struggle – a decision only fully implemented in 1980 – it had not abandoned its fundamental political premises. The same debates – 'what kind of alliance?', 'bourgeois democratic or socialist revolution?', 'armed struggle or peaceful confrontation?' – reemerged in the midst of the civil war.

## The People Are Our Mountains: The Popular Forces of Liberation

*'The organization was clear from the beginning that it was the people who would take the cause into their hands, that the people are themselves the authors of the armed struggle . . . that the people were going to make the war and that the armed groups should not convert themselves into an elite, into heroes uprooted from the masses who would save the people the work of making the revolution.'*[19]

The FPL, so decisive in the revolutionizing of Chalatenango in the 1970s, was founded on 1 April 1970 by eight dissident members of the Communist Party. The distinctive politics which it developed are inseparable from the political biography of its founder, Salvador Cayetano Carpio, better known by his *nom de guerre*, Marcial. He ranks as one of Latin America's most outstanding revolutionary figures.

Marcial, a baker by trade, described himself as 'a product of the class struggle itself '.[20] He led the Bakers' Union to victory in a 1944 strike, at a time when unions were still illegal in El Salvador, and experienced the turbulent political events of that year when the popular movement toppled the dictator Hernández Martínez but remained too weak to avert the 'constitutional' solution which left the army in power.

124

In 1947 he joined the Communist Party.

The Party agreed to his returning to trade union work in 1963, and during his period as General Secretary of the Party between 1964 and 1970, he presided over an extraordinary upsurge in trade union militancy, culminating in the general strike of 1967. Deeply impressed both by what he saw as the failed opportunity of 1944 and by the combativity of the Cuban workers during a visit in 1950, he helped to forge a new type of trade unionism. In 1963 the Party had influence with only eight unions, and even that was largely formal in that it involved only the leadership. Marcial laid the basis for the Salvadorean Unitary Trade Union Federation (FUSS) which was to grow, with 41 affiliates, into the country's largest trade union federation.

His stress on winning support from the rank-and-file unionists by working beside them and helping to pioneer more combative tactics such as sit-ins, brought him into increasing conflict with the rest of the Party leadership. He saw the successful mobilization of 30,000 workers in the 1967 general strike as confirmation that workers' struggle around their economic demands was a profound source of political education. The Party's Political Commission described the strike as adventurist, stating that 'during the period of accumulation of forces it is not possible to allow decisive battles, only partial ones'.[21]

A rift was growing between Marcial and the rest of the leadership. He became increasingly critical of their tactical concern to keep the struggle within legal limits, which he argued was preventing them developing peasant unions and was inhibiting work with the urban unions. He described the Party as the 'fireman', 'pouring cold water on the combativity of the masses until it lost them the capacity to be their vanguard'.[22]

The general strike was followed by the teachers' strike of 1968. As the struggle intensified so did the dispute within the Party. But it was not only the timidity of the Party's political line against which Marcial fought. He also opposed a tendency growing in some sections of the organization towards militarism. After an abortive attempt to form clandestine armed groups of four or five people in 1961, the party had largely abandoned the idea of armed struggle. But there were those who wished to continue with armed actions and who criticized the emphasis on trade union and mass work. Marcial was as much opposed to this as he was to the legalism of the leadership. Though he had become an advocate of the importance of armed struggle following the experience of the Cuban revolution, he was emphatic that this should not be counterposed to mass political work. 'The Party', he wrote in December 1969 in a last attempt to transform the strategy of the organization he led, 'has to combine mass struggle and military struggle and not fall again into the area of one to the exclusion of the other. Neither to convert itself into guerilla *focos* nor to attend only the mass movement.'[23]

The year 1969 was a turning point for Marcial. The Party had supported the Salvadorean government in the brief war with Honduras. When he wrote the document quoted above outlining the need for the Party to ready itself for armed struggle, the political commission ruled against calling a congress to discuss the proposal. They argued that 'if the congress is called, adventurist and leftist ideas may triumph and there is the danger that the Party will adopt an adventurist policy, because the grass roots are not educated.'[24]

Marcial left the Party in March 1970. Many of the ideas that would shape the development of the FPL had evolved during his experience in the mass movement and in the ideological struggle within the Party. He remained a committed Leninist and founded the FPL in the belief that it would become the true Marxist-Leninist party. He remained, too, a supporter of the Soviet Union, although he always insisted on the autonomy of the Salvadorean process. His strategic ideas were also influenced by the experiences of armed struggle in other revolutions, particularly that occurring in Vietnam, from which the FPL's conception of 'prolonged people's war' is largely derived. One contemporary account of the Vietnamese experience highlights this aspect:

*'Although it has not given theoretical form to its struggle, South Vietnam has introduced a new type of guerilla war, adding to the historical experience of the Chinese revolution. In South Vietnam the guerilla war is conceived of as a war of the masses, with the organized participation of the entire population, rural and urban, with militias, village committees, and a revolutionary political party as the axis of the guerilla struggle; it is not simply a struggle of guerilla detachments supported by the masses, one in which the masses do not participate with their own organizations, as was the case in Cuba.'[25]*

These are some of the conclusions that Marcial drew from that struggle though he also recognized the need to develop a strategy in accord with Salvadorean reality. Marcial once talked in the 1960s to Che Guevara about the Central American revolution. Che believed that the armed struggles taking place at that time in the mountainous areas of Guatemala and Nicaragua pointed the way forward for Central America. But Che had to agree that El Salvador had no mountains to act as a sanctuary for a guerilla movement. The most mountainous areas of the country – Chalatenango, Morazán and north of San Vicente – were also densely populated, with many pathways connecting the villages. Most of the land was cultivated, leaving very little vegetation which might conceal guerilla forces. Because of its inappropriate terrain, Che concluded at the end of their discussions that El Salvador could only play a secondary role in the regional struggle, dependent on the logistical support from neighbouring countries. 'It wasn't because of chauvinism that we rejected this proposal', wrote Marcial, 'it was that we saw that El Salvador was a volcano in eruption, that, in addition, the class struggle in El Salvador had different characteristics to other Central American countries. In El Salvador, the greater part of the population is proletarianized, and that is an element which must be taken into account.'[26] 'The people are our mountains', Marcial used to say.

The geographical problem was resolved by launching the work in urban areas where clandestinity was easier to achieve, and combining military activities with political work. The FPL called itself a political-military organization, considering itself a new type of Marxist-Leninist organization, because it stressed the need to make clear to the people the two aspects of the struggle. They were very keen to avoid the error of militarism. 'From the beginning, we were very clear that the military is only the prolongation of the political by other means, by armed means.'[27] The FPL believed therefore that the mass movement had an importance in its own right and was not there simply to give logistical backing to the guerillas:

*'We did not wish to repeat the experience of Guatemala. In Guatemala they formed support groups amongst the peasantry, not for the mass struggle, but around the logistical function, as support for the guerila. We, precisely because of the more integral conception that we had, and the concern not to separate ourselves from the masses (although formally we had to give up the public positions of leadership of the masses) tried, nevertheless, not to become detached from them.'*[28]

From the beginning Marcial and his comrades faced certain dilemmas in building the movement. Orthodoxy told them that the first task was to build the Party and political cells from which the military organization would emerge. But they also believed they had to prove their revolutionary capacity. They began by building armed commandos, and carried out a number of actions before announcing their existence publicly in August or September 1972.

During this early period each member of the armed command had to organize 15 collaborators selected from people involved in the mass movement, such as union activists. The best of these were chosen to organize support groups, not for logistical purposes but for political work with the population. By 1974, the organization felt it had proved sufficient military capacity, and had an adequate urban base in the student movement and amongst teachers (and to a much lesser extent the urban working class), to allow it to turn to the countryside, where hitherto the left had been unable to break the control of the oligarchy and its armed apparatus.

127

At the same time as the mass movement developed, the FPL increased its military actions and began to build popular militias to defend the population, carry out acts of sabotage against economic targets, and attacks on members of ORDEN and the death squads. These activities were intended to encourage militancy amongst the people in their own fight for economic demands, and gradually prepare them for the popular armed struggle.

Once the transition was made to the countryside, the FPL soon acknowledged the need to work with the radical church. Its position on the church was clarified in 1975 in a letter to the progressive clergy which describes how class contradictions affect the church itself and argues that it is unrealistic to expect the hierarchy to support the revolutionary movement.

The letter represents a very significant attempt by a Marxist-Leninist organization to come to terms with the phenomenon of radical Christianity. The organization was evidently anxious to answer any accusation that they were taking advantage of the work done by the radical priests and pointed out that they worked anywhere in the rural areas including those dominated by more conservative forces. The letter was also directed at the base of the organization itself, where there were fierce and often dogmatic debates on the relationship between Christianity and Marxism. The letter is worth quoting fairly extensively:

*'We start from the premise that to be Christian is not opposed to the duty of fighting for justice, for the liberation of the people from exploitation and misery . . . we consider the incorporation of the peasants and workers, who are fundamentally Christian, absolutely necessary to the revolution – a strategic condition.*

*The FPL carries through this belief in practice. Wherever there is a Catholic activist who wishes to make a leap in his revolutionary work and who fulfils the requirements of our organization, we have no reason to reject him, to close the door and prevent him from realizing his aspirations to serve the revolutionary cause. In raising them to a higher level of political activity, our objective at the same time is that their religious work is not discredited. On the other hand, it is necessary to say that every revolutionary, as he moves towards an understanding of the real world, fills the gaps, weaknesses, deficiencies and errors in his knowledge with a scientific foundation which places both understanding and action behind the collective interest.*

*The work of the organization in growing sectors of the countryside is strategic work, aimed at winning a fundamental sector actively for the revolution. Without this it cannot succeed.'* (Estrella Roja, no.2)

The letter had quite an impact and, particularly as the repression grew in rural areas, the FPL was to influence a number of priests working with the base communities. Many of them, if they did not commit themselves to the FPL as such, became very involved in the work of the popular alliance, the Popular Revolutionary Bloc (BPR), which was identified with FPL political strategies.

Of central importance to the FPL's politics, and one which until the death of Marcial in April 1983 divided it from the other revolutionary organizations, was the question of class alliances. The FPL believed that the only class capable of carrying through the needed revolution was the working class in alliance with the poor peasantry.

It did not reject all alliances with other classes. The FPL believed that the essential question with respect to any alliance was which class led and stamped the bloc with its own interests. For the FPL, there was only one way to guarantee that the interests of the working class and poor peasantry prevailed in the revolutionary struggle: they must deepen their own alliance, building a true Marxist-Leninist party.

The related view, that the FPL was the only organization capable of converting itself into the true workers' party, led to many accusations of sectarianism from other organizations. This was undoubtedly a problem during the 1970s in the FPL, as well as in other organizations of the left. As the organization grew and began to influence large sectors of the mass movement, understanding of the debates was often unsophisticated, reduced to slogans and a belief in the inherent superiority of the FPL. This youthful enthusiasm and excess, together with the widespread repression which eliminated many cadres in the course of the 1970s, contributed to damaging divisions within the opposition movement.

But not all the principles on which the organization based itself were carried through in practice. Its strategy based on building a movement under working class hegemony had to face the test of reality. Like most Third World countries, El Salvador has a small and still mostly unorganized working class, a large peasantry and a radicalized middle class with disproportionate influence in the midst of the largely illiterate and uneducated masses. Further complications are added by the fact that the country's rulers had already made their own attempts to control the vital working class movement through compliant unions and cruder repressive methods. The FPL's penetration of the Salvadorean union movement was also hampered by the fact that the more class-conscious workers in El Salvador had been won over early on to the Communist Party's more gradualist and electoral politics. The FPL had a large base amongst the peasantry and the radicalized middle class (in particular students and teachers) some time before their influence in the workers' movement took off in the late 1970s.

Another problem the FPL faced was its relationship with the mass movement. The organization aimed at a constant interaction between revolutionary 'vanguard' and the masses, between armed struggle and other forms of struggle, between open work and clandestine work. Such an interaction was very difficult in the repressive conditions of El Salvador. In practice, most members of the mass organizations had no formal affiliation to the FPL through a party structure, although individual clandestine links existed. Part of the problem lay in the sheer pace at which the mass movement grew. The movement grew incredibly fast, making it very difficult to achieve the balance between building a military apparatus and a strong political organization. At different points in time, the FPL found itself giving emphasis to the one to the detriment of the other, and in fact, the party's theoretical adherence to a Leninist party structure was never fully implemented in practice.

All these problems and imbalances could perhaps have been worked out within a strategy of protracted war, but as the pace of events quickened following the Nicaraguan revolution of 1979, they created considerable difficulties. The FPL had to take drastic measures to create an army in 1980, militarizing much of the political organization it had built up amongst the masses.

The FPL was not of course acting alone in all these years. There were a number of other revolutionary organizations active at the same time, and the divisions between them all had their impact on the coherence and effectiveness of the revolutionary movement as a whole. These organizations are discussed below, although the full history of the Salvadorean left cannot yet be written.

## The People's Revolutionary Army and National Resistance

The 'People's Revolutionary Army' (the ERP) was formally established in 1972. Its origins were much more heterogeneous than those of the FPL. Some of its early adherents came from the student movement, influenced by the radical anti-communist ideas circulating in the European student left of the late 1960s. Others came out of the youth wing of the Christian Democrat Party, the Social Christian Youth, and the youth of the Communist Party. There were also a number of Protestants, including two Baptist Ministers. A few anarchists were also among its early members. Its most prestigious member, the poet Roque Dalton, had been a member of the Salvadorean Communist Party.

They were mostly of a younger generation than the FPL and of more middle-class origin. Joaquín Villalobos, the present leader of the ERP, was 19 when he helped build the first nuclei for the armed struggle in 1970, while Carpio was 50 when he left the Communist Party to set up the FPL. Few had any experience of mass work and it is not surprising that the initial leadership, headed by Sebastián Urquilla and Mario Vladimir Rogel, developed an almost pure form of militarism in the tradition of the *foquista* guerillas of Latin America in the 1960s.

The experience of the 1972 elections led to some reconsideration within the organization and for the first time it began to discuss strategic questions; the characterization of the period and the development of an appropriate political line. In particular, the ERP began to consider the danger of fascism and the need for a structured response which involved the masses. The idea of 'national resistance' emerged in the form of committees against fascism. However, when in 1973 the ERP decided to take up mass work, it found that its federal structures (which were the result of the political heterogeneity of its founding groups), made it very difficult to implement a coherent political line. In practice, the military leadership, which did not favour political work, came to dominate the organization.

In response, those who took the 1972 reassessment seriously and wished to develop the concept of national resistance began to extend their activities, and the two main tendencies within the ERP began to polarize. At the end of 1974, the military wing moved to assert its supremacy. However, it now had to confront an influential and organized internal opposition. Events moved quickly and tragically. On 10 May 1975, two leading figures of the national resistance, Roque Dalton and 'Pancho', were executed by the ERP leadership. The FPL intervened to prevent a complete bloodbath within the organization. The events were to scar the Salvadorean revolutionary movement for many years.

The ERP subsequently went through a process of self-criticism. Between 1975 and 1977 they removed some of the hardline leadership and set up a Marxist-Leninist party, the PRS (Salvadorean Revolutionary Party). In February 1978 they set up their own mass front: the Popular Leagues of February 28 (LP-28).

The ERP continued to reject the FPL's strategy of prolonged popular war in favour of insurrection, maintaining that a revolutionary situation had existed in El Salvador since 1972. In practice, their relationship to the mass movement was still dominated by military traditions and an insurrectionary strategy which made the building of the army the overwhelming priority. The ERP chose Morazán – like Chalatenango, one of the poorest departments of El Salvador – to be zone of control from early on, as the following account by Comandante Juan Ramón Medrano shows:

*Our work in Morazán began after 1974 . . . The first of our cadres who began to work with a structured programme was Amilcar (Rafael Arce Zablah) . . . In this period, our party, particularly through Amilcar's knowledge of the zone, put forward the objective of making Morazán a zone*

131

*of control . . . and we worked towards this from 1974. From the beginning, it was not very difficult to form a consciou∴ness which was political and not gremial [restricted to union demands], due mainly to the previous work of the church . . .*

*The first cadres of the organization who began the work in the zone along with Amilcar, were Santo Lino Ramíres, that is Chele Luis, Aquiles and two other comrades who for different reasons are no longer there, and myself. In the last weeks of 1974 and the first days of 1975, there was a proposal to form a mass front, first in Morazán and then in La Unión, where there was the most development of the peasant leagues . . . The policy of organizing a mass front was not done on the basis of a trade union schema, but with clearly political demands. This allowed us to grow rapidly in Morazán, and from the months of May and June 1975, we began to develop the proposal for the formation of* military committees *[emphasis in the original]. This corresponded to the movement in which the organization made a turn and began to concentrate on military organization, and it is for this reason that Morazán has had a military organization for five years already.*

*The policy of developing military committees enabled us to create a strong military structure in the department of Morazán. From the beginning we began to develop plans for the defence of the zone, and from 1975 we began to make an early type of explosive . . .*

*In this period the work developed peacefully, since until the first days of 1978 there was no confrontation. It was from the last days of 1977, and the first months of 1978, that the first strong demonstrations of the political work began, with the activities around the death of the comrade Juan Ramón Sánchez and the capture of Father Ventura. These two events led at the end of 1977 to an important demonstration of more than 1,000 people in Osicala, against the capture of Father Miguel and demanding his freedom. Never before had anything like it been seen in the zone.*

*From the first days of 1978, the population of Morazán began to live the political struggle more intensely . . . the LP-28 had a special development in Morazán, more rapid than anywhere else in the country. We must remember that there was already a political structure of the Military Committees of the ERP with their armed propaganda. The LP-28 were at the beginning an unarmed organization with their own structure. From the beginning, we conceived the mass front as a structure with a certain autonomy, with its own platform of struggle. Nevertheless, very rapidly the development of the repression in Morazán led to the very accelerated creation, first of the self-defence teams, then of the militia teams of the leagues. Both have now fused with our revolutionary army in the defence of the zone.* (Interview with Comandante Juan Ramón Medrano of the ERP).[29]

The interview illustrates the differences between the ERP and the FPL in the conception of the war and the role of the mass movement. The

132

impoverished and discontented as that of Chalatenango. (Though some interesting differences exist between the peasantry of the two regions: that of Chalatenango was never as isolated as that of Morazán; most *Chalatecos* worked several months of the year as wage labourers outside the department and many were tenant farmers for the rest of the year rather than smallholders as in Morazán.) But no independent peasant movement emerged in Morazán. The ERP organized and politicized the population and created the LP-28, their mass front, with their insurrectionary strategy in mind and with their military structures already dominant. There is no doubt that the ERP's strategy enabled them to build an impressive and effective military force; but the ERP's strategy allowed no time for the politicization that transforms rebellion into revolution.

The National Resistance (RN) separated from the ERP in 1975 to form their own revolutionary party and an armed unit, the Armed Forces of National Resistance (FARN). They kept a base of peasant support in the Suchitoto area where they set up the *Movimiento Revolucionario Campesino* (Revolutionary Peasant Movement) and were able to win over an important sector of the organized urban working class. The RN concentrated their efforts on workers in certain strategic industries, such as electricity and port workers, and won over the unions in these industries.

In theory, the RN appeared to be close to the FPL on a number of issues. It also rejected militarism and the *foco* tradition; it did not believe in absolute party control of the mass organizations; and it also aimed to build the Marxist-Leninist party on the principles of democratic centralism. Like the FPL, it rejected the Communist Party's idea of a national democratic revolution as a prior stage to socialism. Instead, it also spoke of 'the intermediary phase of the popular democratic revolution in which the power of the state is consolidated in favour of the worker-peasant alliance prior to the transition to socialism'.[30]

But the RN had a number of major disagreements with the FPL on practical as well as on some major theoretical points. It condemned the FPL's policy towards the popular organizations for 'its infantile leftism' and 'all or nothing' approach on wages and land questions. The radical leadership of the FPL-influenced alliance, the BPR, for instance, was criticized for encouraging land invasions by the peasants which were seen as an 'agrarianist deviation'. The RN argued that while the peasant unions associated with the FPL (FECCAS-UTC) achieved some of their demands on paper, they could not get them implemented, a sign that peasant 'strikes' were not an adequate form of pressure.[31]

The nub of the criticism was that the FPL supported and encouraged popular combativity in the abstract without sufficient consideration to particular tactical as well as strategic ends. It reflects

133

ERP undoubtedly mobilized and won support from a peasantry as fundamental disagreements between the two organizations. The RN rejected the FPL's commitment to a prolonged popular war in favour of 'revolutionary war and insurrection'. The RN's objective was to build the guerilla army and prepare the population for insurrection. But it also believed that an urgent and immediate task was to build a broad front against the growing danger of fascism in the country. This involved constructing alliances with all anti-oligarchic and anti-imperialist forces in El Salvador, which, it maintained, included progressive sectors of the army. In practice, the mass movement would have to subordinate certain immediate demands to this tactical end.

The RN, along with the FPL and the ERP, rejected the Communist Party view that there existed in El Salvador a national bourgeoisie capable of overthrowing the 'feudal' oligarchy and carrying through a national democratic revolution. But they believed that their principal enemy was the coffee oligarchy, the dominant faction of the Salvadorean bourgeoisie closely tied to the US. A broad range of sectors (including parts of the army) could unite to overthrow it and build a popular revolutionary government as a prelude to socialism; an analysis broadly shared by the ERP in their theoretical treatise on the development of Salvadorean capitalism known as *El Grano de Oro*.[32] The FPL, though it agreed that some sectors of the bourgeoisie were more powerful than others, argued that no 'national' project was possible because their interests essentially coincided and were dependent on an alliance with the US. It rejected a revolutionary strategy which implied sacrificing the momentum of the mass movement in the interests of tactical alliances with sectors of the armed forces or the bourgeoisie, considering it an illusion that these forces would in any case join a popular project. It argued that what the ERP and the RN saw as fascism was merely the counter-revolutionary strategy of the bourgeoisie as a whole.

These, then, were the debates which were to have their resonance inside the awakening peasant movement. The FPL's stress on the politicizing effect of the popular struggle and on the need not to limit that struggle by subordinating it to alliances with other classes, found an echo in the experience of the peasants as they built their own organizations in Chalatenango; the FPL was to win a dominant political influence in that department.

## Mobilizing the People: The Popular Organizations (FAPU and the BPR)

FAPU, which was the first attempt to unite a number of radical organizations in a common front, had emerged in the early 1970s, initially to fight against the high cost of living. Amongst the organizations present at its formation in 1975 were FECCAS, the Salvador Allende United Front of Revolutionary Students (FUERSA), the National Association of Salvadorean Teachers (ANDES), and the Salvadorean Unitary Trade Union Federation (FUSS). Also present were some students from the Catholic University (UCA) and the peasant leaders of Suchitoto. The main revolutionary organizations were represented through their links with these bodies. The Revolutionary Workers' Organization (ORT) (which in 1976 became the PRTC-Central American Workers Revolutionary Party) also participated through the Liberation Leagues (LL). The University students, who had begun working amongst the peasants of Suchitoto, played a particularly prominent role in the formation of FAPU.

But from the beginning there were strategic differences which prevented FAPU from uniting the various organizations into a single body. The ERP wished to use the movement as the base for an immediate uprising. The decision that FAPU should not be an electoral body and that therefore membership was not open to parliamentary parties, led to the withdrawal of FUSS and thus of the Communist Party in October 1974. The RN (through FUERSA) and the FPL (through the students of the UCA) were engaged in an ideological battle over fundamental theoretical and strategic issues).

This eventually led those organizations (notably FECCAS) which came to accept the FPL view to withdraw from FAPU and set up an alternative front; the BPR (Popular Revolutionary Bloc) in 1975 (see below). The RN decided to continue working with FAPU, but in the meantime José Alas, who had helped call the meeting, withdrew:

**I had not the right to decide for the peasants what revolutionary line to follow. The importance of my work was in the cultural field, in the cultural change of the peasantry, their new vision of the land and of work, their participation in evangelization and in political life. And afterwards, the peasantry had to feel free to belong to the organization which it chose in the political field.**

But the revolutionary movement was now being built in El Salvador, and positions were being taken.

The debates between the FPL, the ERP and the RN that were occurring at this time, took place at a rarified level of differing analyses of Salvadorean society and of the trajectory towards revolution. But these political debates were not purely the preserve of the intellectuals who generated them. They had practical implications for the peasants of Chalatenango and elsewhere, for the kind of organization they would seek to build and strategies they would pursue. The work of the church had encouraged the peasants to identify their own interests and gain confidence in their capacity to pursue them. For them the choice was whether to forge ahead with their own organizations, making allies where there were common aspirations and shared political practices; or whether to submit to the tactical objectives of the politicians and ally with classes of which they were deeply suspicious.

These apparently abstract and theoretical discussions therefore had important reverberations in the grassroots of the mass organizations sufficient to create the divisions that prevented FAPU from uniting it. Through the influence of FUERSA and the RN, FAPU had drawn up a project for a law against the high cost of living. The students in the Catholic University objected to the basic goal it outlined: the defeat of escalating fascism in order then to defeat the bourgeoisie. They proposed instead that the defeat of the bourgeoisie was the only way to defeat fascism, disagreeing with the view that the Salvadorean ruling class could be divided into fascist and non-fascist components.

FUERSA then proposed an organic restructuring of FAPU in order to consolidate its influence. FECCAS was urged to abandon its existing structure and reorganize into cells composed of five members in each *cantón*, which would be linked automatically to FAPU. The proposal was unanimously rejected in discussions in the FECCAS base groups. The debate intensified as FUERSA then sent its members to talk to the FECCAS base groups, trying to persuade them to reverse their decision.

The FECCAS structure provided for a direct supervision of its executive from the base through a national committee, formed by all the general secretaries of the base groups, which met every four months. At the end of May 1975, the national committee meeting at Suchitoto decided that FECCAS should leave FAPU. The teachers' union ANDES made a similar decision.[33]

Less than two months later, in July 1975, a rival to FAPU was born: the Popular Revolutionary Bloc (BPR). The BPR, which became the largest of the 'popular organizations' that emerged after the failure to create a united organization, was closely linked to the politics of the FPL. Its importance in our story is that Chalatenango was to become a solid base for the BPR/FPL political alignment.

The BPR was formed following a massacre of some 20 students from the National University during a demonstration in San Salvador on 30 July 1975. A group of priests and sisters decided to hold a funeral in the cathedral for one of the victims. Over 70 people representing different mass organizations were present and they occupied the cathedral in protest at the killings. There was an intense debate within the cathedral, between FAPU, the parliamentary opposition parties and the organizations associated with the FPL. These latter included FECCAS, the UTC (a peasant union based in San Vicente and Chalatenango), the teachers' union ANDES, the student group UR-19, the secondary school students' group MERS, and the shanty-town dwellers' group, UPT. Together, the supporters whom they could

136

mobilize represented a majority and their views prevailed. On 3 August everyone left the cathedral, and on the 5th the FPL-aligned groups called a meeting to announce the formation of the BPR.

The BPR was by no means simply a 'front' for the FPL. Indeed, perhaps one of the most striking things about the FPL is the creativity of its approach to the dilemma: 'mass party' or 'vanguard organization'? The FPL's strategic conception of 'prolonged popular war' placed great stress on the development of mass organizations through which the peasants and workers could fight for their own demands.

The FPL considered that the immediate needs of the workers and peasants could not be ignored during the protracted struggle towards the ultimate goal. They did not in any case share the view that there was a conflict between the two, and believed that as long as there was revolutionary leadership, the struggle for immediate demands could increase rather than hold back political consciousness.

*'The struggle for immediate interests must be a means and not an end in itself. A means which permits sectors of the working class (and other progressive classes) to acquire the first steps in organization and discipline, which allows them to have elemental class confrontation with their exploiters; and through them, to see the causes and roots of their exploitation, the links between the state and the exploiting classes, and in this way to understand their need to drive on the revolutionary struggle which will end the system of exploitation and oppression. In this way, the struggle for immediate interests is not counterposed to the struggle for revolutionary objectives, but becomes the necessary step, essential and inseparable from it.'* (*Estrella Roja*, op. cit.)

The FPL therefore encouraged the peasant union of Chalatenango to fight for better conditions, and to develop new, more combative forms of struggle. The FPL used its influence and the medium of the BPR to link the peasant movement with struggles elsewhere in the country.

The FPL had no prior plan that Chalatenango would become 'its' liberated base area. It saw the organization of the peasantry as an important political process in its own right and the subsequent development of popular militias and a people's army as part of a strategy of prolonged popular war in which the final confrontation would involve an organized mass uprising. The belief that this was a prolonged war was based on the view that 40 years of political and military domination could not be changed overnight. Prolonged popular war would allow for gradual incorporation of the masses into the struggle; over time a situation of military disadvantage for the popular forces would become one of balance with the government forces, and eventually one favourable to the revolution. The strategy of *guerra prolongada* was thus an essential element in the FPL's rejection

of militarism and short cuts to revolution and in its belief that the people must be the authors of their own history. Having rejected the idea of a quick insurrection or *putsch*, the FPL argued that time was needed to build a mass movement capable of taking power. But, as events unfolded, the movement grew at a speed which outstripped the FPL's ability to develop its own organization. The party remained, in Marcial's words, a party of cadres. No time was available to create a cell structure at the local level. This had significant implications for the development of the struggle.

FPL cadres worked with the peasant unions, FECCAS and UTC, and were expected to share the way of life and the dangers daily facing the peasants from the authorities. A number of these cadres became well-loved and respected members of the peasant communities, such as Andrés Torres in Chalatenango and 'Eugenia' in Aguilares. But they were also expected to respect the peasants' own leaders: they could not vote at union meetings themselves nor take leadership positions. In this way the Salvadorean revolution threw up many outstanding peasant leaders of its own, many of whom did join the FPL.

The peasant movement, which developed in Chalatenango and other places where FPL influence was strong, thus did so with considerable influence from the FPL, but it was not under their control. We can pose the question: 'Why did the FPL remain a catalyst and not come to control the peasants' movement in Chalatenango?' The answer is partly given above: an insistence by the FPL that the movement must be made by the workers and peasants themselves. Also, however, the speed of events left the organization in a curious parallel with the other catalyst, the church. Their militants were thin on the ground in relation to the task to be done – it was up to the peasants to make their own revolution.

# 5
# PEASANTS
# ORGANIZED

## The UTC — Early History

In Chalatenango it was the Union of Rural Workers (UTC), not FECCAS, which organized the peasants. It was, from the start, a combative and radical organization and in that respect its origins are very different to those of FECCAS. Chalatenango is more isolated and less important economically than Aguilares-Suchitoto, and the department seems to have attracted little attention from any of the political organizations which emerged in the 1960s except when elections came round. The Christian Democrat Party, which had won some voter support in Chalatenango during the 1960s, came to be seen after 1972 as the opposition which had failed. The party was very urban biased and without the channel of FECCAS did not sink deep roots amongst the peasantry of rural Chalatenango.

The UTC did not therefore go through the process of internal debate which led FECCAS to reject its links with the Christian Democrat Party. It also emerged in a different political climate to the first FECCAS. The political-military organizations had appeared and the opposition movement was becoming more radical. The FPL gained an early influence amongst a number of peasant leaders and they contributed to the organization's militancy. Important too, was the actual experience of the union as it confronted landowners and government in a bid to improve the living standards of its members. The torture and killings of union members and their familes fuelled the anger of the peasants in a way which strengthened their commitment to risk all in the struggle for a better life.

The 1972 electoral fraud was a potent stimulus for many of the early members of the UTC:

**My name is María Serrano. I was born in Arcatao, I am 33 years old, a daughter of a widow. At nine years of age I began to work as a maid until I married at 16. What the parties were saying at that time was nothing but sweet-talk. It didn't correspond with what I was experiencing at all; how full the people were with poverty, the misery of need. I was active in the Christian Democrat Party until the age of 22. Then in 1972, I participated for the last time in the**

141

elections. These fraudulent elections showed me that there was no
way out for us from this misery through elections. In 1974, when the
UTC emerged here in Chalatenango, Facundo Guardado asked me
to a meeting that took place in Arcatao. The meeting took place in a
football ground under the vigilance of the *Guardia*. I joined the
UTC, working within the organization at consciousness-raising and,
together with other people, organizing meetings; all very slow work,
but work which must be done. The meetings had to be illegal as
repression was hard. (María)

The peasants began to drift away from the 'semi-official' organizations,
searching for radical solutions to their problems:

I used to belong to the UCS because we were looking for an
organization to get involved in. Those from the UCS appeared in the
early 1970s, talking to us of Jesus Christ, nothing else. They were

142

aligned to the Christian Democrat Party. I became a member of the UCS in 1974; there was no other group then. When it came to asking the UCS for help with problems we had in the village over a family being evicted, they didn't help. They just talked nicely to us, but in practice they did nothing. So in 1975 we decided to organize ourselves in the UTC. But those from FECCAS, people like Apolinario Serrano, had arrived by then. We chose the UTC rather than FECCAS because FECCAS was in Aguilares, not here in Chalate. The UTC was really what its initials said: the protection of the workers in the countryside.

When we formed the departmental executive committee in April 1975, we didn't even know how to write an agenda and at first we had no idea what to do. Justo Mejía was the president at the time, Gonzalo Molina, Ramón Guardado, María Julia, Santos Martínez: six of us meeting every day. It was easy to organize the people as at that time many village committees existed already. They were organized through the celebration of the Word, where we used to discuss our situation, whether it was the will of God or not . . . five of the six were *celebradores*. (Evaristo)

Another peasant leader gave a capsule history of the formation of the UTC:

The people here, in order to complement their economy, have to go to the large estates in other departments during harvest time, in Santa Ana, San Vicente, Ahuachapán and La Libertad, to cut coffee, sugar cane and cotton. They bring back money to survive. From about 1970, they began to organize cooperatives, which were a means by which to seek loans from the government in a more organized way – for fertilizers and seeds. It was a big advance. Cooperatives were set up in La Ceiba, near Las Vueltas; also in El Jícaro, Arcatao, and Las Flores. These cooperatives had their pre-cooperative groups in the villages; there was an organized network. They requested economic help from the government and began to get some because of the formal and organized way they presented themselves. The peasantry began to have less difficulty in feeding itself.

It was so effective that the cooperatives began to develop other projects, such as requests for schools, roads, drinking water and clinics, taking advantage of an important moment for Chalatenango, the Molina government project; *'a school a day, a football ground a week'*. It was very difficult for the government to refuse the requests, and some places such as Ojos de Agua, Las Vueltas, Las Flores and Nueva Trinidad, where you could never buy medicines before, began to get clinics.

From 1973 onwards, the church began to give Christian education. There was a real need as the area is very big and there

143

were only three priests in all this zone. The population itself began to think of having a catechist from here, from the community, to educate our children, to understand the Bible readings better and not be deceived by the Gospels or apathetic to them. Catechists were elected from the communities, received courses in Christianity in some colleges. A whole network of catechists was set up, who celebrated the Word of God, gave catechism to the children and pre-baptismal talks. This meant the mother and father didn't have to take the child all the way to the parish convent which was some walk away.

The development of the interpretation of the Word and the Bible readings was so great that it came to unite the peasants, make them feel more like brothers, with more fraternal and social relations between them. So much so, that when problems arose, the solutions which were given were arrived at in community. For example, if a man fell ill and had a family of ten to maintain, and if the illness came at the time of planting or cleaning the corn field, the community would go and do it for him so that the family wouldn't suffer hunger the next year. If a man died and left his family in a bad state, the community would ensure that his family didn't die of hunger. The same was true if someone was captured or imprisoned.

This gave the peasants a sense of identification, of security and unity in what they were doing. No longer did they conform with what the boss or the dictatorship said. But the peasants, the people, had to liberate themselves. What kind of liberation? How? When? And who was to lead it? This was a problem which had to be considered as things developed. But the first step had to be an organization which encouraged the peasants to participate. And once the organization existed and made demands, it was pretty important they were met successfully. This would give the peasants security and make them feel capable of confronting not only the problems in the community, but also the government authorities. They would begin to feel part of society, that they were important, that the economy of the country depended a lot on them; for instance the coffee, cotton and sugar harvests.

As in Chalatenango, cooperatives were set up in San Vicente too, such as in La Cayetana. In that part of the volcano of San Vicente, they organized coops, but the problem was that most of the volcano is the property of the landholders who wouldn't sell them the land. They had trouble organizing efficiently, as they needed the land. The people there began organizing Christian communities (it was a very Christian place) and they began to confront the same problems as we did in Chalate. We were discussing which form of organization we should build at the same time. But it was in San Vicente, where they formed the first bases of the UTC: La Paz, Opico and La Cayetana, where seven days later there was a

144

massacre and they killed seven *compas* [comrades]. They gave us
the way forward in our search to give our organization a name. We
asked for advice from Andrés Torres Sánchez, a peasant who
managed to go to university, and who we knew through the
cooperative movement. When we told him our situation, he decided
to come to live here and help us resolve our organizational
problems. We also brought someone over from La Cayetana and La
Paz to tell us about their experiences. In this way we moved towards
the formation of the UTC.

The UTC was formed in November 1974. Amongst those who
set up the organization were Facundo Guardado, Justo Mejía (who
was one of the oldest, about 45 years old), Santos Martínez,
Gonzalo Molina, Ramón Amaya, Julián Mejía, Antonio Morán, and
Gerardo Dubón (who was 16 years old). Of these, only Facundo and
Santos Martínez are still alive. We visited the villages and talked to

145

the people. The little we knew we could explain in a way they would understand. People were very enthusiastic, they could see that what we said was the reality. The churches where we spoke would fill up with people; in Jícaro, Concepción, and Jocotillo. When we talked of the UTC, we could see that people liked it and saw it was what was needed. ('Caravina', UTC peasant leader)

A powerful impetus for change was the experience of confronting problems collectively:

All those who were organized helped each other, it was the only way to cope with our dire situation. If someone's cornfield was overgrown, we went there – all of us in the organization – to weed it together. We made a collective bean field which served to help those *compas* who were unlucky, someone who had had a bad harvest, for instance, or who had a sick member of the family, so that we could give him money to buy medicines.

The UTC had groups in all the hamlets, each with their directorate, a general secretary, an organizational secretary, one of propaganda, of conflict, one of social assistance. The directorate was elected by assembly vote; three nominations usually. The assembly met once a week. We always oriented ourselves through the UTC, we realized that without an organization we were worth nothing against the oligarchy. We had a very clear idea of why we were fighting; we used to talk about 'primitive' society, how the Indians had lived, the arrival of the Spanish, and then how, over time, people had developed. We wanted to understand our history. (Walter)

The peasants' thirst for their own organization was strong. The UTC spread like wildfire throughout Chalate, from the *pueblos* to the outlying villages. In fact, this thirst had led a number of peasants to believe for a short while before the UTC appeared that ORDEN was the organization they had been waiting for:

Many of the *compas* of the UTC joined ORDEN for a few days first – because we thought it was the organization which would respond to the needs of the people, that's what we heard. It was people who had been judges or *alcaldes* in the nearby villages who began it all. I can give names; I remember a *Señor* called Humberto from Potonico. He began to organize the people and he spoke of demands, but we soon realized that ORDEN represented the interests of the rich and that it came to sow discord in our villages. But some of the poor peasants thought it might solve their problems, and a pass from ORDEN was a guarantee before the authorities that you weren't a subversive: it was the only way the peasant could be respected. So ORDEN gathered support in many of the villages, but we soon realized that this wasn't in our interests. We organized the UTC and many left ORDEN. We argued the case with the few who remained, making them see why it wasn't in their interests. Some preferred to stay there but we converted many who became honest *compas*. (René)

---

The government had been keeping a close watch on peasant organization in this department for two reasons: because it's a frontier region and still tense after the 1969 war, and because the government distrusted the objectives and intentions of the movement which was brewing up in the countryside. The government couldn't understand the movement where people mobilized every Sunday in one or another village, holding meetings with celebrators of the Word, the catechists who were working closely with the people. There was always music. The regime wasn't happy about this and began to organize vigilante groups, like ORDEN, who controlled the catechists and tried to denounce us. The *comandante* of the village or the municipality would go to the communities and hamlets and talk about ORDEN, that it was a better means of keeping order amongst the population. So many did join ORDEN. Its role was to inform about what was happening in the hamlet, if unknown people were walking about there, for instance. Later, ORDEN took on the task of informing on those who organized the meetings or any other activity, telling the leaders of the hamlets who in turn gave the information to the army.

Those who were members of ORDEN usually had a small piece of land and security over it, because the *comandante* said that those who belonged to ORDEN wouldn't have to pay taxes and that the authorities wouldn't bother them, nor take their arms away. But there were also those who had absolutely nothing and who joined ORDEN. Those who stayed in ORDEN did so basically because they had an identity card which protected them: without a card they'd say you were a subversive, that you should be dead. And so many people died, they often weren't organized or anything, they were just walking around without an ORDEN card. I too belonged to ORDEN in 1974, for one year before working in the UTC.

Once the authorities became aware that the UTC existed and as it became active after 1975, repression really began here. They began to arrest people on the roads who they thought were members of the UTC, just on suspicion. The local *comandante* would interrogate them to see what activities they were involved in. Then, the government began to install National Guard posts here in Las Vueltas, Ojos de Agua, Las Flores, Arcatao, Nueva Trinidad, San Isidro, San Antonio de los Ranchos, Conacaste and Potonico. That is, a load of little towns which had never had National Guard posts. The most that used to come to those places were three or four guards for the local festivals, to keep order. But when they put in 30 or 50 guards in each one of these places, then there were difficulties. The threats began, and whoever was arrested might be killed, and then they gave more autonomy to the ORDEN groups so that they could kill people. There were cases of ORDEN members killing people, not for political reasons, but for purely personal reasons, but they had the authority of the repressive forces. They just said they were subversives and killed them. This made the peasant population more combative, more willing to confront the enemy. (Victor)

In Aguilares, where FECCAS had its strength, there was often a real battle in certain villages between the peasant union and ORDEN for influence, even amongst the poor peasantry or semi-proletariat who formed the main base of FECCAS.[1] In Chalatenango, after some initial

interest in ORDEN, most of the poor peasants were won over to the UTC:

**It was very rapid, almost all the peasants of Chalate joined and the few who didn't — it was because they were very close to the enemy and the enemy didn't allow them to, although it is everyone's right to organize. People might not get organized in some places, for fear of the enemy, but in the villages where the control of the enemy was less strict, the organization grew very rapidly; in six months it had established itself. (René)**

ORDEN was able to attract peasant support in a number of ways. It gave security and a certain degree of power within a village. It allowed its adherents to carry arms and they were protected by the authorities. This became increasingly important as conflict grew in the rural areas. Affiliation might also bring job security to wage labourers, and to a more limited extent it might increase opportunities for employment, as members of FECCAS were blacklisted and work given to politically 'safer' peasants. Affiliation might bring material rewards in the form of the resolution of certain immediate problems, such as access to credit, agricultural materials and technical assistance.

A number of different factors seem to have shaped the outcome of the ideological battle between the radical peasant movement and ORDEN: social class, community structure, and the prior influence of the different political and social organizations and institutions. The situation of war and consequent dislocation of communities made it impossible for me in 1984 to conduct a systematic analysis village by village. But many insights can be gained from previous studies of the growth of FECCAS in Aguilares and elsewhere.[2] However, there are some important differences between Chalatenango and Aguilares which caution against an automatic transfer of all the conclusions. There are rather more owners than renters of land in Aguilares, and because of the presence of the sugar estates a higher percentage of landless unemployed, but greater opportunities for seasonal and permanent employment within the area. In Chalatenango, where agro-export estates and other sources of employment are largely absent, the peasantry is much more homogeneous from village to village.

In Aguilares, those most ready to become politically involved (whether with FECCAS or ORDEN) were the semi-proletariat. Those most difficult to organize were the *colonos*/wage labourers, who stand in a much more dependent relationship to the landowners. This class difference is shown in the table on page 151. In Chalatenango, the situation was similar. It was undoubtedly the semi-proletariat who formed the largest social base for the UTC, but in that department they were in any case the majority of the peasants.

As the political situation polarized still further and repression mounted in the late 1970s, an apolitical option became less viable. The

| Membership of FECCAS/ORDEN according to social class | | | |
|---|---|---|---|
| | **Middle Peasant** | **Semi-proletariat** | **Wage Labourer** |
| FECCAS | 19% | 52% | 29% |
| ORDEN | 31% | 31% | 38% |

*Source:* Cabarrús 1983[3]

| Political involvement according to social class | | | |
|---|---|---|---|
| | **Middle Peasant** | **Semi-proletariat** | **Wage Labourer** |
| FECCAS/ORDEN | 25% | 42% | 34% |
| Apolitical | 29% | 27% | 44% |

*Source:* Cabarrús 1983[4]

*colonos* and others who had thought it better to hold onto what little they had and keep their heads down, increasingly had to choose sides. The table above shows the sources of support for FECCAS and ORDEN in seven villages around Aguilares in 1977. FECCAS recruited disproportionately from the semi-proletariat. ORDEN drew almost equally from all classes of the peasantry, and was able particularly to attract the *colono*/wage labourer and sectors of the middle peasantry who feared the turmoil among the poor peasants below them. The table opposite shows that the semi-proletariat were the most politicized of the social groups.

But the competition between ORDEN and FECCAS cannot be analysed purely in the mechanical terms of social class. A key factor was also the influence of the political parties – the UNO (National Opposition Union), the united opposition formed to fight the 1972 election of the official PCN party – and of the church.

The comparative neglect of much of Chalatenango by the parties, until the church began its conscientizing work, may have contributed to the growth of a peasant union in a department noted for its combativity from the beginning. The variety of ideological positions had had less opportunity to take root before the church began the process of conscientization. The main characteristic of the peasants of Chalatenango prior to the period of organization seems to have been a widespread passivity, with cooperatives constituting the first limited efforts at organization in the late 1960s and early 1970s.

A number of other factors affected the political path a peasant might take, according to Cabarrús' study. These included: the social dynamics and relationships within communities; their geographical position with respect to sources of employment; and their location in relation to urban centres, which offered social distractions away from the appeal of political activity.[5] In Aguilares, kinship relationships within each community played a particularly important role. These were frequently the source of power within a community and would often determine acceptance or rejection of the organization. Conflicts were frequent between different families with land problems at their root. Particular families, or individuals related to them, gained strong leadership positions within a community through their capacity to secure benefits for it from the outside world, such as credits, study grants, roads and wells. FECCAS found it sometimes gained support in a community through the support of a family in conflict with another family linked to ORDEN.

FECCAS could hardly compete with ORDEN on the basis of government patronage and hence material goods. But its strength lay in the inability of ORDEN to solve any of the fundamental problems facing the peasants. 'ORDEN was an apparent solution to an economic problem which had no solution.'[6] As conditions deteriorated, it was not just a road or a well that was at stake, but survival itself. The fundamental economic demands for land, jobs and better conditions on the *fincas* could not be met by ORDEN. These required radical political change; FECCAS and the UTC were able to show that, united and organized, the peasants could fight for it:

When demands were first put forward by the UTC there were only slow improvements. For example, when we asked to be given *tortillas* on the *fincas*, we didn't get them in the year that we demanded them, but in order to confuse our common stand, the following year they put it forward as a suggestion of theirs, not ours.

We achieved something; some reduction in the prices of inputs. And some landowners, though not here in Chalate, gave land to the peasants. But more importantly, we gained the will and the faith of the peasants in their own capacity, and the fear they had of the dictatorship and the oligarchy was channelled into action. The peasants with their machete or their stick in their hands, seeing how the whole Ministry of Agriculture was retreating in a heavily defended building, said, 'Why do they have armed guards, when we don't have any and came here only to demand such and such a thing? If they shoot at us they are cowards.'

In 1975, when the organizations were mushrooming, we as the UTC also participated in the mobilizations of the 30th July. That day there was a massacre of the students. When later the dead were being taken to the cathedral, the population cried like fathers and mothers, as though their son had died; and they went to the cathedral to denounce what had happened. (Manuel)

152

## Apolinario Serrano, 'Polín'

'Apolinario Serrano and I were friends and used to talk quite a bit. He told me about his life as a poor peasant, how he felt rooted amongst his people, and how Marx's writings had illuminated things for him, convincing him to throw in his lot with the people. He was loved by all; men, women and children. He gave up his house and the piece of land that went with it, to the people. That was Apolinario, he sacrificed himself for the people.' (Quique, activist of the UTC)

'. . . *he was a man much loved, of great hope for achieving justice for the peasantry. I believe one of the most serious errors and one of the injustices that most cry to heaven has been committed. The people are deprived of their hopes and of the voices that denounce their oppression'*. (Archbishop Romero on the death of 'Polín Serrano, October 1979)[7]

Apolinario Serrano was born in 1943 in the *caserío* of El Líbano, in the municipality of Suchitoto. His parents died when he was young and he was brought up in considerable poverty by his grandmother. He never went to school but worked on the family's small plot of land and on the sugar cane plantations in the summer months. He began working with church communities in Aguilares in 1970, and joined FECCAS in 1973 at a time when the peasant union was in a period of stagnation. 'Polín' played a major role in the transformation of FECCAS into a combative peasant organization, independent of the electoral politics of the Christian Democrat Party. In 1974 he was made secretary general of the organization. In this position, 'Polín' encouraged the alliance with the UTC, visiting Chalatenango and forging close links with peasant activists there. He was elected secretary general of the FTC when it was formed in 1978. During these years he became a committed revolutionary and joined the FPL. He was aware of the importance of linking the peasants' struggle to those of other sectors, and he was one of the main people behind the development of the BPR. 'Polín' was captured and then killed on 29 September 1979 in Santa Ana near the *Cuartel de Caballería* (cavalry barracks), along with three other members of the FTC.

One of his comrades in the FPL, *comandante* Nadia, wrote the following about him:

'He began his struggle for the land in Aguilares. He was always a man sensitive to the problems of his class. Because of this and his involvement in the church, he became a member of FECCAS, where he slowly but surely developed into an outstanding leader. He became secretary general of FECCAS without being able to read or write. [Later] . . . he learned to read very well. Writing took a lot of manual dexterity which he never developed. He was an exemplary comrade in all respects, combining both peasant and proletarian ways of thinking and acting. He had a small piece of land which he gave to FECCAS.*

*He said that everything which tied him to private property was a regression in his development . . . He dedicated all his time to revolutionary activities. In FECCAS he showed not only organizational ability, skill for analysis and in identifying revolutionary principles and a great honesty, but also intelligence in the application of revolutionary ideas and work methods. This led him later on to join the FPL . . . He was a member of our revolutionary council and was elected to the permanent leadership, the central command. Within the command he was responsible for the national commission of the masses . . . He learned to read and write so that he could give more to the revolution. He used this to educate himself and later to help as an instructor in our cadre school. He expressed himself very easily in meetings.*

*As "Polín" came out of the Christian communities, he had many ties with priests. He had much access to Monseñor Romero and a deep respect of the principles of the church. He adopted Marxist-Leninism but always respected the religious beliefs of the people, the structures of the church, realizing that there was a need for the church to be more and more on the side of the peasants. In this sense, he had a lot of influence on Monseñor Romero.*

*He always had something funny to tell us. Once, he was reading Marx and he got enormously excited. He called a comrade and told him, "Look, this old fellow needs to come and give us some talks here."*

*One proof of his sacrifice are his reports to the central command . . . "Polín" presented the best tables and summaries of his work. He had to make great efforts to present his work with precision; no-one has yet presented reports as clear as his; as complete or as precise. He was 34 years old when he died in September 1979; he was going to get married that month . . ."[8]*


## Justo Mejía

Justo Mejía was born on 12 July 1932 in the village of La Ceiba in the *municipio* of Las Vueltas, Chalatenango. He went to school in the village when he was eight years old and reached third grade. At thirteen he worked with his parents as a farmer near Guarita on the border with Honduras. At eighteen the economic situation of his family was so desperate that, together with some friends, he went to Santa Ana in search of work. A year later he went to work on the banana plantations in Honduras, but returned to El Salvador at twenty. He lived a dissolute life, drinking a lot at this time, but at 27, following the death of his mother, he settled down with Guadalupe Mejía who bore him nine children. He worked as a farmer and small tradesman, and joined the Christian Democrat Party during the 1960s. At 39 years he joined a peasant cooperative as manager. He became radicalized at this time and began to meet with various inhabitants of his village to discuss how the community could struggle for its rights. In 1974, he participated in some church-run courses on agrarian reform and the history of the country, and a year later helped found the UTC in Chalatenango. He was secretary general of the first departmental council and at the end of 1975 joined the national leadership. He played a major role in the development of the UTC until his death on 9 November 1977. He was captured, tortured and murdered by four members of the National Guard on the road from San Fernando to Chalatenango.

## The UTC and FECCAS

Throughout the late 1970s the unions were able to attract support because they took up major issues and actively campaigned around them with some notable success. FECCAS and the UTC also grew because they were the peasants' own organizations. For many of the peasants of Chalatenango, the UTC distinguished itself by being 'theirs'; the poor peasantry ran it, and had their own leaders. Indeed the Salvadorean peasant movement produced a number of remarkable leaders, many of whom learnt to read and write within the organization:

**What influenced me most politically was learning to read and write. A sister in my place began teaching me and later I slowly learned more by myself. It changed my life because reading books left me thinking about change. A book called the *Cartilla* – for the teaching of the ABC – religious books, the New Testament and others were the first books to teach me a better understanding. Another thing that influenced me was the injustice of the landowners towards the poor and the activities of the repressive organizations. Through studying I came to know the exploitation all around us, by the landowners, the authorities, the church even which charged first one *colón* then five, twenty-five and one hundred *colones* for a wedding, or a christening. (Quique)**

Many of El Salvador's leaders have died in the struggle. Two who will be particularly remembered are Justo Mejía, the first Secretary-General of the UTC, and Apolinario Serrano, 'Polín', Secretary General of FECCAS and subsequently of the FTC (Rural Workers Federation) which united the two peasant organizations. Their stories are recounted in the box on pages 153-4.

The emergence of peasant leaders and the role of outside collaborators is particularly interesting. Outsiders, especially urban intellectuals, were not readily welcomed by the peasants. They had to win acceptance, through sharing the hardships and risks of the peasants. But when they did, they earned much respect. Andrés Torres was an intellectual, though of peasant extraction. No-one knew he belonged to the FPL until he was killed in 1977. Then the FPL acknowledged him as a member and the reaction of many peasants who

155

knew and loved him was to identify more closely with the FPL, which had proved itself through the work of Andrés as close to their interests:

Andrés was a humble *compa*, honest and sincere. He advised us, never showing tiredness nor anger with anyone. He worked in all the hamlets, organizing people. I told him about problems we had, about people who would betray each other and he would advise me.

We didn't know much about the political-military organizations at that time, we sometimes saw FPL propaganda but we had no idea that they had commandos and saw no link between what they were doing and our own organization. It was then, in 1977, that Andrés Torres was killed in Santa Tecla. And when his picture appeared in the newspaper with the letters, FPL, on the wall behind him and it turned out that he was one of the best militants of the FPL, everyone who had known him, either personally or from things he had said, was very surprised. People's attitudes began to change, many wanted to follow his example. FPL propaganda increased at this time, and its proposals tackled many of the problems we were facing in the communities. That was when we began to make contacts with the *compas* of the FPL, to find ways of getting close to the organization, and from then on our union became more politicized. But I would say that it was the death of the *compañero* which really affected the peasants, especially those who had worked with him and identified with his example, his ideas, his struggle. That was one of the things which helped the FPL make roots amongst the peasants. (Caravina)

Cabarrús' description of the planning of a strike in 1974 by FECCAS illustrates the role played by outside collaborators in the peasant organizations:

'The role of the collaborators was to coordinate discussion. They analyzed the situation and contributed – with great caution, due to the mistrust of the peasants – their opinion. The task of deciding on the work to be done depended on the initiative of the peasants. In the case in hand, the "strike" was planned at the peasants' own wishes, as it was they and not "the students and priests" who would pay the consequences. This element of mistrust enabled the peasant movement to maintain in practice a peasant style of acting, recognizable in the way of preparing both a march, dispersal and food supplies.'[9]

The peasants' contact with the students and teachers who would collaborate with them in this way increased with the formation of the BPR, and their influence is visible in the language and vocabulary the peasant movement began to adopt as it became more structured and institutionalized. This was Marxist in origin, though:

'every elegant and complicated word was explained slowly (to the peasants), *in a process similar to the education in the catechism to Indians at the time of the conquest. In a short time, the peasants were using continuously and with great boldness words which did not form part of their lexicon. They also often "adapted" certain terms: for the peasant, there wasn't a "proletariat"* (proletariado), *what there was in El Salvador was a "pooretariat"* (pobretariado), *a sector in which they naturally felt themselves represented.*'[10]

Apolinario Serrano's comment to friends is an amusing illustration of how some of the peasants responded to Marxism (see box on page 154). When he first saw some of Marx's writings he was so impressed that he suggested the old fellow be asked to give the peasants a talk! Where Marxism as they encountered it articulated their situation, many peasants readily took up its words and phrases, while those who came to lead the movement often gained a more sophisticated understanding. Among the peasant leaders of Chalatenango, many felt a sympathy for Marx and Lenin because, from the little they knew, what they said seemed relevant to their situation:

**I wouldn't say I was a Marxist-Leninist, though I would like to be one. I don't have the knowledge. What I know is that Marx was a great scientist. He said that to survive, human beings need to eat and to eat they must produce and we're Leninist because we put what he said into practice. Marx and Lenin taught us that it's not the peasant alone who will change things, but the workers and students too. But I really know nothing.** (Enrique)

The influence of Marxist ideas is reflected in the movement's documentation. FECCAS published its *carta de principios* (statement of principles) on 8 October 1975 after a lengthy process of discussion by all its members. It is a very important document in the history of the peasant movement and indicates how far FECCAS had travelled since the early days when it was under the influence of Christian Democracy:

'*FECCAS is **a political organization of the rural workers.** Not in the sense that the dominant classes and their reactionary government gives to the word "political", identifying it with the parties, elections etc, or with dirty games, deceptions, lies etc (a common thing in the bourgeois and petty-bourgeois parties). FECCAS is not political in that sense. FECCAS is a political organization only in the sense that it aims **to defend and promote the true, immediate and fundamental interests of the wage labourers and poor peasants** in as much as it aims to organize those rural workers to fight with strength and combativity for its interests and to participate directly in the radical (root) change of the capitalist system and total liberation from imperialism.*' (FECCAS, *carta de principios*, 1975, emphasis in original)

FECCAS also opted, as did the UTC, to base its organization on the

157

principles of democratic centralism, which it defined as:

'. . . *a form of organization in which there is, at the same time, a strong* **centralization** *of the leadership of the movement and a constant, responsible and conscious* **participation** *of all the bases and members of the organization . . . given the importance of our objectives and the difficulty of realizing tasks in the present conditions of the country, FECCAS must be structured in such a way that all its members can participate to the maximum in the work and daily struggle, in the plans and activities of the organization. For this reason, our struggle seeks to permit and encourage the members to examine everything, to ensure that the agreements made are carried out, to elect their own leaders and control their work, constantly criticizing it. This is how FECCAS understands democracy.*

*But this active participation of all members, does not diminish the importance of the work of the* **leadership.** *The leadership of our organization is carried out by a body elected for that purpose. Its election is made from below to above. Once named, it has the responsibility of guiding the organization correctly. But, as we have pointed out, the orientation of its activities and the solution of the problems will be discussed by the bases, and all the members must bring their criticisms. Thus, the leaders are not above our organization, but under its control.'* (ibid.)

158

The base of the organization understood this official position in very simple terms. One peasant explained: 'Centralism is when there's no time; democratic is when there's time to discuss something.'[11]

## Federation: the FTC

'. . . The development of the historic work of this department has been difficult. When we began the struggles of the rural workers, we said that we aren't willing to organize ourselves into just any organization; first we must analyze and discuss which organization most represents our interests. We aren't willing to be deceived in the way the electoral parties have tried to deceive us. In the early days I said, "my aspirations have been and will always be, to see an organization come out of our suffering, created by the peasants of Chalatenango themselves, an organization which we know has revolutionary principles and which defends in practice the interests of the rural workers".

For this reason we organized the UTC. It was the beginning of a hard struggle. We began with few and it is our duty today to remember those founding comrades who are responsible for what the UTC is in the department today. From the beginning, FECCAS helped us to consolidate the UTC and we hope that one day soon we will be one organization. For more than a year, we have been carrying out our struggle together, with this aim in mind.' (An extract from the speech of Justo Mejía to the first departmental council of the UTC, 'Heroes and Martyrs of Chalatenango', in November 1977 shortly before his capture and murder by the National Guard.)

Over time, FECCAS and the UTC drew closer together, eventually uniting to form the most combative peasant organization the country had ever known, the Rural Workers Federation (FTC). The alliance between the organizations was not forged easily at first. Some members of the UTC were initially suspicious of FECCAS' origins in the Christian Democrat movement and there was some resistance to an organic link. The two organizations moved closer together through joint activities and because political fraternity was established through membership of the Popular Revolutionary Bloc, BPR:

**The unification of FECCAS and UTC joined the peasants at a national level. Immediately the organization grew in Cinquera, Suchitoto and there were demonstrations in Arcatao and Cojutepeque. But the previous creation of the *Bloque*, in July 1975, was a major catalyst for this growth too. It integrated the students', teachers' and workers' organizations. The peasant leaders of FECCAS had approached the UTC to coordinate their actions and managed to organize a protest demonstration in response to the repression of the students. I don't know how many people came**

159

from Chalate, but we were thousands. Many came from Arcatao, which was the furthest away; that was really something, that so many came from there. We all managed to arrive the same day and we went to the university where they gave us somewhere to stay. We were very proud, we had never entered the university before, and here we were entering as if it was our house. When we returned home we told the others that we had been in the university and people had received us well, everyone was very pleased.

That was the first time in our history that the Central Cathedral had been taken for six days. It permitted a growth of the revolutionary movement into what was later to become the *Bloque*. After that, the BPR represented the major political force in the country, as it responded to the aspirations of the people. It was toward the end of 1976 and early 1977 that the most decisive development took place in the form of demonstrations and protest actions, land invasions as in Cinquera, San Vicente, El Paisnal. The struggle was carried out first through a legal petition to see how we could rent the land, but this was denied to us. We tried all channels, but it was impossible, they didn't listen. (Vidal)

Awareness of the coincidence in objectives between the two organizations led their leaderships to promote a discussion amongst the base on a strategic alliance. A letter was distributed outlining the proposal to all the members. As a result the National Councils of the two organizations voted unanimously in favour of the proposal in February 1976. The organizations still kept their own structures, however, but this proved very cumbersome, slowing down decision-making and repeating roles in each organization. In 1978 the decision was taken to form a single body, and the First National Council of the FTC, the Rural Workers' Federation, 'Andrés Torres Sánchez and martyrs of the popular revolution', approved a new structure integrating the organizations. Below, a peasant describes the emergence of the Federation:

Over the years, the methods of FECCAS and the UTC changed in that we no longer allowed ourselves to be led by the parties as before. When we saw that they only went for the most elementary democratic demands, and that the UTC followed a line that gained us direct experience, we followed that. So from 1975 onwards, our people lived a process of increasing bitterness as they pushed ahead with the basic demands against the landowners. The struggle for the land had gained strength by 1976, also demands for lower land rents, and demands to the bank for agricultural credit, and reductions in the price of agricultural materials and loans . . . This struggle was channelled into the Union of Rural Workers, the UTC. But FECCAS too had moved away from being a manipulated organization and had become truly representative of the agricultural workers, and which had a certain clarity about its immediate objectives.

So after having organized ourselves in the UTC, we realized that FECCAS was suffering the same forms of repression as us. At the next opportunity we formed an alliance to create a united front for our demands. When FECCAS made their petitions, we were automatically present there too. At the end of 1975 a joint platform was worked out for the BPR, a scale of wage increases during the sugar, coffee and cotton harvests. It also demanded that workers on *fincas* receive better food and medicine for the sick, adequate housing during the harvest and wages to be paid in cases of sickness. The fusion of FECCAS and the UTC took place in 1976, but both organizations continued wilth their own structures and representatives. The peasants had agreed that there was to be one organization, as both had the same objectives and ways of struggle. So the federation was born. (Manuel)

*'Stop the repression against farmworkers! BPR'*

# 6
# PEASANTS AND POLITICS

## The Struggle Begins 1975-1977

We have seen how FECCAS was radicalized initially through the influence of the church's pastoral work, culminating in its decision to join the BPR in 1975 and the publication of its statement of principles in October of that year. At the same time, the peasant leaders, many of them Delegates or *Preparadores* of the Word, began an intense process of recruitment, visiting the different *cantones* and setting up bases of the organization, usually from the Christian base communities where they existed. By about 1976, the organization had some 2,000 members and 500 sympathisers in 66 bases, not just in Aguilares – though with 23 bases this area was the organization's strongest – but also in a number of areas in the departments of San Salvador, Cabañas, Cuscatlán and La Libertad.[1] There is no similar numerical data available for the UTC though it spread rapidly throughout Chalatenango and large areas of San Vicente.

The goverment's reaction was limited at first, though there were plenty of signs of things to come. In June 1975, six members of one peasant family were killed by government forces in the community of Tres Calles. In July a campaign was launched against the Alas brothers which culminated in an order for their arrest by a Suchitoto judge accusing them of 'instigation to rebellion against the government, for anarchic anti-government activities'.[2] (The brothers managed to stay alive and in 1977 they finally fled the country.) At the end of July 1975 the massacre of students took place in San Salvador.

More ominous signs of the future pattern of repression came in August of the same year, when the first of the death squads appeared: the Anti-Communist Liberation Armed Forces, or FALANGE as it called itself. The FALANGE called for a return to the 1932 methods of General Maximiliano Hernández Martínez and launched a campaign of murder and bombings aimed at urban trade unions and opposition parties. It was probably a specialized unit created by ANSESAL, the military security agency, using funds from the landowners' associations.[3]

By December 1975, FECCAS felt strong enough to organize its

163

first national demonstration in Aguilares. Some months later, in July 1976, the anniversary of the students' massacre, the BPR held its first demonstration. There were 3,000 peasants present from FECCAS and the UTC in a demonstration involving some 10,000 people. Shortly afterwards it began a campaign against the Agrarian Transformation law.

In November 1976, FECCAS and the UTC presented a joint proposal to the Ministry of Labour, demanding better food and work conditions, and an increase in the agricultural daily wage to nine *colones* and three *colones* for meals. To support the demands, they held four demonstrations in Zacatecoluca (La Paz), Cancasque (Chalatenango), Quezaltepeque (La Libertad) and Ilobasco (Cabañas). In Quezaltepeque the peasant movement had its first confrontation with the authorities. When police arrested a demonstrator, a commission of six was organized to secure his release, but a policeman shot at the commission and the crowd of some 2,500 people, wounding a number of people. The crowd, some carrying pistols while others grabbed stones, stormed the town hall and released the peasant and seven other prisoners while the police fled through the back entrance.

Tensions, already high in the rural areas, were fuelled by another incident on 5 December 1976. The dam at Cerrón Grande was almost complete and as the waters rose peasants were being forced out of their homes. The owners had sold their land to the government and ignored the fate of the peasants who had lived on it. A group of some 250 peasants sought an interview with Francisco Orellana, one of the landowners. During the meeting his brother was wounded by shots, which some witnesses claimed were fired by Francisco himself in panic. The incident immediately aroused the landowners' deep-seated fears of the 'masses' and they launched a campaign in the press to denounce the 'hordes' of FECCAS and the UTC who had attacked Orellano's *hacienda* under the instigation of 'third world priests, native and foreign, who . . . keep impelling farm workers into violations not only of the laws but of the fundamental principles of Christianity'.[4] On 11 December the army launched a military operation in the north of the country, in Aguilares and El Paisnal, and in Las Vueltas and Las Flores in Chalatenango, taking over villages and intimidating the population in a show of strength.

The authorities now began to organize themselves in Chalatenango, and new military posts sprang up in the region. The peasants in turn began to consider their own security and each branch of the UTC elected someone to take responsibility for the defence of members, such as warning systems during meetings. Even at this time there were some who could no longer sleep in their homes at night for fear of a visit from ORDEN or the National Guard. In the coming years this was to become increasingly common. I met one 16-year-old boy, Lito, in Chalatenango, who told me that he had begun attending

164

*National Guardsman arresting peasant, Chalatenango*

Kenneth Silverman

meetings of the UTC in 1976 at the age of eight when all his family began to participate. When it became known to the authorities, the family was harrassed and eventually at the age of ten, he and his brothers began to sleep in the hills. He still attended school until he was 12, but after school he would go straight to the hills for the night.

By now the peasant movement had taken root in El Salvador and was growing in numbers and combativity. But, although it had become a movement of national importance, its main base of support was still confined to certain geographical areas and the linkages with the urban workers were still embryonic, given the weakness of the organized labour movement. The forces ranged against the peasants were immense. The oligarchy and their military allies were now largely united in their fight against the common enemy, while the left-wing opposition was weakened by continued divisions which took the popular movement along different political paths. This situation led

165

the BPR to issue a very cautious statement at the beginning of 1977 urging realism on its supporters:

'. . . the popular masses, principally the agricultural labourers and poor peasants, have begun to join organizations which accord with the fundamental interests of the proletariat. Nevertheless, it should not be forgotten that we are in a stage of the revolutionary process in which, on the one hand the forces of the bourgeoisie are dominant at all levels – economic, political, ideological – and on the other, given the ideological and organic dispersion of the left in our country, the popular masses are presented with various alternatives, and for that reason the development and consolidation of the Prolonged Revolutionary War of the People cannot be achieved overnight and much will depend on interpreting correctly each moment and conjuncture and developing correctly the tasks that the process is demanding in its different moments and stages.'[5]

The ERP and the RN were heartened by the popular response to yet another electoral fraud in February 1977. Thousands of people flocked to the Plaza Libertad in the capital, organizing a permanent protest vigil against the ballot-rigging which had once again deprived the UNO (National Opposition Union) of victory and installed yet another military president, General Romero, to safeguard the interests of the landowners. The people erected barricades around the square and the protest was only dispersed when government forces moved in on 28 February, resulting in an estimated 100 dead, 200 wounded and 500 arrested. The RN described this mobilization as a 'pre-insurrectionary' event, but the FPL, while acknowledging the growth in combativity, continued to take a cautious view. Much political work remained to be done, the FPL argued, especially among the urban working class, and military preparations were needed, such as the building of a popular militia to meet the coming repression.

The repression came quickly. The previous year, in September 1976, FECCAS and the UTC had begun a campaign against the refusal of landowners to rent part of their land at affordable prices. They had first of all presented a number of petitions to the Ministry of Agriculture, invoking the Land Renting Law (Ley de Arrendamiento de Tierras) with the expectation that they could gain land for rent ready for planting in April of the following year. However, the Ministry remained silent, and the peasants decided to organize a series of peaceful land invasions on 5 April 1977, during Holy Week. This was an entirely new and more combative stage in the peasants' fight. They took land belonging to the hacienda San Francisco in El Paisnal, where the landowner was evicting peasants who had long rented land from him; the hacienda Guajoyo in Tecoluca, the hacienda Platanares, Zacatecoluca (La Paz department) and the hacienda San Francisco, Tejutepeque (Cabañas). Two land invasions took place in

*National Guard*

Chalatenango; the peasants took over the idle land and began planting at once:

**In Chalate two land invasions took place; I was in charge of one. In the village of Jicarito, people met with those from Portillo del Norte. They had already decided on a plot which was only used to rear cattle. Justo Mejía and I were made responsible for the invasion as we knew the area. But I said it wasn't going to be only us who would invade but all the people; so we met with those from Jicarito and El Portillo, and we showed them that a real land invasion was nothing to play around with but a serious business. So we had about five meetings and finally they said, alright, go on then, do it, we support you. This was in 1977. We organized it well. I told them the first thing would be to gather here in Portillo, to go down together towards Cancasque in a demonstration to hold a meeting there in front of the town hall. From there we would go on to invade the plot. We did this and then began preparing the land we had taken, planting maize. We did it all without arms, although the *Guardia* was nearby. We kept this going for some months, but then gave it up.**

167

The *Guardia* had evicted people from land in San Francisco and they were coming towards us. And as it was a long way from Arcatao and many *compas* would be taken by the *Guardia*, we thought about it and decided that without weapons, we would just have to leave the land. We returned another time in the same year, and again, until the *Policía de Hacienda* came and massacred us. (Quique)

On 17 May, government troops launched a large-scale operation to evict the peasants who had taken over the land in El Paisnal. Two thousand troops came with helicopters and armoured troop carriers and took over the entire region, surrounding Aguilares in the early hours of 19 May. A peasant sleeping in the church tried to ring the church bell to alert the town but was shot and killed. The troops broke down the church door, stripped and blindfolded the peasants and Jesuits who were there and threw them to the ground. Then they smashed windows and shot open the tabernacle, scattering the communion wafers on the floor. The pastor of Chalatenango, who had been visiting Aguilares, was arrested and beaten. Soldiers moved through the town, ransacking houses, and later announced that one soldier and six civilians had been killed in an armed encounter. Eyewitnesses corrected the numbers: at least 50 townspeople had been shot dead and hundreds taken away by the army.

On 26 August, the security forces struck again in Chalatenango. Forty or fifty members of the National Guard and Treasury Police arrived at the village of El Salitre in the early evening and began to search the houses. They seized Serafín Vásquez, a Delegate of the Word, on his way back from a literacy class and took him to a house where classes in Christianity were held. A young peasant, called Pablo, lived there as his own home had been flooded out when the Cerrón Grande dam was built. The security forces killed them both with machetes and then arrested another Delegate, Felipe de Jesús Chacón, as he got off the bus on his way home. His body was found with a bullet in the head the next morning. He had been badly tortured, his scalp cut off, the flesh stripped from his face and his body hacked with machetes. Chacón's son, Juan, was a leader of the BPR and he himself had been a coordinator of the base communities around Tejutla.

# The Church Under Attack

The attack on the church had begun in earnest. Between 29 November 1976 and 31 May 1977 there was a press campaign which included 63 paid adverts and 32 editorials against the church.

In January 1977, two Jesuit students working in Aguilares were expelled from the country. At the end of the month, a Colombian priest, Mario Bernal, who worked in the parish of Apopa, was kidnapped and taken to Guatemala. In the following days a Belgian priest, Guillermo Denoux, was tortured and expelled; a member of the American Maryknoll religious order, Bernard Survil, was also expelled; and Rafael Barahona, a Salvadorean priest working in the parish of Tecoluca in San Vicente, was arrested and tortured for two days by the National Guard and finally released with a fractured skull.

February 1977 was a momentous month in many ways. In the midst of this wave of repression which brought the church into direct confrontation with the government, a new Archbishop came into office. Oscar Arnulfo Romero had been chosen because he was considered a conservative and a politically safe choice for the post. *La Prensa Gráfica* published a brief interview with him on 10 February in which he said: 'We must keep to the centre watchfully in the traditional way, but seeking justice', though he also said that a priest who takes a stand for social justice should not be considered a subversive.[6] In fact, Romero had already begun to change some of his views; in mid-1975, for instance, he had secretly attended talks by Father David Rodríguez, whom the Bishop Aparicio of San Vicente accused of being communist. Father Rodríguez had come to talk to members of his clergy and after hearing three of his talks, Romero had concluded that he was just applying the gospel to El Salvador and told the Bishop of his opinion.[7]

Just three weeks after the new Archbishop had taken office, on 12 March, Rutilio Grande was shot dead along with two companions on his way to say mass in El Paisnal. Grande had come under increasing attack from the right for his parish work. Many Delegates of the Word played leading roles in FECCAS and although the union meetings were always held at a different time to the religious celebrations, to the right the two were synonymous. Grande himself had never resolved his personal dilemma. He believed that the evangelical work was something much broader than any particular political project and that his team should not become directly involved with the peasant organization. But he recognized the peasant union as a legitimate union body with human rights which had to be defended. In these words from one of his last sermons, spoken on 13 February 1977 on the occasion of Mario Bernal's expulsion from the parish of Apopa, he expresses his anguish at the growing violence against the church and his parishioners:

'*I am very much afraid that, very soon, the Bible and the Gospel will not be able to enter our frontiers. Only the covers will reach us, as its pages are subversive – against sin, of course . . . If Jesus of Nazareth was to return, as in that time, coming down from Galilee to Judea, that is, from Chalatenango to San Salvador, I dare say that he would not get as far as Apopa with his preachings and actions . . . They would stop him in Guazapa and jail him there.*'[8]

169

The right, however, placed responsibility for increasing peasant militancy with the parish team and the Jesuits as a whole. Marxist clergy, it claimed, had subverted the peasants. The Eastern Region Farmers' Front (FARO), submitted a statement to the US Congressional hearings on the 1977 presidential elections in which it stated:

*'Everybody knows it, and FARO published it, that the Jesuits have organized and exercise demagogic control of FECCAS and UTC; that those organizations committed acts of violence in Quezaltepeque where a humble market vendor was killed; that members of those organizations started the disturbance at Hacienda Colima which ultimately led to the death of an outstanding citizen, Guayo Orellana; that leaders of those organizations carried out acts of violence that ended in killings in the Tecoluca parish area; and that those organizations together with other organizations also under the demagogic control of the Communists . . . rioted in the streets of San Salvador shouting "Death" and slogans threatening violence and bloodshed.'*[9]

Rutilio's death shook the Salvadorean church hierarchy as well as its base. In particular it shook the new Archbishop who had known him well. He refused to participate in government functions until the killing was investigated.

The Archbishop came increasingly to identify with the cause of the poor. This was to have an extraordinary impact on the popular movement, inspiring many thousands and convincing the more cautious of the legitimacy of the peasants' struggle. Romero's message was spread across El Salvador through the archdiocesan radio, YSAX, which broadcast his Sunday sermon. One biographer has written:

*'I know someone who worked for a company that calculated the size of various audiences for advertising agencies. She dug up confirmed figures for radio audiences in El Salvador. The first finding was that the bishop's Sunday sermon had by far the largest audience of any programme in the country. The figures are quite clear. His audience was 73 per cent of the countryside and 47 per cent of urban areas - and the sermons lasted at least an hour and a half. It was the time when our bishop's voice could be heard coming from houses, cars, and the transistor radios of persons walking down the street. But not everyone felt safe turning the volume up. A friend told me that soon after Bishop Romero's sermons started, the sale of earphones in his store doubled. The* campesinos *especially, were aware that it might be dangerous to be known as someone who listened to Bishop Romero on the radio.'*[10]

The sermons would always begin with theological teaching on the scriptural readings of the day, then these would be related to the reality of El Salvador, and finally there would be church announcements including a reading of every documented case of persons who had been killed or tortured or disappeared. If there was a major event, Romero would present a 'pastoral position' on it. One writer has called these sermons a kind of 'oral newspaper', whose impact was so great that the YSAX transmitter was bombed ten times during three years, from 1977 to 1980.

Even the more conservative bishops had rallied to support the new Archbishop following the assassination of Rutilio Grande. But the repression continued and intensified after the FPL had kidnapped Mauricio Borgonovo, the foreign minister, demanding the release of 37 political prisoners. A new death squad had declared itself now, the White Warriors Union (UGB); the FALANGE was no longer heard of. Many of the attacks on the church were attributed to the UGB although they were often carried out openly by government security forces. The UGB called on the government not to negotiate on the Borgonovo kidnapping and threatened an 'eye for an eye' if he was killed. UGB handbills began to circulate, 'Be a Patriot, Kill a Priest!' This is exactly what happened. Borgonovo was killed when the government refused to negotiate, and on 11 May Father Alfonso Navarro was found dead. Father Navarro had been one of the founders of the new pastoral work with the peasants in Opico until he had been transferred to an upper-class parish in the capital.

On 21 June 1977, shortly before General Romero was due to take office as president, the campaign against the church reached its peak. The UGB told all the Jesuits to leave the country within thirty days or they would be systematically killed. But El Salvador was now receiving international attention as human rights became a theme of Jimmy Carter's presidency. Congressional hearings were held on the persecution of the church in El Salvador and when General Romero took office on 1 July, he had to take steps to protect the Jesuits.

But in the five months prior to the president's inauguration, two priests had been killed, two tortured, one beaten, two imprisoned, four threatened with death, seven refused re-entry into the country and eight expelled.[11] A number of priests had been forced to flee, such as Rutilio Sánchez who had had to leave his parish of San Martín and seek refuge in the seminary. Following the security forces' operations in Chalatenango in August 1977, Archbishop Romero opened his sermon in a nearby chapel with the words: 'These days I have to walk the roads gathering up dead friends, listening to widows and orphans, and trying to spread hope.'

## The Worker-Peasant Alliance 1977-1978

The Salvadorean government was under some pressure from the Carter administration following the assault on the church. In his first few months in office, President Romero did not attempt to prevent workers' and peasants' demonstrations in San Salvador. The national press, in a brief period of openness, took announcements of their activities from unions and popular organizations. The BPR organized a demonstration to commemorate the second anniversary of the students' massacre on 30 July. Between then and 15 November, there were about 11 BPR demonstrations in the capital and in other areas, particularly Santa Ana, Aguilares and San Martín, either denouncing repression or in solidarity with harvest workers or other workers. FAPU organized two demonstrations in July and November in support of a series of workers' strikes.

The guerilla organizations were also increasingly active at this time. On 12 July the FPL assassinated ex-President Colonel Osmín Aguirre, who had been involved in the massacre of 1932; on 29 July they killed two local commanders in Chalatenango; and on 16 September they killed Dr Carlos Alfaro Castillo, the rector of the University of El Salvador and a powerful landowner. About 35 bombs went off in different parts of the country on 21 August, 27 of them placed by the ERP. On 21 September the ERP took over four radio stations to transmit a revolutionary communiqué, and in November they clashed with soldiers on the outskirts of Osicala in Morazán. On 11 August, the RN kidnapped Dr Carlos Emilio Alvarez, a member of one of the country's most important coffee families. As the mobilizations continued and increased from July to November so did the repression, and Chalatenango was particularly affected. ORDEN was of increasing importance in identifying peasant activists, but the armed forces were more and more directly involved in the repression.

Despite this, FECCAS and the UTC organized two more land occupations, one on 10 August in the *hacienda* El Sitio in Tejutepeque, and the other on 7 November on the *hacienda* La Paz near Opico in San Vicente. The main campaign from October onwards centered on wage claims by the agricultural workers on the plantations where harvest time was just beginning. FECCAS and the UTC together with ATACES (the peasant union organized by the Salvadorean Communist Party) presented a claim to the Ministry of Labour for a minimum wage, 11 *colones* a day in each of the coffee, cotton and sugar cane harvests (compared to the 8, 6 and 5.50 *colones* respectively paid for the 1976-1977 harvest). The coffee growers had recovered from a slump in world prices in 1971-1975. According to the IMF, their net income after tax had increased fivefold in 1976 and in 1977 was likely to be three times higher again, recovering in a year all that had been lost during the slump.[12] FECCAS and the UTC added claims for better work conditions to the wage claim. The box opposite is the text of an FTC leaflet which illustrates the demands of the peasants working on the plantations. The Ministry of Labour failed to respond and on 27 October two peasants were killed in a demonstration organized by the

172

## FECCAS/UTC Publicly Denounce Irregularities on the *Finca* 'La Gomera'

FECCAS, the UTC and members of the BPR, send our most fraternal and revolutionary greetings to all workers on the *finca* 'La Gomera', *cantón* las Granadillas, department of La Libertad. It belongs to Ana Vilma Avila, who is guilty of ill-treatment and irregularities towards these workers:

1 At the weigh-in, the workers are being cheated out of up to one *arroba*, and are paid at the most 1.85 *colones* per *arroba*.
2 The food is of bad quality, the workers are given hard and rotten beans, *tortillas* of badly ground maize, and the food is handed out very late (between 2 and 3pm).
3 On Sunday 9 September, all workers had to go picking yet again, without being told what they would be paid.
4 The workers in the drying yards have to work for eight hours and have been promised eight *colones*.
. . . We are calling on all workers on the 'La Gomera' to put the following demands to the exploiter, Ana Vilma Avila:

1 Payment of 14.25 *colones* for a working day of eight hours or of 3.60 *colones* for the *arroba* of picked coffee, with no difference between sexes and including those working in the yards.
2 Payment of 14.25 *colones* for the Sunday (*Séptimo*).
3 A Christmas bonus for all workers and time off over Christmas and New Year.
4 Good and sufficient food or payment of 4.50 *colones* for the three daily meals and distribution of food at mid-day.
5 An end to cheating at the weigh-in.
6 Free medical treatment for all workers.

FTC December 1979

---

FTC around the campaign. On 30 October, troops took over the towns of Apopa and Cojutepeque to prevent two demonstrations called by the BPR.

But this time the peasants took a new form of action facilitated by a remarkable upsurge in the militancy of the urban workers. Along with a number of striking textile workers, the peasants peacefully occupied the Ministry of Labour in an attempt to get a reply to the workers' request for negotiations with factory owners and the peasants' request to present their case to the Commission for the Minimum Wage. A large crowd of peasants and workers gathered outside in support. Through the mediation of the Archbishop's office, the demands were granted; it was the first concrete step in the forging of a genuine alliance of workers and peasants through the pursuit of basic demands.

The most significant new development in these months from August to November 1977 was the activity of the urban labour movement. From 10 August until mid November there were at least 11 strikes in the electrical industry (*Compañía Eléctrica de Río Lempa* – CEL), the textile industry (El Léon factory, *Sacos Cuscatlán*, INSA), the clothing industry (*Fábrica de Guantes*, EAGLE), the food industry (*Embotelladora La Cascada*, AINCO, *Fábrica de dulces y pastas* DIANA), the mining industry (*Minas de oro de San Sebastián*) and the construction industry (*Nuevo aeropuerto Cuscatlán*). These strikes saw the development of new forms of struggle, with factory occupations and solidarity actions organized through the BPR and FAPU to involve as many other unions and popular organizations as possible.

There had been a number of strikes since 1974 but not on this scale or level of militancy. Between 1974 and 1977 there were 15 strikes involving 5 to 6,000 workers of which eight were successful and seven were defeated.[13] First FAPU and then the BPR had been gradually extending their influence in the labour movement. It had been difficult at first, as Samayoa and Galván point out in an article on the union movement of these years:

*'The popular organizations had to confront the problem of penetrating an area in which the positions of control were already taken. Unlike in the peasant world, virgin because of abandonment, the unions had been in fact subordinated to leaderships which persisted.'[14]*

In particular, they had to challenge the Communist Party, which controlled some of the major union federations, and the United Confederation of Salvadorean Workers (CUTS) which was set up in 1977. Any challenge to Communist Party domination had to be organized in great secrecy given the conditions in the country, avoiding any open conflicts which might draw the government's attention to it. In 1975 the Workers' Committee of Revolutionary Orientation (COOR) had been set up. It worked in semi-clandestinity to foster a new, more militant unionism and gained considerable support amongst the textile workers, particularly in the El León and INCA factories. FAPU set up the Inter-Union Committee in 1977 and had won influence in FENASTRAS, which grouped some eleven unions including the important power workers union, STECEL. By the end of 1977, the popular organizations were making some headway among the more organized workers. But they still faced the major problem of the low level of unionization, by one estimate only 20 per cent of the labour force.[15] Reaching this unorganized labour force was a very slow and difficult process, given security problems, the low educational level of many workers and their precarious economic situation in a country of high unemployment.

By the end of 1977, the government had found a way of circumventing international criticism of its human rights record by 'legalizing' the repression. On 25 November 1977, the government had enacted the Law for the Defence and Guarantee of Public Order which created a permanent state of emergency. Just thirteen days after the new law came into effect, on 17 December, the army, in a five-day operation, 'legally' evicted peasants of the FTC who had taken over land. At the end of January 1978 the National Guard evicted 600 workers who occupied the *Central Azucarera Izalco* sugar refinery, demanding better wages and conditions. Amnesty International severely criticized the new law. It seemed, they said '... specifically designed to restrict the actions of trade unions, the political opposition, and human rights monitors, including members of the clergy who report human rights problems or advise members of the peasant trade unions'.[16]

But the repression was too late. It failed in its intention of intimidating and terrorizing people into passivity or retrenchment. Instead, such was the momentum of the popular movement that it was spurred to greater militancy. Willingness to flout the law whatever the consequences was now apparent amongst wide sectors of the working class as well as the peasantry. During the 15 months of the Public Order Law, there were 40 strikes in violation of it. Factory occupations and the taking of managers and bosses as hostages became a common and deeply politicizing feature of the strikes. Both FAPU and the BPR played key roles in mobilizing solidarity from all their affiliated popular organizations and helped maintain a level of activity and militancy despite the repression. The peasants organized mobilizations in support of the workers, travelling from Chalatenango to picket factories and provide logistical support to the workers:

In September 1977 we participated in the strikes of the workers in San Salvador, in *La Diana*, *Fábrica de León* and others. Here in Chalate every three days we chose a delegation, some 500 people, to go to the demonstration in San Salvador. There they left 100 in one factory, 100 in another, and so on, so that 100 peasants spent three days and nights with the workers. They were relieved by 500 new people. In the meetings everyone raised their hand to go to the demo. We just chose the number we needed, everyone coming voluntarily in this way. (Víctor)

---

By 1977 Facundo Guardado of the UTC and Juan Mendoza of FECCAS were working together in the BPR. Embassies and churches occupied by the *Bloque* in 1978/1979 were made into centres of study. Or the peasants would go to an institute together with the students to occupy the buildings. This unity is very relevant. In this way in 1978 we took the Ministry of Labour in San Salvador and held it for three days and they gave us all we demanded, all of which gave a lot of confidence to everyone. In

**1979, the workers of a soft drink factory went on strike, we went in solidarity with them and many peasants from here went to the city. The workers were pleased and felt strengthened when the rural workers showed solidarity with them.** (Ramón)

In February 1978, FECCAS and the UTC had again taken up the demands of the poor peasant smallholders and tenant farmers and they proposed legislation to lower land rents and prices for fertilizer and other agricultural materials. The minister of agriculture refused to see them, but the president of the Agriculture Development Bank told them to return on 17 March. One hundred peasants arrived on 17 March and found the bank closed, whereupon they marched through the city. The army attacked, killing four of the peasants and wounding 30. A group of peasants fled the scene and took a bus out of the capital. The bus was stopped by the police some eleven kilometers out and five more peasants died and one policeman. 'Our people are hungry', said Archbishop Romero: 'They need land to work, they need to talk with someone about finding a solution to their problems. Dead and wounded are the outcome of that desire.'[17]

Holy week that year brought new violence, this time in San Pedro Perulapán, a rural area some twelve miles east of San Salvador. Tensions between ORDEN and members of the FTC were running high; ORDEN members were looting and burning houses belonging to members of the peasant union, beating men, women and children and soon killing as well. Tránsito Vásquez, a local leader was kidnapped and the next day found decapitated with his head hanging on a tree facing the body. Members of the FTC then forced three of the murderers to beg pardon of his corpse and dig his grave. This was followed by armed clashes between ORDEN members and some peasant activists in which nine peasants died. A few days later the FPL executed five members of ORDEN.

The revenge of the authorities was swift. The army, together with members of the Treasury Police, the National Guard, the National Police and members of ORDEN, launched a military operation aimed at peasant leaders and sympathizers throughout the area. Six were killed, 14 wounded, and 68 disappeared. When a British journalist visited San Pedro a year later in April 1979 she found the National Guard still occupying the village and the women smuggling food to their men who were hiding in the surrounding countryside. The Archdiocese of San Salvador took in the first refugees from the army sweep through the San Pedro area – peasants were now quite frequently forced to flee their homes as a result of army operations – and Archbishop Romero formed a commission to investigate the events. The commission concluded that they 'were provoked mediately and immediately by ORDEN in close collaboration with the security forces.'[18]

176

The BPR peacefully occupied the cathedral in protest at the events. But army operations continued from May to December, particularly around the *municipio* of Cinquera, together with numerous attacks by ORDEN and the National Guard, all against members of the peasant union. At least eight peasants were killed in this period and many more arrested and tortured.[19]

## The Question of Violence – 1978-1979

By 1978 the need for an organized form of self-defence from ORDEN and the security forces was evident in all the areas where the peasant organization was active. The peasants had been evolving various methods, but the step toward using armed defence and the armed struggle as such, was a considerable one. Vidal describes how the peasants of Chalatenango began by stealing small pistols from members of ORDEN, during the clashes between ORDEN and FECCAS-UTC that were increasingly common:

**We saw that it was necessary to create a defence force for ourselves, but we had no arms. So our defence began with the minimum we had, with stones for example. We would hit the enemy with stones when they came, and while they were delayed for a moment, the people could get away. Or with the *corvo* or the machete, we took a revolver from the ORDEN man. In this way we have succeeded in capturing arms by the most simple means; with a stone we captured a machete, with a machete we seized a .38 or a .22, and with this we even managed to get a rifle.** (Vidal)

Members of the BPR would sometimes carry small arms on demonstrations, although for many the issue of taking up arms was difficult to reconcile with the Christian message and this provoked some discussion. But the situation was becoming increasingly desperate for the peasants:

**I didn't experience the repression personally at first, I knew how to keep a low profile. But I had continued to go to church and soon anyone who went to a celebration of the Word was a subversive to the enemy and they watched him. But I would not stop going; the martyrs of history have always given me strength to confront this kind of situation . . . If they could struggle, then why couldn't I risk my life, and so I did. And then came the rise in repression: on 9 September 1979, the troops came, and we all left for the mountains; we went to a hill, the Cañada. There was a village up there in the hills where we took refuge and didn't return again. And there in the hills we began to think of the need to defend ourselves, because until then we hadn't used any kind of arms, but since then, yes.**

**You see, what happened was that at first we met in hamlets in**

## Chalatenango: Most Punished Zone

'. . . *Chalatenango is the most punished zone, particularly Arcatao and Las Vueltas, places in which the population has been persecuted and killed, and the region has been left almost deserted.*'[20]

From 2 July to 27 November [1977] incomplete lists recorded a total of 38 people arrested by the security forces and/or by ORDEN. Some of those arrested had later been freed, but usually after being beaten up and even tortured. Of the arrests, 28 had taken place in the department of Chalatenango . . . In the same period members of the security forces and/or ORDEN beat up five people, all of them in the department of Chalatenango. Still during this period the same forces searched the houses of peasants on seven separate occasions in various municipalities in the department of Chalatenango, without, of course, any legal authority. On another three occasions (once in the department of Chalatenango and twice in that of Morazán), entire *cantones* of chief cities of municipalities were occupied by soldiers for one, two or three days, with consequent house searches and arrests. There were also cases, still in the department of Chalatenango, of the harvests of small landowners being destroyed, or, where the harvest had already been gathered, of the crops being stolen — acts carried out by members of the security forces or of ORDEN. Finally during this period, seven peasants were killed by members of the security forces and/or ORDEN in the department of Chalatenango, one in San Vicente, and another in Cabañas. Three women, one of them a girl of ten, were raped by national guardsmen in the department of Chalatenango. In some cases, leaders of peasant organizations were affected, and in many, grass-roots members of the same organizations. Two of those killed were active Catholic catechists, and one of those beaten up was a priest. The priest was arrested and tortured for several hours during one of the military operations in . . . Morazán.

So while the government maintained a relatively respectable facade in the capital, the repression of farm workers went on, but in a more intelligent and selective way than during the final months of Colonel Molina's government . . . The department of Chalatenango was selected to complete the repression begun under the previous regime in the department of San Salvador and San Vicente. Between the three of them they account for the greater part of the peasant organizations' local branches.[21]

Yesterday I was at San Miguel de Mercedes (department of Chalatenango), simply doing my duty encouraging the Christian communities that are developing there. The military guards at both sides of the entrance to the town kept many people from arriving, and they had to go back. They made me get out of the car too, and they searched it. They even suspect the bishop! And afterward they said it was for my security. If it was for my security, I thought, why are they so suspicious of me seated in a car? And I said to them: 'Why don't you let those people that you have stopped go in with me? I'll walk with them'. They were women. The guards wouldn't let them enter. Afterwards I had the chance to find the people at San Antonio de los Ranchos, where they were waiting for me, because they were eager to speak with their shepherd.[22]

We have lived through a tremendously tragic week. I could not give you the facts before, but a week ago last Saturday, on 15 March [1980], one of the largest and most distressing military operations was carried out in the countryside. The villages affected were La Laguna, Plan de Ocotes and El Rosario. The operation brought tragedy: a lot of homes were burned, there was looting, and — inevitably — people were killed. In La Laguna, the attackers killed a married couple, Ernesto Navas and Aurelia Mejía de Navas, their little children, Martín and Hilda, thirteen and seven years old, and eleven more peasants . . . Last Sunday, the following were assassinated in Arcatao by four members of ORDEN: peasants Marcelino Serrano, Vicente Ayala, 24 years old, and his son, Freddy. That same day, Fernando Hernández Navarro, a peasant, was assassinated when he fled from the military . . . Amnesty International issued a press release in which it described the repression of the peasants, specially in the area of Chalatenango. The week's events confirm this report in spite of the fact the government denies it . . . It would be interesting now to analyse what these months have meant to a new government that started out with the intention of bringing us out of these horrific situations. And yet if what it aims for is to cut down the leaders of the people's organization and impede the process which the people want, no other process can take place. Without roots among the people, no government can be effective, and it has no hope if it seeks to establish itself by blood and suffering.[23]

**various areas in Chalatenango. But then, the authorities weren't carrying out the aggression. It was ORDEN, the paramilitary organization, which tried to get on top of the UTC. Sometimes ORDEN would stone the houses of those who were members of the UTC, killing women and children. But then the authorities got organized, and the National Guard and the army began to patrol the area.** (Herman)

Security and defence now had to be organized in every village and this often meant carrying a weapon to fight back if attacked. There had been armed clashes between the peasant activists and ORDEN members already, for instance at San Pedro Perulapán. The peasants always stressed how this step had only been taken after all the peaceful attempts to present their case had failed, and many had suffered arrest and torture and had lost members of their family as the repression intensified:

**Towards 1979 the repression got worse: we had to leave the house because they were invading and killing, terrorizing the people. In the**

## Repression of the Guardado family

In Chalatenango, it has sometimes been dangerous just to bear the name of someone associated with the peasant movement. This seems to be the case with the Guardados. Not all the Guardados recorded below are from the same branch of the family but the following, almost all of them from the department, have lost their lives.

| | | |
|---|---|---|
| Pastor Guardado | 3.2.1977 | Murdered in Cancasque |
| Moisés Guardado | 3.2.1977 | Murdered in Cancasque |
| Herminio Guardado | 3.2.1977 | Murdered in Cancasque |
| José Angel Guardado | 25.3.1977 | Murdered by National Guard and Treasury Police in Cancasque |
| Abraham Guardado | 28.3.1977 | Murdered by National Guard in Las Flores |
| Máximo Guardado | 19.5.1977 | Murdered during military occupation in search of peasant organizers in Aguilares |
| Miguel Guardado | 26.8.1977 | Murdered by National Guard and National Police in Tejutla |
| Osmaro Guardado | 6.3.1978 | Taken by National Guard in La Laguna, tortured in prison, since then disappeared. Protests by the family the following day were received with gunfire, three people killed |
| Salvador Guardado | 28.7.1978 | Murdered in Tamarindo |
| Jesús Guardado | 29.9.1979 | Secretary General of FECCAS, murdered by 'White Warriors' Union' |
| Próspero Guardado | 31.12.1979 | Murdered in La Laguna and Cancasque |
| Víctor Manuel Guardado | 31.12.1979 | Murdered in La Laguna and Cancasque |
| Josefina Guardado | 31.12.1979 | Murdered in La Laguna and Cancasque |

*Sources:* Amnesty International, Salvadorean church and news publications.

hamlets, the people organized their own security, without arms but by eyesight – with a shout the sign would be given to the others so that they fled when the enemy came. The enemy, after having taken a place, stayed there so that we couldn't rest day or night. During these retreats we suffered hunger and rain, and the *compañeras* had to take care of the children in the mountains. In this way we suffered a lot. And as the whole village left, the place remained empty. They burned our houses, and **ORDEN** took our animals. What the enemy didn't take with them, they set alight, like the maize; and when we came back we didn't find anything; the little that had cost us so much to obtain was now being enjoyed by **ORDEN**. (Fausto)

---

I had five children who were killed by the enemy; my *compañera* was four months pregnant and had a miscarriage because of an attack. In 1979 my father was killed by the army; five days later they killed my mother by putting her on a stake and machine-gunning her. My mother-in-law, too, they cut her ears off, the nose, cut all her face down to the bone. Later, in 1982 they also killed my girl who was two years old. (Walter)

---

I was taken and tortured by the *Policía de Hacienda* in 1976; we were celebrating the Word. Me and other *compas* were taken for holding the celebration and 'were disappeared' for 72 hours. They finally let us go but only after many threats so that we would know that if we continued this they'd come to take us from our houses and make us really disappear.

I was arrested again in 1977, on 17 February. I was captured near the cemetery in Jalapa by members of the army. They put a .45 to my head and kicked me in the stomach and asked me lots of questions. I spent four hours with them and then they passed me to the National Police in the same town who also interrogated me. They said I had killed someone and they knew me well and they left me without food and water. The second day they took me to the barracks of the National Guard. They took me in a lorry, threw a mattress over me and two guards sat on top of me. At ten kilometers I let out a shout because I was burning, they had put me on top of the engine of the lorry. When we reached the barracks, I could hardly stand. I was then interrogated again, they beat me and took a statement and then they tied me to a wire-strung bed where I was kept for two days and two nights. There they came to interrogate me with electric shocks.

I didn't really feel fear, I knew what could happen to me. They said to me, 'Look, you have eight children, you won't see them again'. 'That's alright', I said, 'I've seen and been with them, that's enough'; another said, 'Look, your wife is going to get another man'. 'That's natural', I said, 'I wouldn't worry about that'. Others came and put a pistol to my head and said I was going to die, 'That's alright', I said, 'death means nothing to me'. Then they put me in a cell for another two days but continued to torture me. They said I had to answer 'yes' to all their questions, but I said I would only

181

answer 'yes' when the answer truly was 'yes'. They then asked me a series of questions and I answered 'no' to every one, and with each answer they kicked me four times. The only accusation was that I had been in a demonstration; they kept asking me how many demonstrations I had attended, I said one, and they asked me who had organized it. Then they sent me back to the cell and said, 'you didn't say anything, but at night we are going to come and cut your head off'. I didn't sleep, expecting them to come at any moment. But nothing happened. I was nine days in the cell and then I was taken to the National Police in San Salvador for 31 days before I was released. Then I rejoined our struggle. But I came out with eyesight problems, and I lose my memory often in the middle of a sentence and I can't walk too well either. (Enrique)

Some peasants had begun to look toward the FPL as offering the clearest way forward in the situation. While only a few joined the guerilla forces as such, a number participated in the popular militias.

After the land invasions, I began to think that we couldn't achieve anything any more without armed struggle. I thought there was no other alternative because for many years we had been living with the promise that they were going to give us something, but we hadn't achieved anything at all. (Quique)

---

The idea of armed struggle emerged when all peaceful means had been exhausted. One could see that the enemy didn't care at all for legal and peaceful means. In the beginning, they laughed at us when we held demonstrations, they called us stupid. But later, when members of ORDEN, those assassins, were kidnapped, just with little pistols, with popular means, then the armed struggle really began. (Fausto)

The countryside was by now very polarized. On the one hand the government had created ORDEN, a peasant based, primarily repressive organization. It also tolerated another peasant organization, the UCS, which sought to improve peasant welfare through cooperatives and other activities. On the other hand, there were FECCAS and the UTC and some small peasant organizations, which sought radical change in society to make it respond to the needs of the poor peasants. The polarization and the increasing level of rural violence provoked heated debates within the church.

The relationship of the church to the popular organizations and the question of violence were two issues which highlighted the different positions within the church. Archbishop Romero took up the theme of the relationship of the church to the popular organizations in a pastoral letter which was published on 26 August 1978 signed also by Bishop

Rivera. He strongly supported the right of the poor peasants to organize, but did not consider all forms of organization to be legitimate, especially when they provoked conflict and confrontation between peasants, a veiled reference to ORDEN:

'. . . *our peasants are being divided by precisely that which unites them most deeply: the same poverty, the same necessity to survive, to be able to give something to their children, to bring bread, education, health to their homes. In order to escape from their shared misery, some let themselves be seduced by advantages which pro-government organizations offer them, for which, in exchange they are used for repressive activities, including denunciation, terror, torture and in some cases murder of their own brother peasants.'*[24]

Two days after Romero's letter, Bishops Aparicio of San Vicente, Barrera y Reyes of Santa Ana, Alvarez of San Miguel (who was also the military vicar), and Bishop Revelo, published their own letter. They condemned FECCAS and the UTC and Marxist-Leninist organizations, declaring that priests and religious should not collaborate directly or indirectly with them.

FECCAS and the UTC produced their own reply to the accusations, but a number of priests took up their defence.[25] The question of violence was more problematic. Archbishop Romero condemned all forms of violence, including repressive state violence and what is called 'revolutionary violence' unless it was a legitimate act of defence used as a last resort. But, he stated in his third pastoral letter of 1978 '. . . the peace in which we believe is the product of justice.' In the ensuing months, his views showed a slight but perceptible shift. His fourth and last pastoral letter of August 1979 referred to Pope Paul VI's statement on the right to insurrection in the 'very exceptional case of evident and prolonged tyranny'. Shortly before his assassination in March 1980, he was to state:

'*Profound religion leads to political commitment and in a country such as ours where injustice reigns, conflict is inevitable . . . Christians have no fear of combat; they know how to fight but they prefer to speak the language of peace. Nevertheless, when a dictatorship violates human rights and attacks the common good of the nation, when it becomes unbearable and closes all channels of dialogue, of understanding, of rationality, when this happens, the Church speaks of the legitimate right of insurrectional violence.'*[26]

# Towards Civil War 1979-1980

The country was plunging towards civil war. The archdiocesan legal aid office, which had begun documenting the repression during 1978, noted 1,063 arrests for political reasons, 147 people killed by the security forces and 23 disappeared. The majority of the victims were

peasants. Priests also continued to be killed: in January 1979, Father Octavio Ortíz, who worked with the base communities in the poor suburbs of the capital, was killed by the National Guard; in June, Father Rafael Palacios, who worked with the base communities in Santa Tecla; and in August, Father Alirio Napoleón Macías, pastor of San Esteban Caterina in San Vicente. After the killing of Father Ortíz, 380 priests and 600 nuns marched through the streets of the capital on 30 January 1979 with a banner reading 'No More'.

The popular movement continued its mobilization. The BPR pressed the claim put forward by the FTC in September 1978 for a minimum wage for harvest workers of 12.1 *colones* for an eight-hour day, for adequate food and for a medical dispensary on each estate to look after the workers' health. FAPU organized 'peasant brigades' which staged a series of *tomas* or brief takeovers of some of the *cantones* in the Suchitoto area during April and May 1979. The peasants held meetings and distributed propaganda.

The workers' movement, too, gathered pace at the beginning of 1979, with some 30 strikes involving about 20 unions in the first three months of the year. In March the STECEL power workers cut off the country's electricity supply, to press not only their own demands but also those of other workers on strike at the same time. The sheer pace of events and the audacity of the popular organizations' challenge to the government inevitably had an influence on the workers and both the

185

BPR and FAPU were gaining considerable influence within the trade union movement.

The political-military organizations, who were trying rapidly to improve their military capacity, linked a number of their actions to the strikes. By the end of 1978, guerilla actions were occurring on average once a week. On 3 March 1979 the FPL executed the manager of a shoe factory. In the same month they shot a number of policemen as an act of solidarity with the striking workers of the Constancia beer factory, a number of whom had been killed during an army encirclement of the factory.

May saw a new wave of popular activity. In April five leaders of the BPR had been arrested, including Facundo Guardado, one of the founders of the UTC in Chalatenango and now secretary-general of the BPR. The organization occupied a number of churches and embassies in order to draw international attention to the arrests. The security forces began to shoot at demonstrators who had gathered in support, and the FPL took reprisals against a number of policemen. On 8 May police opened fire on a small demonstration which had stopped in front of the Cathedral, still under BPR occupation. In front of the cameras of a number of foreign journalists 25 people were killed and 70 wounded. The government was forced to release two of the BPR leaders, but denied holding the other three. The BPR's campaign escalated. On 20 May, churches were occupied in Apopa, Suchitoto, Aguilares, San Antonio de los Ranchos (Chalatenango) and Santa Ana, as well as in the capital. Archbishop Romero appealed to the government either to charge or release the three leaders. The government's response was further repression. During May 115 people were killed, 92 wounded and 55 arrested, of whom 30 disappeared. About 30 members of the teachers' union ANDES were killed in June, and a further 123 people in July.

September saw even greater levels of popular mobilization than the demonstrations of May. Buses were burnt, buildings attacked, factories occupied and thousands took to the streets in demonstrations. The president's brother was killed by the guerillas, while 100 opposition members were killed in street clashes in the space of three weeks. On the 20th of the month, an alliance was formed which included the Christian Democrat Party (PDC), the social democrat MNR, the LP-28 and FENASTRAS, the main affiliate of FAPU. This was known as the *Foro Popular*. Only the BPR remained outside the grouping which put forward a common platform for free elections, political pluralism, economic reforms and respect for human rights.

Much has been written about the event which followed; the coup of October 1979. The most revealing account of the coup is that of a *New York Times* journalist, Ray Bonner, who in his book *Weakness and Deceit, US Policy in El Salvador* gives a blow-by-blow account of how a handful of younger officers were outmanoeuvred in their bid to shift the path of government towards one of reform and accommodation to the popular movement. Those who emerged victorious from the coup were not the younger officers who had originally plotted it, but members of the senior command, deeply conservative and trusted by the US embassy and the oligarchy. The overthrow of President Romero was nevertheless seen as a necessary step in the face of mounting popular pressure, and an increasingly sophisticated guerilla movement encouraged and emboldened by the July victory of the Sandinistas in neighbouring Nicaragua.

But the ascendance of the most conservative wing of the armed forces was not immediately apparent. One of the leaders of the reformist group of young officers, Colonel Majano, was a member of the first Junta. He had already developed some links with the UCA and the traditional opposition parties and they were approached to join the new government. They seized on what they felt was an opportunity both to introduce reforms and to pre-empt the growing movement on the streets. The military were also anxious to deal with the popular movement, but through repression rather than reform. The first Junta after the coup was therefore formed out of the false hopes of the liberal opposition. The PDC had five ministerial posts, the UDN (Salvadorean Communist Party) five and the MNR four. Guillermo Ungo of the MNR was a member of the Junta itself, along with the rector of the UCA, Ramón Mayorga. The other three members of the Junta were Majano, Mario Antonio Andino, representing the private sector, and Colonel Jaime Abdul Gutiérrez, included at the prompting of the US.

The opposition members of the government were mostly members of the *Foro Popular*. The other popular organizations did not, however, withdraw immediately from the *foro*, though the LP-28 was not present when it decided to support the Junta. In any case events quickly destroyed any lingering expectations in the alliance. On 16 October, one day after the coup, troops took over six factories which had been occupied by striking workers, most of whom were members of the BPR. Ten workers were killed and many arrested. Six days later, six members of FAPU were shot when the security forces attacked. Six days later, six members of FAPU were shot when the security forces attacked a funeral march for two members of the organization. A week later, the LP-28 held a march in support of demands of the BPR and FAPU and for the release of political prisoners; 86 people were killed by the army and 200 wounded. At the end of October, 29 students were killed on a BPR demonstration. The LP-28 and FENASTRAS withdrew from the *foro* on 24 October.

The ERP had responded to the coup with a call for an insurrection and almost immediately occupied a series of shanty towns. Fifty of its members lost their lives in battles with the army. Subsequently, the ERP admitted it had not been the moment for an insurrection but justified its action as necessary to maintain the mobilization of the masses. They characterized the Junta as 'Romerismo without Romero', in effect a US-backed right-wing coup to preserve the dominant classes' hold on power, though making use of some new tactics. After the failure of the 'insurrection' it drew closer to the other political-military organizations in pressing the Junta to carry out the reforms it promised.

FAPU had not itself joined the *foro* but FENASTRAS, its largest affiliate, had. FAPU had believed that the *foro* could express the interests of the popular movement but that it had been betrayed by the Christian Democrats. It now emphasized continued popular mobilization to unmask the true nature of the October regime. It called for the strengthening of organs of dual power through the formation of local committees in rural and urban areas. At the same time it believed the revolutionary movement should take advantage of splits in the armed forces and it had some expectations that the Majano faction could be won over to the popular movement.

Although this position continued to divide FAPU from the BPR, the two movements shared an immediate tactic of forcing the Junta to comply with its promises to the popular movement. As one peasant from the FTC explains:

**During the harvest season of 1978/79 the FTC had no control over the political activity of the peasants. When there was a problem on the *fincas* with the owner or the administrator, because he cheated them, there were many people who threw sacks and baskets on the street, sat down and said, 'We'll demand that they pay us and we won't work, we can't go on like this'. Even people who weren't organized. It was then, in October 1979 that Romero fell. Then the Junta came with their project of agrarian reform. We decided to take advantage of the situation and to begin with land invasions. So it turned out to be a problem for the junta, because if they repressed us then the reform became a lie, if they didn't then we'd have the land, you see. Because the whole political project of the junta rested on the agrarian reform and the nationalization of the banks, all was inevitably linked with production which in turn depended on the organization of the farm labourers. And when this project crumbled, the junta began to disintegrate. The enemy began to repress the land invasions. The repression became generalized so the agrarian reform project and democratic mask of the junta fell. (Manuel)**

The BPR reiterated its adherence to Prolonged Popular War, and continued to build the popular movement through struggles for immediate demands, though it did not rule out the possibility of an insurrection at some future time. In November 1979 it called for the

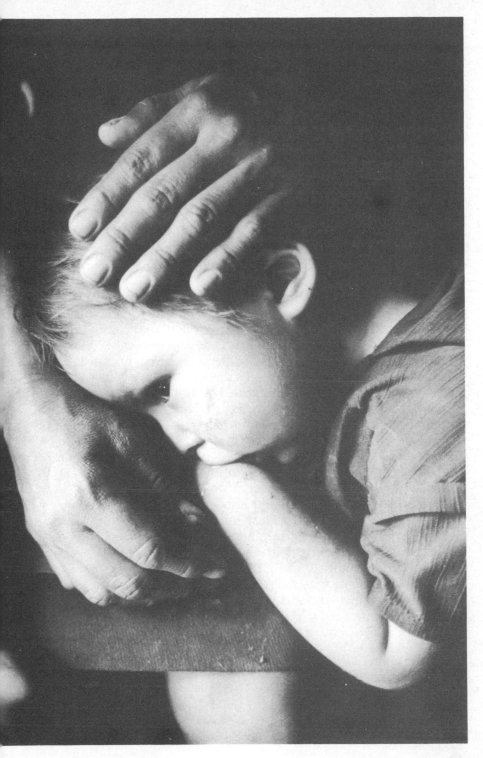

organization of popular committees in each town and *cantón* to demand cheaper housing and lower prices on basic goods, and stepped up the campaigns of the trade unions and peasant unions affiliated to it.[27] All the popular organizations called for the end of the repression, the dissolution of ORDEN and the release of political prisoners and an explanation of the whereabouts of the 'disappeared'.

The BPR occupied the Ministries of Labour and Economy between 24 October and 6 November, forcing concessions from ministers, who as members of the *foro* had put forward many of the same demands as the BPR. The BPR offered a 30-day truce to fulfil the agreements. But the civilian members of the Junta proved powerless. ORDEN was ostensibly dissolved but in fact continued in existence under a different name, the FDN (National Democratic Front). None of the economic or social reforms were carried out and the repression continued. When the truce elapsed in December, the BPR organized a wave of occupations of various cotton and sugar estates demanding the implementation of agreements.

The beginning of 1980 brought with it the resignation of Ungo and Mayorga from the Junta together with 37 ministers, which left the PDC as the only civilian party supporting the government.

The level of popular mobilization was by now huge. On 22 January the largest, but also the last, mass demonstration in Salvadorean history took place. It was organized by the Revolutionary Coordination of the Masses (CRM), an alliance formed on 11 January between all the mass organizations. The CRM included the UDN, or Salvadorean Communist Party, which had begun to revise its strategy after its 7th Congress in April 1979, creating an armed wing, the Armed Liberation Forces (FAL). A quarter of a million people took to the streets on 22 January to mark the 48th anniversary of the 1932 uprising. The march was attacked as the FAPU contingent turned into the cathedral square. Forty-nine people were killed and hundreds injured.

The message was clear: repression was still the right's response to the popular movement. The revolutionary movement was entering a new phase. On 23 February the CRM issued a political platform reflecting the new unity of the left, 'the programmatic platform of the revolutionary democratic government'. It was built around democratic, anti-dictatorial and anti-imperialist demands and represented a minimum programme for the united front in construction. It was a programme drawn up with the mass movement at its strongest; it was a unique moment in El Salvador's long war.

22 January 1980. The popular movement takes to the streets.

*Members of the popular militia looking across the hills of Chalatenango*

# 7
# PEASANTS AND REVOLUTION

## Preparing the Offensive — March 1980 to January 1981

**No-one had any inclination to take up arms, but when they saw the treatment of the people, the catechists especially, by the *Guardia* and ORDEN, it was as though you had lit a little fire, and with each little twig you put on it, the flame rises even stronger. In the same way, the people were seized by the heat and decided to fight.** (Vidal)

To many observers, El Salvador seemed on the verge of a popular insurrection at any moment in the first six months of 1980. The murder of Archbishop Romero in March outraged the Salvadorean people and many who had hitherto stood on the sidelines of the struggle now joined the popular movement. Some have maintained that if the revolutionary organizations had been prepared to lead such an insurrection at that time, the Salvadorean revolution might have already been won, at a time when the Carter administration in the US would have been less able or willing to prevent it through direct intervention.

However, the revolutionary movement was clearly in no condition to take such a step. There were two problems in particular: lack of unity between the different organizations and lack of military capacity.

Although the guerilla forces had increased their military skills and experience considerably over the years they still did not constitute a guerilla army, nor did they have the means, either in arms or logistical back-up, to create one rapidly. In September 1979, the State Department had reported to Congress on the strength of the different guerilla organizations. It estimated that the FPL, the largest of the organizations, had 800 men, the RN had 600 and the ERP was considered the smallest 'terrorist' group.[1] Even if these figures are not completely accurate, and they probably underestimate the military capacity of the ERP if not its numbers, they give some idea of the situation and certainly reveal that the guerilla forces were not yet a serious military threat. This is how one *comandante* of the FPL described this period in Chalatenango:

*Shrine to Archbishop Romero, Cathedral, San Salvador*

I come from this department . . . I was here when the mass movement began . . . I worked in the town first, but in 1980 I came straight to this place, El Jícaro. At the beginning of 1980 there were about 30 men here with ten weapons, that was what we had then, that's the seed from which we've grown. We had other camps, such as at San Antonio too. . . . we could have had plenty of men but the problem was there were always fewer guns than there were people. We also had guerilla camps in La Cañada — that's what it was like then, a lot of people with no weapons. (Comandante Felipe)

But the revolutionary organizations could not devote themselves solely to developing the army; a major preoccupation was the building of unity between themselves. The CRM had brought the popular organizations together, but this unity was still fragile. The LP-28 broke it in February by failing to inform the others of its intention to take over the Spanish Embassy. FAPU was blocking the entry of the MLP (linked with the PRTC) into the CRM on the grounds that it had to prove its capacity to mobilize the people and it was not able to join until May 1980.

But a significant step in the direction of greater unity of the opposition forces took place in April. A coalition of professionals, unions, the National University, small business associations, the social democrat (MNR) party and the Popular Social Christian Movement (a split from the PDC), formed the Salvadorean Democratic Front (FDS). Five days later it joined the CRM to create the Democratic Revolutionary Front (FDR) which adopted the Programme for a Democratic Revolutionary Government drawn up by the CRM in January.

Unity amongst the guerilla forces was slower to evolve. A first step towards a unified military apparatus was the formation in May of the United Revolutionary Directorate (DRU). But tactical and strategic differences still prevented full unity. The RN argued for an insurrectionary line, and was having secret meetings with a sector of the officer corps believing it was possible to win over a substantial sector of the army to such a move. The FPL maintained that there should be no full-scale mobilization until victory was certain. But the momentum for insurrection was growing and was difficult to resist. The FPL would have found itself isolated if it had not gone along with the tide.

Preparations for an offensive were begun. During the crucial last six months of 1980 the revolutionary organizations began building a guerilla army and testing the readiness of the city for insurrection. History may well look back on these months as the most politically significant of the Salvadorean revolution.

On 24 June the FDR called for a 48-hour general strike to demand the end of the state of siege and repression. Eighty-five per cent of El Salvador's economic activity was brought to a halt as 150,000 workers joined in, nearly 50 per cent of them state employees. Popular neighbourhood committees were active during the strike, distributing food and organizing self-defence. The FDR wished to follow this up by another strike two weeks later but FAPU objected and only supported the three day strike called for 13 August on the last day. This undoubtedly weakened its impact, but other problems arose from the more decisive response of the armed forces and business sector. The latter threatened to sack anyone who joined the strike while the government put thousands of troops onto the streets to help keep businesses open.

The army had shown its strength in the urban areas, and the opposition forces their weakness. The situation was complicated by differing expectations amongst those opposition forces. The organizations who had formed the FDS hoped for a strong display of strength which would force negotiations, heading off civil war and the more radical options favoured by the revolutionary organizations. The RN still believed that a split in the military was imminent, which would alter the balance of forces but should not be prematurely provoked. The RN seemed to be taking its own path, organizing a 20-hour strike of STECEL, the power workers' union, at the end of August, and then in early September withdrawing from the DRU while FAPU lost its executive position on the CRM.

However, by mid-September the fortunes of the reforming wing of the army, led by Colonel Majano in the junta, had clearly waned. The RN's hopes for a split were dashed, with the hardliners in the army very much in power and able to oust Majano in December. On 21 October, the RN rejoined the united guerilla command which now called itself the Farabundo Martí National Liberation Front (FMLN).

By now the war of attrition which has so characterized El Salvador was in full swing. The assassination of Archbishop Romero in March had heralded a wave of repression, which in the words of Ray Bonner, 'reached a magnitude surpassed only by the *matanza* and was far worse than anything imagined under General Romero'.[2] By the end of the year its victims numbered 13,000, the vast majority workers and peasants. Amongst the more notorious events was the killing of 600 peasants trying to cross the Sumpul river in Chalatenango (see box, page 197). The army was now mounting regular large-scale sweeps through areas where the guerillas were strong. Many peasants fled their homes and the guerillas began the difficult task of turning the able-bodied into an efficient fighting force while surrounded by enemy army posts.

The toll of the repression on the revolutionary movement was more than numbers can convey. Many leading cadres in city and countryside lost their lives. Some of the most devastating losses are well known, such as the killing of six leaders of the FDR on 28 November, including the president, Enrique Alvarez, Juan Chacón of the BPR, Manuel Franco of the UDN, Humberto Mendoza of the MPL, Enrique Barrera of the MNR and Doroteo Hernández of FAPU. Many more died who had key, but unpublicized roles in the popular organizations, and the BPR was undoubtedly the worst hit. The labour movement in the capital was particularly badly affected by the repression, losing a great many of its most experienced leaders.

The popular movement was weakened not only by the right-wing terror unleashed with such ferocity during 1980, but by the sudden loss of many members incorporated into the guerilla army. The mass

## The Sumpul Massacre

(Testimonies given to *Socorro Jurídico*)

I was fishing near the Honduran border when a load of Honduran soldiers appeared, three hundred and fifty of them, and they positioned themselves on the banks of the river. A lieutenant from the Honduran army started interrogating people on that side of the river, they wouldn't let anyone in who wanted to come in from El Salvador. On the morning of the fourteenth, I was making my way towards the river to cross the frontier and take my wife to Honduras. But I couldn't because already on the banks of the river on the Salvadorean side there was shooting and helicopters were flying around. Honduran soldiers seized about a hundred Salvadoreans who were trying to escape across the river from the Salvadorean National Guard. They drove them back to the Salvadorean side, I heard lots of shooting: they were all dead.
(José Guardado Ramírez)

I left with five of my children, we kept on running through Salvadorean territory, always downstream. My wife was coming behind with another child but I didn't really know which way she was coming. To get us all across the river, I left three of them, the three smallest, over on the other side and then went back for the other two still on the Salvadorcan side. The National Guard was coming up right behind them. And then my little girl, my three-year-old daughter, started to panic when she saw me going back to El Salvador to get her brothers. She tried to follow me back across the river . . . but then the bigger ones got hold of her and stopped her throwing herself back into the river to follow me where she would have drowned. So then I could go back to get the others who were already half way across in the middle of the river because they'd seen the soldiers coming up behind them were getting so close. I put those two on a little path up ahead and went back to get the other three up. They had got stuck . . . but my wife was still on the other side of the river with the other daughter. There was no time there was just no time to go back and get them because the soldiers were just above and I couldn't get through the hail of bullets. I'd gone back twice but I couldn't help my wife and the other little girl. I couldn't get them across. So I went on with the five children until we got to a village. We slept the night near there in a thicket and I didn't have anything, just nothing in the way of clothes to put on the children. For my little girl, to protect her from the insects, I took off my shirt and arranged it round her to keep them off. But the other children and I were eaten by insects the whole night.
(Eduardo Flores)

organizations, which had become such an effective means of political mobilization, were sapped of much of their strength as their membership was drawn into the army, and political work was abandoned in favour of military priorities. However, lack of arms made it difficult to incorporate everyone who wished to join into the guerilla army. Many people who might otherwise have joined the struggle found themselves with no clear options in a situation of increasing rural terror from the armed forces. Some chose to flee their villages, heading for refugee camps in neighbouring Honduras or refuges provided by religious and other humanitarian organizations within El Salvador. The number of officially registered displaced in El Salvador rose from 2,000 in January 1980 to 197,199 by January 1981. During this period the war had moved to the countryside and Chalatenango found itself at the centre of the ensuing conflict. The testimonies which follow are the peasants' account of life in Chalatenango in the months leading up to the offensive of January 1981.

José recalls the increasing repression in the department as the army tried to dislodge the guerillas from their bases in the area:

**As organization and participation in political activities increased in our department the repression took on a more cruel character. The dictatorship not only sent armed patrols to the hamlets to threaten the people, it now invaded with thousands of soldiers, killing people, burning their homes and robbing the people of their animals. It was a persecution to the death. The objective was to intimidate the peasantry, force them out of their homes and into refugee centres where they could be kept under control. They were afraid that the guerillas would use the new political awareness of the peasants to install their military bases. To prevent this was the dictatorship's first objective and it led to massacres, like that of 13 May 1980 in Yurique, where they killed many people who were occupying a piece of land. . . . They burned all their houses and the crops. And they gave the people three days to leave. It was then that some people began to emigrate, some to Honduras, some to Soyopango and other areas, because they were afraid of being killed. But others stayed here and began to work as they could at first, and then the *compas* of the organization began to go and find people and bring them together again. For the peasant, it is the most painful thing to have to leave his or her home, see it burned to the ground and the people killed. It was then that the peasants became truly militant, demanding to be incorporated into the armed struggle.** (José)

Víctor and Abel explain how many peasants joined the armed struggle:

**During 1980, most people were thrown off their land by army operations and so we began to fight back. We had to look after ourselves. All we wanted to do was sleep in peace. We had to stay vigilant the whole time and if we heard any noise we had to run . . . gradually we began arming ourselves. With a knife we got a .22 and we used that to capture a .38, and with the .38 we got a G-3, that's**

how we got arms. The first guerilla posts were set up in El Alto, El Jícaro, Los Amates and Portillo del Norte. The recruitment took place in the same places. The people wanted to join a guerilla camp; they certainly didn't have to be forced to join. The militia and the guerilla began to grow as the military preparations got underway and people arrived to give military instruction. These small groups would ambush the armed forces when they came into the villages to repress the people, and succeeded in capturing more arms for the militias which strengthened their operations. People were gaining more political understanding too, especially the women, who were much more politicized in comparison with the early 1970s. (Víctor)

---

Repression increased during 1980 when the CRM was formed out of all the sister organizations of the FMLN. That day was the last time we went to San Salvador, when we witnessed the great massacre of our *compas*. It was after that that we organized the popular liberation army or guerilla columns. We recruited all the young people to give them political and military training and divided the country into sub-zones of military fronts and sent them to different ones. We had realized that we could no longer work in the city as the enemy had too strong a control over it. Camps were set up as we prepared the offensive of January 1981. At this point there was a slump in political work, because all the most experienced people had to go into the armed forces. And our political work with the people, well, we sort of put it to one side because we had to see to what was more immediately important. We saw we had made a bit of a mistake when three months later everyone had joined the military. (Abel)

# War and Revolution

The uprising of January 1981, intended by the FMLN as a 'final offensive', has frequently been described as a failure and even an error in conception. The objective of the offensive was, according to Villalobos of the ERP:

'. . . *not to wipe out the army, but to stir the masses to revolt and, on the basis of the mass uprising, pass on to the application of different tactics which would range from the prolonged siege of garrisons with the support of the masses, to measures which would oblige the army to disperse and then we*

199

*would attack it as it moved. For San Salvador, for example, our proposals were not to occupy the military garrisons but to harass them, while other units sparked off uprisings in the poor quarters. Once this had been achieved we would try to get the army to move into the poor quarters to recapture them and we would attack it at that moment.'[3]*

However, the uprising did not take place as expected. The repression of 1980 had taken its toll. Fighting lasted about a week and the FMLN reported some 43 major actions. In only one instance did part of any army garrison come over to the FMLN, in Santa Ana, where Colonel Bruno Navarrete led a mutiny against the local commander and took 100 troops into the guerilla camp. Elsewhere the army remained united and resolute, a factor which inevitably also discouraged the population from joining the insurrection.

As the FMLN retreated it was forced to admit that the action was precipitate and henceforth described the offensive as 'general' rather than 'final'. But, in hindsight, the implications of January 1981 were less serious militarily than some commentators supposed, and of rather more consequence in political terms.

Militarily, the offensive had involved actions in many parts of the country which had generalized the war. Coordination between columns and fronts had been inadequate, but important first efforts had been made in that direction. The offensive did, however, precipitate increased US involvement in the Salvadorean war. Its failure, which coincided with the inauguration of President Reagan, convinced the new US administration that it could win a rapid victory over the FMLN with minimal involvement. El Salvador became the 'test case' of the administration's determination to halt 'communism' in its backyard and in other traditional spheres of US influence. But the administration badly underestimated the capacity of the FMLN.

The failure to achieve the initial objective now forced the FMLN into a sustained effort of military preparation. 'Because in the short term', said Villalobos, 'after January, we couldn't launch a counter-offensive with insurrectional aims. It was obvious that what we needed in that moment was the development of our military strength. The six months after January were a period of resistance, of consolidation of the rearguard, of development of our forces and of advance towards a stage of higher quality in the military terrain, which had its first expression in the campaign of July and August.'[4] It was a crucial period of mostly defensive activity, when the FMLN had to both recover from the January offensive and turn itself into an effective fighting force. The guerillas had to confront large-scale army operations in their main base areas of Morazán and Chalatenango; control over the Guazapa volcano, the guerilla front closest to the capital, was also fiercely contested. By July 1981, the FMLN had managed to hold on to Guazapa and extend its control in its rearguard,

*Guides and messengers*

enabling it to dominate increasing areas of the northern mountain range. Elsewhere, the FMLN held only very small patches of territory often in very exposed and highly populated rural areas, where new recruits were trained with the support of the local population.

By July 1981, the FMLN was able to begin offensive actions, capturing large amounts of arms and ammunition and scoring their first major military success in the taking of the town of Perquín in Morazán. There were steps to improve the level of coordination between the different fronts and in planning acts of sabotage. By the end of the year there were more military successes in Chalatenango and Morazán, and an increasingly confident FMLN tried once again to prepare for a large-scale offensive to coincide with the elections of March 1982. But it was apparent that a strategy based on 'the great offensive', insurrectionary explosion, or single decisive battle was not appropriate to the war. Subsequently the FMLN abandoned such expectations and adapted itself more realistically to the gradual accumulation of military strength. By October 1982, the FMLN had recovered from the setback of March and launched a new offensive with much improved coordination, gaining more territory and causing very high casualties amongst the Salvadorean army.

The commitment and high morale of the guerilla forces, together with popular support in certain key areas, compensated to a considerable extent for the inhospitability of the terrain to guerilla warfare. The weakness of the 'enemy' army undoubtedly also contributed to the success of the guerillas. The low morale of the troops, many of them teenagers forcibly recruited into the army, contrasted strongly with that of the guerilla forces. More importantly, the FMLN was able to ensure a supply of weapons and ammunition from government soldiers who preferred to hand them over rather than die in battle. The Reagan administration soon found it was supplying both sides in the war.

The Salvadorean army proved very inept in the early years in other ways. Its officers, more interested in political power and the accumulation of personal wealth than the art of war, fought what has been called a 'nine-to-five war with weekends off'. In February 1982 a US military officer complained to journalists:

*'General Guillermo García, whose prior battlefield experience was nil, is trying to fight set-piece battles, marshalling regimental-strength units against a mobile enemy that evaporates into the hills. His offensives take such elaborate preparation that the guerillas know where the units are heading three days before they start out. When the full panoply is on the road, with planes flying cover, a few sharp fights take place, with the exposed soldiers generally taking the worst of it. The army combs the area for guerillas, claims to have cleared the zone, then returns in triumph to San Salvador. But nothing has really happened'.*[5]

The US gradually escalated its military assistance and involvement in the war as the guerillas went from strength to strength. They sought links with the few talented and professional officers and trained special brigades in more effective counter-insurgency techniques, such as small patrols to penetrate behind guerilla lines at night. Although it had little success in its bid to professionalize the Salvadorean army in the first few years, the US was probably decisive in ensuring that it did not actually collapse as the FMLN gained strength. But the Reagan administration found it difficult to win the necessary public and congressional support to enable it to swing the balance in favour of the army. The Salvadorean army continued to use tactics of pure terror against the population which resulted in high civilian casualties and international condemnation, but no major victories over the guerillas.

In 1983, the US promoted a new plan based on the counter-insurgency strategy developed in Vietnam and aimed at winning away the guerillas' social base. Plan CONARA was launched in San Vicente in May involving resettlement of farmers in hamlets (strategic villages in military terms), providing them with food aid and seeds while carrying out a military offensive against the guerillas and their suspected supporters. The operation was to be combined with a new emphasis on a locally-recruited civil defence force and small mobile anti-guerilla units to keep the FMLN out of the area. As the 6,000 troops marched into San Vicente to implement the strategy, the guerillas simply faded into the hills with many of their civilian supporters and spent June to August planning their response. It came in September when the FMLN launched blistering attacks in Tenancingo, Tejutepeque, El Triunfo, Nuevo Edén de San Juan and elsewhere. Several hunter battalions specially trained by the US to put the FMLN under constant harassment were themselves routed by the guerillas and counter-insurgency bases considered impregnable soon proved unable to contain the guerilla forces. The FMLN now took the military initiative, controlling an estimated 25 per cent of Salvadorean territory by the end of the year, with at least as much again in dispute.

The frustration of the army led them to escalate the aerial war against the guerillas. The bombing of Tenancingo at the end of September 1983 illustrates its frustrations. The FMLN had attacked the town on 25 September. When the army commander found himself unable to hold back the attack, he called for an A-37 strike, despite the fact that the government soldiers had already surrendered. The bombs hit a large group of civilians fleeing the town, even though two Green Cross volunteers had waved a flag to indicate they were civilians. According to testimonies taken by the Archdiocese Office for Legal Protection, 175 civilians died in the bombing.

On 30 December 1983, the FMLN scored its most spectacular military victory so far, when it took the country's fourth largest army garrison, El Paraíso, in Chalatenango. The garrison had been modernized under US supervision and was considered unassailable. One hundred government troops were killed in the battle and the guerillas captured large quantities of weapons and heavy artillery (see page 223). The following day, guerilla forces destroyed the Cuscatlán bridge, described by the Salvadorean defence ministry as the most important bridge in the country, the only link to the eastern part of El Salvador. The FMLN was forcing the army away from the mobile war of attack advocated by the US advisers, into a static war to defend certain strategic positions.

The military achievement of the FMLN was considerable. The accounts below of the war in Chalatenango build a more detailed picture of just how remarkable the achievement was. Not only was a strong guerilla army created in extraordinarily adverse conditions, but the civilian supporters of the guerillas in the countryside bore the brunt of a terrible war of attrition, yet many continued to live in the FMLN controlled zones rather than flee to refugee camps or San Salvador. Their continued support in the face of much hardship has been a crucial factor in sustaining the guerilla army. Below, *Comandante* Ramón of the FPL, interviewed in March 1984 as he prepared an attack, describes how he became a *comandante* and the progress of the war:

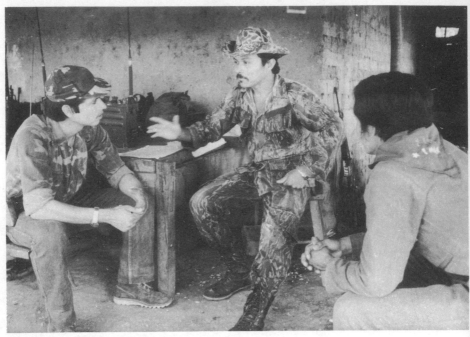

*Comandante Ramón (centre)*

The step from being an agricultural worker to becoming *comandante* is a big one. But the people give you everything they know, so that you learn. I never had any intention of becoming a *comandante* or *jefe* when I began to take part in the struggle, but only to make a contribution to the struggle of the people. I began work with the mass organizations, I was in the UTC for a while, organizing demonstrations and protests. In 1978, I asked to be a guerilla and began clandestine work. All the guerillas are from the people, the guerilla army is born out of the people's feelings. The guerillas are mostly peasants and workers and there are some students and professional people such as doctors. The majority of the guerillas in the combat zones come from those areas, that's how we can move about so easily, because we know the terrain.

We began by living secretly; from there we went on to have camps; and now we've got mobile units which are a proper army. It has cost the revolutionary movement very dear to form this mobile army with its military capability and firepower in such a small country where there are no mountains, where there's no place to hide. But our people have shown great heroism which you can see in our brigades: the Rafael Arce Zablah brigade and the battalions in Chalate and Cuscatlán.

I learned military strategy directly in daily practice. I didn't go to military school, for example, but got my experience during combat,

204

saying to myself, if this combat was like that, then the next one has to be better, learning from experience all the time. In this way we formed our own ideas of military strategy. And on this basis I led a number of successful operations, without realizing what one puts into it. One day they told me I'm now a *comandante* — great! Lately it has become necessary to deepen our understanding. We have some courses in military strategy. They are organized on all the fronts; some are for new recruits, some are for *comandantes*.

There are many aims to our present campaign. The first is to hit the enemy garrisons really forcefully and wear away the enemy army and seize their weapons. We also want to expand our theatre of operations and the area under our control which is also how we win popular support. When we gain territory, we win over the people and that helps the revolutionary movement.

The weakness of the Salvadorean army is obvious: we have managed to smash its fighting capacity. The Atlacatl and other elite brigades trained by the US have greater firepower than the other troops and therefore higher morale, they are also organized for immediate response. But even these have lost their mobility under our attacks. There have been many important operations where we have even acquired 120mm mortars, like at Tejutepeque, Tenancingo and recently with the annihilation of the Fourth Infantry Brigade in Chalatenango. Something else which demoralizes the enemy troops is that we take prisoners of war and set them free. As to whether we get help from abroad, we can say to the whole world and to our people that we began the struggle with only a couple of .22 rifles, pistols and shotguns and have got all the weapons we have now from the enemy, one by one. The evidence is in the lists of arms and ammunition we have captured from each operation. Here in El Salvador there is no foreign help. Here it's the people who are helping us. It's the Salvadorean people who are giving their lives and their food to help the guerilla in their struggle.

The life of a guerilla may be hard, but this is a question of conscience. Our principle is: first the revolution and afterwards personal interest. This manages to strengthen you. For example, I haven't seen my mother for a year and a half, and a brother not for the last five years. I've just had a note from him, where he tells me, 'I only hear your voice on the Farabundo Radio, but don't know how you are'. It's just like that, in this war these things happen.

The people here have maintained a sense of humanity, of human warmth, in the midst of the war. If all the peasants are by nature humanitarian, then in the organization this is being deepened. Here solidarity, fraternity are strengthened, you always have your thoughts directed to others, not just to yourself. This improves you. Everyone who comes here feels good because it's a pretty different way of life. For example the soldiers who come here when they surrender say, 'this is a very different life to that with the bourgeois army'. A *comandante* here for instance, doesn't have any special privileges. I live with my people, eat what they eat. There are times when they worry about me not eating as I wait to be the last. (Comandante Ramón)

The FMLN retained the military initiative until the first half of 1984. The January 1981 offensive had proved only a temporary setback to the FMLN in military terms. But its political effect was of more consequence in the long term. Essentially it changed the nature of the war, at least as far as the FPL was concerned. The FPL's conception had always been that of a war by 'the entire people', in Giap's words, and the aim was to incorporate the people into the war at different levels. A powerful regular force composed of mobile strategic units, the Popular Liberation Army (EPL), would be the decisive military instrument against the enemy army. The EPL would be supported by zonal guerilla units with mobility in particular areas. But the fundamental force responsible for incorporating the mass of the population into the war and preparing for the mass insurrection was the Popular Liberation Militias (MPL), local forces whose role would be to organize the self-defence of the population and carry out acts of sabotage in coordination with the EPL.

The war was also seen as a struggle which would encompass the entire country, depriving the enemy of military space to operate, wearing it down in a process of continuous offensive. The FPL acknowledged that in the geographical conditions of El Salvador, the early establishment of fixed battle fronts from which to advance and establish liberated areas would be impossible until the final phases of the war. The rearguard needed to supply and support the guerilla army was therefore not conceived of as a well-defined geographical area but as a dispersed and rather amorphous base of support resting primarily on the mass movement and its organizations in various parts of the country. Hence, considerable importance was given to political work amongst the population both prior to the emergence of the revolutionary army and by that army itself as it advanced through different areas. The FPL maintained that what Giap calls the 'people factor' (see box on page 207) would compensate for the geographical disadvantages with which they operated.

These premises of the revolutionary war were part of a strategy of prolonged struggle, the expression at the military level of the fundamental political principles of the organization. The offensive of January 1981 represented an abandonment of the notion of a prolonged war in favour of insurrection, and although its failure led the FMLN as a whole to return eventually to a more long-term view of the war, the conditions were now very different to those before the offensive. In the first place, the FMLN had now become a primarily rural-based

### 'The People Factor' — Vietnam and the FPL

The people's armed forces are the revolutionary armed forces of the labouring people, of the workers and peasants. They fight to defend the interests of the people, the class, and the nation . . . Our military art is that of a small nation, whose armed force is still weak in equipment and technique but which rises up to fight against an enemy who is materially much stronger. This is a military art, whose characteristic is to defeat material force with moral force, defeat what is strong with what is weak, defeat what is modern with what is primitive, defeat the modern armies of the aggressive imperialists with the people's patriotism and determination to carry out a complete revolution. . . . The people's war generally takes place in conditions when our side enjoys absolute political superiority over an enemy materially stronger than we are. Considering the revolutionary character of the war and the balance of actual forces, our military art has determined the following strategic orientation: to promote a war by the entire people, a total and protracted war. . .

. . . We attach the greatest importance to the role of the rear in a war. As soon as the question of armed struggle was posed, another question was also posed — that of having places where our people's armed forces could be hidden, trained, supplied, strengthened, and could rest. While revolutionary struggle was developing, we created a rear where there had been none, developed it, beginning with political bases among the masses, and now have a relatively complete system of popular national defence. We can say that in the early days when our Party made the decision to prepare for an armed struggle, we did not have a single inch of free territory; at that time, the only rear we had was our secret political bases, and the complete loyalty of the people who had become conscious of their revolutionary cause. It was from these secret political bases that our Party — our first guerilla units were then concentrating on armed propaganda, political activities being regarded as more important than military activities — endeavoured to build up secret bases for the armed struggle, and gradually came to wage partial guerilla war and to create a free zone . . . Looking back at our people's armed struggle through successive periods, we can fully grasp the strategic significance of the rear in relation to the war and draw this conclusion: from the viewpoint of the people's war, the building-up and consolidation of the rear must be carrried out in every aspect. *The political, economic, and military aspects are equally important, but most important is the political factor, the 'people' factor. That is why in the last war, with the support of the people, we succeeded in building up relatively safe bases, not only in inaccessible mountainous regions, but also in the midst of the vast, open delta region, criss-crossed with rivers and studded with enemy posts.* (Italics in original)
(General Nguyen Giap, 1970)[6]

The armed struggle in our country is the method of struggle that is maintained throughout the entire process until victory. The popular armed force is formed by the people, armed and organized in their own regular or irregular armed forces, in their own army, which defeat the enemy's army . . . the revolutionary strategy that corresponds to the concrete conditions of our country is the strategy of prolonged people's war, the global strategy used by the exploited against the anti-popular war that the exploiters are developing . . . This strategy . . . involves the correct combination of the violent with the peaceful struggle, the illegal with the legal, the mass with the guerilla struggle, economic and political, armed and unarmed. It is the strategy in which the people join the struggle, strengthening their forces, winning space, wearing down the enemy's forces, gradually altering the balance of forces, creating the political and organizational instruments needed for the final defeat of the enemy, with the mass armed struggle maintained as the fundamental element . . .

(FPL, policy document)[7]

movement, cut off from the capital, San Salvador. Its base of support there, so strong in the late 1970s, had been severely weakened by the events of 1980.

In the countryside, the FMLN began, following the 1981 offensive, to establish a logistical rearguard. Although it could not establish fully liberated areas in the classic sense, it did succeed in setting up definable zones of guerilla control. Such bases were clearly essential to sustain the guerilla army, given the failure of the offensive to generate a mass insurrection. But for the FPL it was a move away from the idea of a mobile army supplied and supported by the organized population throughout the country.

The FMLN retained much support and sympathy in many regions other than the zones of control, but the political work outside those areas was now much more difficult given the intensity of the repression. The need to build the guerilla army had already affected the mass movement and although some effort was subsequently made to redress the balance and renew political work, the activities which had helped build the mass organizations in the 1970s were no longer possible. At the same time as political activity became more difficult, military priorities became increasingly pressing. The demands of the war, for instance the building of an effective guerilla army to take on the enemy army, became in practice more immediate than the pursuit of revolution through the political mobilization of the entire population. The FMLN did succeed in creating an impressive military force, which by 1984 looked increasingly like a regular army with battalions and even brigades. But this eventually became vulnerable to the aerial war unleashed that year by the 'enemy army' under US instruction, as will be seen in the last part of this chapter. But first the story of how Chalatenango, known by the FPL as the Apolinario Serrano Front, came under guerilla control.

## The 'Liberation' of Chalatenango 1981-1983

This is how one peasant woman described the January 1981 offensive in Chalatenango:

**At the end of 1979, when we left our homes, we began to organize the popular militias. I was in them, the head of a militia group in a brigade. We went on a few small operations. Then I joined the guerillas for a time. I really liked it. I took great satisfaction in overcoming the physical difficulties. We set up battalions about this time, but they were only that in name really, because it was just ordinary people who were in them. I was in the political commission of a battalion and by 1981 I was the political head of a detachment for the offensive. I took part in the seizure of a radio station in Chalatenango . . . at that point we didn't have any arms, we didn't have any weapons except enthusiasm. Each of us had a .38 pistol so you can see what kind of arms we had . . . Everyone thought it was ridiculously funny, but it was a miracle they didn't kill us all . . . take the provincial army HQ with a .38, yes that's suicide! But in that operation our forces captured a G-3, a FAL, a small quantity of other arms and a cannon which we hadn't blown up, real weapons . . . we had to leave on the double carrying all that stuff. A number of *compañeros* died in that operation fighting just with pistols, but they died in the most heroic way.**

**That operation taught us many things. We didn't win a military victory but we found out what we were lacking, what we needed, and that of course was an army. So we knew we had to start building one and that's what we did . . . it was very exciting. But on a personal note, there's something else I remember about how that operation was for me — I cried for the whole 22 days it took, and everyone else laughed at me. It was because, well, for the 12 or 14 years we'd been married, my husband and me, we'd never been apart. I could have died for him, I missed him so much. Anyway, I left the guerillas after a time to do political work, organizing the people. It was a problem at the time that many people were leaving political work to join the guerillas. We were all guerillas in 1980, all of us . . . and it was only the old people and children who stayed behind; in any case I too was getting too old for it. (Beatriz)**

Chalatenango came under guerilla control only gradually. The younger peasantry in the area mostly went into the guerilla army, while their parents played a crucial role in support functions. At first it was a hazardous, clandestine operation, in which the population sustained guerilla camps often situated no more than half an hour's march from an army post. Self-defence and alarm systems were organized with great care by the population, as the army and National Guard now mounted large-scale operations to dislodge the guerillas and their supporters. This is how a member of the FPL who played an important role in Chalatenango at this time describes his experiences in 1981:

After the 1981 offensive we began to confront a higher level of war. In other words, not only did we find that we had managed to arm and organize hundreds of combatants who had abandoned the political struggle of the masses and joined the military units and militias, but also the enemy had made strides in counter-insurgency warfare and it launched military invasions against our zone which were far greater than anything of the past. In January and February 1981, we began to confront enemy invasions which involved thousands of troops and which now entered using artillery and the airforce as a support. Do you know that at the end of February 1981, beginning of March, we had a meeting of the party organization in the northern front in a place which was being mortared by the enemy; we counted 80 mortars a minute. It was an incredible thing, a terrible thing, we just weren't used to that kind of attack. Nor did we have much experience at that time in dealing with the army invasions. And that year, 1981, we experienced a number of invasions. I myself was in five and I didn't experience them all. I was involved in the military actions to defend the population and also in the organization of the people to get them out of the area as well as to solve the food problem, because the enemy destroyed everthing when it invaded, all the crops, the houses, the little that the people had. We didn't start from zero. Many people had experience in organizing their own self-defence. Not only had they taken part in demonstrations in San Salvador or in Chalatenango itself or in other big towns, but they had had to defend themselves in their own small villages. When I first went to Chalatenango in 1979 security was already well-organized. There were alarm systems, for instance, if a patrol was spotted a firework would be let off and then everyone would know they had to go and hide in a pre-arranged place.

We organized the people into small units of 15 families each. Each family group elected its own leadership which looked after the problems of security and self-defence, supplies, production and health problems. These were the most urgent needs at the time. These family units were the nucleus of what later became the PPLs (Local Popular Power). The food problem for the people and the guerillas was solved in two ways. There was production itself; our people played an exemplary role in this respect. They continued to cultivate the land, even in those conditions. They grew maize and beans and some vegetables, just to solve immediate problems. The

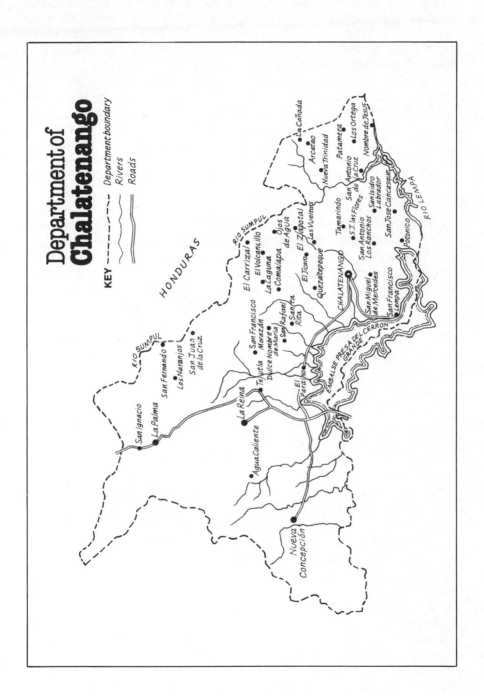

# Department of
# Chalatenango

KEY
– – – – – Department boundary
Rivers
Roads

HONDURAS

RIO SUMPUL

San Ignacio
La Palma
San Fernando
Los Naranjos
San Juan de la Cruz

El Carrizal
El Volcancillo
La Laguna
Comalapa
Ojos de Agua
El Zapotal
Las Vueltas

La Cañada
Arcatao
Nueva Trinidad
Patamera
Los Ortega
Nombre de Jesús
San Antonio de la Cruz

Tamarindo
S.T. las Flores
San Antonio Los Ranchos
San Isidro Labrador
San José Cancasque
Potonico
RIO LEMPA

San Francisco Morazán
San Rafael
Santa Rita
Dulce Nombre de María
El Jícaro
Quezaltepeque
CHALATENANGO
San Miguel de Mercedes
San Francisco Lempa

Tejutla
El Paraíso
EMBALSE PRESA DEL CERRON GRANDE

La Reina

Agua Caliente

Nueva Concepción

other form was by taking over land which had been abandoned by ORDEN members who lived on the periphery of our zone. We grew food on this land and made use of the cattle that still existed in the area to give milk to the children. We resolved most problems through the participation of the people.

The enemy still had many army posts in Chalatenango at that time. Antonio de los Ranchos was the only town where the enemy had withdrawn its soldiers. But the enemy still had posts, and well-manned posts at that, in Las Flores, in Nueva Trinidad, in Arcatao, in Las Vueltas, the heart of the zone, in La Laguna . . . At that time we lived with the enemy; it was a very difficult situation. The example of Chalate is a reflection in miniature of the history of the revolution as a whole. Because we had to defend the population, resolve all the material needs and at the same time raise the military capacity of our fighters to take on this force, installed in the heart of our villages; and then expel it, defeat it, annihilate it if possible.

At that time, the popular militias often had camps of their own. One of our contributions was to change people's conception that the militias had to be in camps separate from the population. We believed that as a paramilitary force, they had to be part of the people, living with them and sharing their problems and resolving them together with the people.

In the wake of the January 1981 offensive, the guerillas began to shift their actions from ambushes and harassment of army patrols to attacks on local garrisons, forcing the soldiers to abandon the posts while appropriating their arms. The creation of the vanguard units (*unidades de vanguardia*) enabled the guerillas to operate from fixed positions and was the major development in 1981. Below, *Comandante* Rigoberto of the FPL describes the situation of the guerillas in Chalatenango in July 1981:

'*There are two types of camp in Chalatenango at this moment — a camp is a place where a combat unit is based. Those for the vanguard units, the seed of our popular army, and those for the local guerilla units who are linked more to the population and participate more in the social life of the community . . . usually, the population live around the camps, or rather we build them in the heart of the people, because that's how our guerilla movement was born.*

*Up until the offensive which we began at the beginning of this year, the National Guard and the army moved through this department with a certain freedom. Where they passed, they left a trail of blood and terror. But after the general offensive, the enemy was forced to remain in the barracks and it can't now move here except with a lot of artillery and air support, and thousands of soldiers transported from Santa Ana, Sonsonate, Sensuntepeque, and even with the help of the Honduran army. Our fighters on the other hand move around with full freedom, like it was their own house. Until now*

212

*then, the army and the security forces have had various posts throughout the department, but everyday they are more isolated, more desperate because they can't leave their barracks, they cannot move around in vehicles, they don't have electric light nor drinking water, we've blocked the roads, often they can only get food by helicopter . . . If they stay in their barracks we advance and gain control of more territory, if they leave, we ambush them and cause many casualties. Now we have stepped up our occupation of towns and attacks on enemy barracks. We have attacked the barracks of Chalatenango and simultaneously about thirteen posts, amongst them San Antonio de la Cruz, Cancasque, Las Vueltas, Arcatao, Dulce Nombre de María, San Francisco Morazán, Concepción Quezaltepeque, Ojos de Agua and others. We have captured arms, munitions and even mortars . . . we are in the strategic stage of the general offensive towards the taking of power.*[8]

Captain Felipe, who played a major role in the military actions which 'liberated' Chalatenango, describes how the guerillas managed to expel the army from large parts of the department by the end of 1982:

**The January offensive was a big experience for us and very good training. We did win battles, but people had no experience or expertise. Before this offensive, attacks had been made on army posts in Patamera and San Antonio de la Cruz in 1980, and we had recovered some arms. People had done a lot of harassing the enemy before all the guerillas in Chalate got together into one organization for the offensive. We didn't have the expertise to form an army, but what the people here had was a fighting spirit.**

**After the January offensive until July 1981 our actions centred on fixed army posts. The guerillas were now structured into proper military units which we began to build in March 1981. These became our vanguard units. When we began to form them, nobody was interested. The people, the fighters themselves didn't see the sense. The basic problem was that our army is mainly peasant based. And the peasants, often people from the area itself, did not want to leave their *cantón* and become a mobile force. But when we had formed the first platoon and had the first victory people's enthusiasm was roused, and now everyone wants to join a battalion.**

**In October 1981, we gathered the biggest concentration of our forces ever on the Volcancillo mountain. The army launched one of its biggest offensives against us. They didn't stay in the mountains but encircled the villages in the area, with forces all along the road from here to the Sumpul river. There were more than 2,000 civilians in the area. The first few days of the offensive were fought at Comalapa, La Laguna and Carrizal. When the guerillas met up with the civilians in the area they had to evacuate them. Around 2,000 were evacuated from Las Vueltas; it took us a whole day. Nineteen**

213

*Captain Felipe*

eighty one was a year of resistance, but we knew it would take time to see the results. It was a difficult year for supplies because we hadn't been able to grow much food. We learned to eat roots, certain plants, like *malanga*, and other shrubs, but the hunger did something awful to you . . .

The liberation of Chalatc really began with the attack on San Fernando in January 1982. It marked a new era in our struggle for liberation. The barracks is about 80 kilometres north-west of Chalatenango town; it was a communications centre from where contacts took place between Honduran and Salvadorean troops. We had destroyed the road to the town of San Fernando and the barracks and neighbouring posts of San Francisco Morazán, La Reina, San Ignacio and La Palma were supplied by helicopter which landed in the small town square. One of our exploration teams had observed the arrival of an 80mm machine gun. It was the chance to wipe out the enemy rearguard and recover weapons. Twenty selected fighters from the vanguard units launched the assault on the barracks at night, although they had marched about forty kilometres and were very tired, while forty members of the militia posted themselves along the access roads to the town. We succeeded in annihilating the barracks and capturing all the arms.

After that, we attacked Nueva Trinidad where wc seized our first 90mm cannon, and in April we took San Isidro. We were constantly under attack from mortars during these operations, in the morning, the evening, midday. We often went for three days or more without food, I remember when we attacked Ojos de Agua and Carrizal in May people had only eaten one *tortilla* in three days. Hunger sharpens people's desire for combat because they know that once they have taken a town there will always be food in one form or another. In those days people liked attacking fixed army posts because we always took over the kitchens and if there was time we would spend two or three days in the town. There was no problem with the bombing at that time, it wasn't like it is now. Also the enemy didn't have the capacity to respond quickly, they were pretty slow.

In May 1982 there was only one trained unit and the beginnings of two more. We didn't give much time to training then, only a month. But these were people who had been selected from the local guerillas and they had already taken part in operations. But the training wasn't much also because actual experience of combat is more important than anything else. It's quite different nowadays when people are recruited without any experience of combat. But they develop quickly, because we always put them in units where there are already old hands, so at the side of the veterans they gain experience very quickly.

In October 1982 we attacked Jícaro and Las Vueltas, Guarjila and other hamlets and military stations. An operation against

Potonico was completely spoilt by lack of supplies, especially boots, but also food. That's what led to the suspension of the operation; we had nothing to eat and no shoes. Later in the month, on the 27th, we attacked La Laguna. By November 1982 the whole of the eastern area up to Arcatao was in our hands as well as the mountainous area of Comalapa, Concepción Quezaltepeque right up to San Fernando. In January 1983 we launched another offensive attacking Tejutla, La Palma, La Reina and Agua Caliente, strengthening our positions so that the enemy could now only enter the area by mounting a very large-scale offensive.

## The Guinda

If hell exists it must be more gentle than breaking the army circle. (Carmen)

---

The years 1981 and 1982 were hard, serious years for the people because they were the years of the great invasions, where the people had to move from village to village. It was the time we spent whole nights walking in the rain, without food or water to drink.

Some people left for Honduras then, others to the city. But it was usually because they had family problems. There were few desertions and many people stayed. And when the FMLN began to liberate the garrisons, this really shifted the spirit of the people. At no point did the people lose heart completely, there was always a group of very combative people who motivated everyone. It was often very bad, but we'd rather die here. There's no reason why we should leave our land. We were born here and we are going to die here. (Quique)

Of the many terrible army invasions of 1981 and 1982, three have stuck in people's memories more than any others; those of October 1981, May 1982 and October 1982. Below, María Serrano describes the 1982 invasions. As the army sweeps through the area, the people retreat into the hills, in mass withdrawals called *guindas*. Many massacres take place during these *guindas*. And while the population hides in the hills, the army burns their houses and crops. Most buildings have been destroyed in Chalatenango, not just houses but also churches, either during the army invasions or through bombing and other attacks on villages in the areas. The photographs on pages 228 and 230 illustrate the destruction of Chalatenango.

Here on the front we have had enough *guindas* to choose from, but of all the ones I have lived through, the most brutal were those of

*Guinda*

May and October 1982. In May the Ramón Belloso brigade invaded.
The enemy began to drop troops into the eastern part of
Chalatenango. Then they surrounded us and on 29 May we found
ourselves in Los Amates with about 5,000 people when the enemy
began to blast shots at us. We started running like mad, it was like a
river of people, and we started running, running. We had to go
through the river Sumpul; but unfortunately, at the time the river
was very high, so that many women and children drowned. And all
the time there was shooting, I don't know how they didn't shoot
everyone. Afterwards, we left to sleep in a ravine, where we spent a
few days, I don't remember how many days, all I remember are the
nights. I remember one particular night, walking to a ravine; we
were so many people that we left a trail so that the enemy found our
path the next day and followed us. As soon as night fell and we began
to walk again to another place, the enemy was there exactly where
we had been the day before; they were trailing us. We hadn't slept
nor eaten. Although the night is to sleep, we used it to walk, and used
the day to hide ourselves. I couldn't sleep because of the tension. I
walked with my shoes broken, and the sand was getting in. I'd been
told that in the October 1981 *guinda* some people's feet were flowing

217

*Comandante Douglas, a key figure in the 'liberation' of Chalatenango*

with blood. How is it possible to walk with bleeding feet? But then I found out myself: my own feet were bleeding.

One morning, we were in a hamlet and the enemy was so close that already the shells were falling close by. Then everyone began to run, everyone was running. When the helicopter began to circle over us, we all ducked down. But we were a huge column of people. How could it be, I asked myself then, that they don't see us? And why isn't the helicopter shooting at us? I soon found out: it was moving the troops to form a circle where we were heading. The breaking of an enemy circle, I can't really explain it, is the most horrible that can happen in a war, because you are absolutely certain that they will kill you. You want to live; the instinct for life overwhelms you. We began to run, they had encircled us. But not horizontally, where we were going, but vertically, so that however fast we might run they were always shooting down on us. In this way our column was broken up. We ran here and there, we went down slopes. There was a rain of bullets, thousands of bullets of all calibre machine-guns; and we were running and running. Along the way they killed many. Women were killed and the children they were carrying, they shot at them too. We had to leave the bodies there, even if it was your own son, you had to leave him because they were shooting right down on top of us, and the bullets were ringing in our ears. There was a moment when we all threw ourselves down to the ground because the shooting was so bad. But there comes a time when you even prefer to die than to go on running, because you can't anymore, your throat is dried up, you have no more strength to run.

When we had run until we could run no more, we collapsed into little ditches, like the ones they make in the cornfields in the winter. And no sooner did we fall in there, than four soldiers appeared and saw the little track we had made, and I don't know why they didn't come to take us or to kill us, we had no more than a revolver. I was sure they would kill us, but they left. There we waited for night to fall so that we could climb out. But no-one knew the place we were in. How terrible the enemy is in the night: the enemy moves and you are moving yourself, everything makes you afraid, the enemy is afraid too, they shoot at anything that moves. We went on running, climbing down a slope, and after a while we came across the first dead . . .

There was a moon and this made it all even more frightening because the shadows kept moving. As we went down the ravine, I heard a sound like a child crying and when we got down there, it was one of the women who had got lost and when she saw us she started screaming: 'they're coming to kill me, they're coming to kill me.' And so we told her that we had come down to hide too. She had a child and I had to throw away her bundle of clothes because she couldn't carry it and the child. Further on down the ravine we found

*The US-trained Atlacatl Brigade during an army offensive*

another woman who came from my village, a friend of mine. She said to us: 'I'm so glad you've come, I couldn't go any further because I've been wounded.' We looked behind her and saw this sort of black thing. It was a pool of blood, she'd been wounded in the leg. At her side were her two children who were asleep. It's really tragic not to have the strength to carry a child. We had to keep on walking. At two o'clock in the morning we crossed the river Gualsinga and we hadn't got any further when someone collapsed from the strain. Further on another woman also died of exhaustion. This is what happens on these *guindas*, both to the young and the old. Some of the nearby troops went away because they thought they had killed everyone. I was walking along weeping with fear and then we arrived at a little village. I could hardly walk by this time. I got there leaning on a stick and walking only on my heels. When we arrived someone gave me five tortillas and a bit of meat stew. There were 35 of us but I shared out the five tortillas and put a little bit of lard from the bottom of the tortilla on my feet.

We stayed there a little while but then went on as the enemy was following behind us. When we saw them, we started to run, climbed up a hill and then went down to cross the Sumpul river to get to Cancasque. We crossed the river at about seven o'clock in the evening. We were just crossing it and a great storm began to come down on us; we had already put up with a lot of rain all these nights when the enemy was following us around. Well, that night, there was a great storm, and I couldn't take anymore, my knees were hurting from rheumatism for all the rain and hunger and lack of sleep. We got to Cancasque pretty wet, and our clothes dried on our skins, because in the flight you lose everything, throw everything away; you want life, you don't want a blanket nor any other thing, you want life.

When we left the ravine, it began to rain again, and it got so dark that with the heavy rain we could only walk by the light of the lightning. I found myself waiting for the person in front of me to walk but when the next lightning flash came, no-one was there, they had already gone. I felt my way blindly and bumped into the next person, but the same thing happened again and again. I have never lived a night so dark and a storm so fierce. Finally we reached a little village where we stayed the following day.

The next night they told us that the enemy was retreating. It's hard, very hard then. After the invasion you have to fill yourself with a good amount of strength because when you get back to the village every house is a hospital because everyone is ill from suffering and hunger. You can't get hold of any drugs, as all the purchasing channels have been disrupted. You can't find anything to eat, which is the worst, and you have to raise the people's spirit, telling them about the situation in such a way that they can accept it. If you say to a *compa*, 'You have to go on', it kills that person. You have to help them, tell them that you are determined and they will say 'me too'. It's terrible coming back after an invasion. You get the impression that they have killed everyone; then the people slowly begin to come down from the mountains, with thin necks and big heads from so little to eat. You tell them, 'It's great to see you coming back'. Everyone comes back looking like a skeleton.

The helicopter is one of the most fearful things for us because it's a machine that moves and can stay in the air to machine-gun groups of civilians. There is one helicopter, a round one, which we call the 'mosquito', it's the most criminal one: it places the bombs with great precision, like the one on the hospital, where it dropped two bombs and killed all the patients and a woman who was looking after her children. I just don't know how the enemy can do this. All these people who have to flee, they're just ordinary people, women, men, children. The enemy doesn't care about this. Once one of the *compañeros* was on the other side of the hill doing reconnaissance and as we were passing that hill, he heard someone say, 'There's a column of women and children going past down below. Shall we shoot?' And the order came back. 'Shoot them'. More than a hundred people died on this *guinda* and many of them were women and children. When the enemy hears a child cry, they throw grenades in the direction of the noise and this is terrible because children often cry from hunger and cold.

In May a woman went up the hill during a *guinda* for the night like everyone else. She heard crying, just like a child's, 'Mummy, I'm cold'. 'Poor little thing', she said, 'we'll go and get it.' But then a *compañero* who was up there, said, 'Hang on a minute, I'll go and see.' It was a cruel soldier imitating a child and there were others there waiting to see if anyone came out. At the beginning of the invasion, almost the whole of this zone was bombed. There was a woman in La Laguna, who was holding her child in her arms during a bombardment. A splinter of shrapnel blew up the child's head and she was left with the rest of it in her arms.


# Guerilla Successes: October 1983 to 1984

The army were unable to mount a successful invasion of the eastern part of Chalatenango during this period, and the FPL could embark on the political experiment and various health and educational projects described in the next chapter. This was less the case in other areas of the department where the army continued to mount operations facilitated by their control over the main northern road through the department to the Honduran border and the branch road to Chalatenango town. Soldiers and guerillas continued to dispute territory around Santa Rita,

*Guerillas display arms captured from El Paraíso*

Dulce Nombre de María, San Francisco Morazán and the hydroelectric plants of the Cerrón Grande and Cinco de Noviembre. But by the end of 1983, the FMLN had control of at least 28 of the department's 33 *municipios*.[9] The destruction of the barracks of the fourth army brigade in El Paraíso, Chalatenango, is the climax of this period. Below, one of the guerillas who participated in the attack describes how it took place:

**We knew that what we were going to do was a big step in the war. We'd never done anything like it before. We arrived at El Paraíso after walking for three days. We were very hungry and thirsty. There were three hundred of us on the mission. First, some of the** *compañeros* **got inside while we waited near the wire fence for them to come back. Then we all went in and it all started to happen. The enemy soldiers were in chaos because they didn't have a clue what was happening and some were even praying. Some** *compañeros* **went up to the door of the barracks and shouted to the soldiers to give themselves up and then they seized four rifles and dug themselves in around it. Then someone got into the barracks which was spraying machine gun fire. The captain shouted that they wanted to surrender but because of the noise of the fighting and the confusion, he couldn't be found. At two o'clock we stormed the barracks. Some soldiers ran away, the rest surrendered. They now only had the watchtowers and trenches which we attacked at six in**

*Women guerilla fighters*

the morning. By one in the afternoon, we had control except for a single soldier who didn't want to surrender because he thought he had enough ammunition to last out. He destroyed almost a whole squadron of ours, killing five of our people and wounding three. So in the end the *compañeros* shouted to him to surrender and when he wouldn't, he was killed.

There were four women guerillas in my detachment. Altogether twelve women took part in the attack on El Paraíso. They took 15 prisoners, some of whom had been trained in the US. They wore berets they had brought back from there. Anyway, when the *compañeras* shouted at them to surrender they came out with a lot of crude jokes and a torrent of insults. They didn't have any political awareness, they were just being *macho* and with that sort of *machismo* they didn't give a damn about anything. The *compañeras* tried to make them a bit more aware and reason with them about the things that we're fighting for. They told them, 'you're not our enemies. We don't see the soldier as our enemy because he's the son of a peasant, he's a worker in the countryside and he's exploited too. And even in the barracks he's exploited and maltreated. Our enemies are the bourgeoisie and US imperialism.'

I myself saw about 70 dead soldiers at El Paraíso, and we also took many prisoners. We had to destroy some of the weapons which we didn't have time to move, 120mm cannons with rubber wheel-rims, a small tank and 15 army lorries. At about three o'clock the enemy began harassing us from the air with indiscriminate rocket attacks, using two or three planes at a time. We piled up all the rifles we had captured into a lorry but we couldn't get them away because of the planes. Then about nine o'clock at night, we heard that the Atlactl brigade was coming to recover the barracks, by 9.25pm it was only 300 metres away. There was only the ammunition dump left to destroy and we set fire to it with petrol. Our morale was very high, we'd shown the enemy a different kind of fighting: as the *comandante* had said, it had been a real battle. Some units went into the hillside and slept there through the night of 31 December. When they saw that neither the troops nor the planes were coming, they dismantled the 50mm machine guns and left by the road to Dulce Nombre de María, using some of the lorries we had managed to take away. Then we had festivities and dances to celebrate our great victory. (Toni)

*Guerillas celebrating victory*

## The 'liberation' of Chalatenango — chronology of events 1981-1985

### 1981
**Mid-July** At least 3,000 Salvadorean troops mount operation to surround Chalatenango. Casualties unknown.
**October** 110 peasants captured in big army sweep around Concepción Quezaltepeque.

### 1982
**January** FMLN take San Fernando and Nueva Trinidad.
**April** FMLN take San Isidro, Potonico, Las Vueltas, Guarjila, El Jícaro, La Palma, San Francisco Morazán, Tejutla, Cancasque.
**End of May** Radio Venceremos claims about 600 civilians killed in army sweep in Chalate which involved 3,000 troops, including the elite Ramón Belloso battalion. Six A-37 Dragonfly jets and four spotter planes arrive from the US.
**October** FMLN begins campaign where they seized and held El Jícaro, Las Vueltas, La Laguna.
**November** Army used 3,500 troops in operation to retake towns. Honduran army also said to be involved.

### 1983
**January** FMLN launch campaign in Chalatenango.
**March** 89 people reported killed in army operations in the department.
**April** 155 people killed.
**May** 60 people reported killed in political violence in Chalatenango.
**July** 30 people killed in large-scale military operation in Tejutla, La Reina, La Palma, San Ignacio and Citalá.
**September** FMLN launch another big campaign.
**October** Unknown number of casualties in intense bombing in northern Chalatenango.
**November** Bombing continues in northern Chalatenango.
**December** Bombing in whole of department.
**December** FMLN attack and destroy army barracks at El Paraíso.

### 1984
**January** Chalatenango town attacked by FMLN, army operation and aerial bombardment follow.
**February** 42 people killed in military operation in Volcancillo area.
**Mid-March** Big counter-insurgency operation to reclaim the department. Bombing raids with 23 casualties recorded at Dulce Nombre de María and La Laguna. 7.5 tonnes of explosives dropped on the population each day.
**April** 19 civilian victims in fighting near Nueva Concepción.
**August** to 4 **September** Unknown casualties in bombardment by planes, helicopters and artillery of Portillo de Norte and San José Cancasque.

**August** 50 people killed and 51 captured by army near Los Cordova on Gualsinga river after 600 villagers forced to flee their homes in army attack on Tamarindo, Haciendita.

**Late October** Army sweep in the department following the peace talks, operation is carried out by new commander of the Fourth Brigade in Chalatenango, Colonel Sigifredo Ochoa.

**November** Armed forces attack on La Laguna with two A-37 planes. Army operation in northern Chalatenango.

**December** Unknown number of casualties in Las Vueltas and La Laguna aerial bombardment.

**1985**

**January** Unknown number of victims in fighting in Nueva Concepción.

**Early February** Army claim it has taken control of seven villages in Chalatenango formerly held by the guerillas, including Tejutla, Citala, La Reina and Nueva Concepción.

**March** Fierce fighting in San Fernando. Casualties unknown.

**April** 2,500 troops reported to be doing sweeps in several departments including Chalatenango.

(Sources: *Socorro Jurídico*, *Tutela Legal*, *Latin America Newsletters*, British and US newspapers, International press agencies).

# Chalatenango 1984-1985: 'Free-Fire Zone'

In 1985, Colonel Ochoa, head of the Fourth Army Brigade, gave a frank account of his objectives in Chalatenango:

*'To help cut civilian contact with the rebels, the program in Chalatenango prohibits civilian movement or residence in 12 free-fire zones. Air strikes and artillery bombardments now are being carried out indiscriminately in these areas, the military leader said.*

*"In these zones", said Colonel Sigifredo Ochoa, pointing to 12 red areas on a provincial map, "there are no civilians. There are only concentrations of guerillas, so we keep these areas under heavy fire . . ."*

*"Our first goal is to clean up the province militarily," he said. "This means we cannot permit civilian contact with the rebel army. We must separate the people from the guerillas and then crush the guerillas. The civilians can return when we have searched the area."*

*"Without a civilian base of support, the guerillas are nothing but outlaws," Ochoa said leaning over a map in his command headquarters. "Without civilians the rebels have no food and cannot maintain their army."*

*Ochoa said that civilians have fled the free-fire zones in Chalatenango to take refuge in Honduras or in the sprawling urban ghettoes of displaced people that ring the capital, San Salvador.*

'The toys
that they send for our children
are the bombs
that they drop from the planes'

(Extract from popular song)

*Relief officials in San Salvador, however, say that civilians do reside in the free-fire zones.'*
(Chris Hedges, *The Dallas Morning News*, 21 January 1985)[10]

The US began to step up its involvement in the Salvadorean war during 1984 and the counter-insurgency operations launched in Chalatenango and elsewhere towards the end of the year were the outcome. The first indication of the more direct US influence over the war was the escalation of aerial bombardment at the beginning of 1984. The planes used in the bombing — mainly A-37s — and the bombs, were all US supplied. The use of bombing against guerilla strongholds is a tactic the US developed in South-East Asia with devastating effect.

Bombardment of guerilla-controlled zones became significant in the last months of 1983 and particularly following the taking of the El Paraíso barracks. Adonai, a peasant in charge of the popular militia of Chalatenango, describes how his mother died in bombing raids in the department at this time.

**Bombardments began to be a real problem in the last days of December and the first days of January 1984. About six or eight people died in the south of the department at this time, near San Isidro. Amongst them was my mother, who was killed on 28 December 1983. At ten in the morning two A-37 and one A-7 arrived, the two covered the A-7 which attacked and the first bomb hit directly the house where my mother lived. There she and a girl of nine years died, four others escaped with injuries though one of them died later on 2 January. On 19 January there was a bombardment of a strategic mountain position and a young, 18-year-old *compañero* died. He was head of the militias in this area. Another woman of 45 died, leaving two orphans.**

The bombing raids escalated further in the weeks prior to the March 1984 election. In the two weeks between 16 March and 29 March 1984, the Archbishop's human rights office estimated that there were 235 civilian deaths as a result of indiscriminate air operations.

The bombings mostly affected civilians, but other tactics employed in the aerial war had serious implications for the guerilla army. In February 1984 US pilots began to fly OV1 Mohawk observation planes over El Salvador; these planes carry infra-red sensors that enable them to detect guerilla movements at night. They were the first regular tactical support the US had given the Salvadorean army and their main effect was to make it much more difficult for the guerillas to concentrate forces for major operations.

The US poured some US$10 million into the presidential elections, and the victory of the Christian Democrat, José Napoleón Duarte, gave greater legitimacy to US policy towards El Salvador. Duarte presented himself as the alternative to the extreme right and the guerillas and was

*Sheltering in 'tatu', home-made air-raid shelter*

*Most of the houses and churches in the eastern part of Chalatenango have been destroyed during army invasions or by aerial bombardment*

230

able to persuade US congressional opinion that he could curb the abuses of human rights of the former and take some steps towards a negotiated settlement of the war. In the meantime, Congress was prepared to acquiesce in vastly increased US military assistance and involvement in the war effort.

Between May 1984 and the end of the year the US appropriated more than US $260 million in military assistance for El Salvador, about equal to the total amount of US military aid to El Salvador over the previous four years. This has greatly increased the technical superiority of the Salvadorean army over the guerillas in the fields of air surveillance, communications, air transport and air firepower.

El Salvador's helicopter fleet was tripled to approximately 50, enabling the Salvadorean army to transport 400 troops to any part of the country in just over an hour. By early 1985, the Salvadorean airforce had received six C-47 'gunships', some already equipped with .50 calibre rapid-fire machine-guns capable of saturating an area 45 yards square with 600 bullets in one second.[11]

The US escalated the daily reconnaissance flights over El Salvador, transmitting the information gathered directly to brigade headquarters in El Salvador. The number of US advisers reached at least 122 during 1984 according to official reports.[12] Many of them worked directly with the Salvadorean high command, giving specific combat instructions and even accompanying Salvadorean army operations into FMLN controlled territory.[13] Fifteen thousand Salvadorean soldiers and officers had received US training by the end of 1984 according to State Department figures, and plans were under discussion for a new army training school within El Salvador. By 1985, the Salvadorean armed forces numbered 45,000, compared to 16,000 in 1981.[14]

The Reagan administration had by 1984 gained influence within a sector of the high command, weakening some of the traditional ties between the officer corps and the oligarchy and establishing a group of more efficient officers prepared to pursue the war according to US methods. Five years of counter-insurgency have produced more experienced and capable officers, while greater army mobility and more rapid response to intelligence information on guerilla positions considerably enhanced the army's effectiveness during 1984 and 1985. The FMLN was forced to abandon its large-scale operations, now much more easily detected, and return to smaller patrols and quick-strike actions over a wider range of territory. It also resumed activities in San Salvador.

The FDR-FMLN launched a diplomatic offensive in February 1984, calling for negotiations around a proposal for a Provisional Government of Broad Participation (GAP). The GAP was the culmination of a process of political realignmnent within the FMLN, leading to more conciliatory positions. The clearest shift took place within the FPL. Marcial opposed what he considered to be an

> **'The only choice left for us'**
>
> The bombings began here last year, the first was on 8 October 1983. Four A-37 planes came and that's when Lito's family was killed. We left the area to try and find tortillas for the children. The enemy must have known where people were going because they followed right behind us. Then came the attack. Another woman and I had to run although I had a fever. As we were crossing a river, the guerillas joined us, we didn't know them, we just kept on going. We were attacked by a helicopter and an A-37, shooting at us with mortar and machine-gun fire. I said to my children, 'we've got to get out of here whether it means life or death'. That's when my daughter was wounded. I couldn't find any way of stopping the bleeding. Then one of the guerillas said to us: 'Look, *compañeros*, you'd better keep going because the enemy's coming right behind.' But he couldn't go any further because we were afraid that if we moved, we would be killed by a bomb, so it was six o'clock in the evening before we could leave. I had to carry my little girl in my arms because she couldn't walk because she'd lost so much blood. At eleven that night she was treated by a doctor in a hospital at the front. The next day they took us to a trench where the enemy bombarded us heavily; but, thank God, then the *compañeros* set up a line of fire to defend the people and so the enemy couldn't advance to where we were because it was getting dark. Then the *compañeros* took us over to the other side. The bombings keep on now every day, in fact I'm surprised they aren't here now. In spite of all this, though, we're going to continue the struggle. It's the only choice left for us. (Norma)

abandonment of the FPL's historical position. But he found himself isolated within the leadership of the party. He committed suicide in April 1983 shortly after Comandante Ana María of the FPL was murdered by one of his supporters.

Unlike the 1980 Programme for a Democratic Revolutionary Government, the GAP did not presuppose the defeat of the enemy army. The Government of Broad Participation would result from a process of dialogue followed by a cease-fire. It would be based on a broad alliance of anti-oligarchic and anti-imperialist forces including the 'non-oligarchic bourgeoisie', with no single force predominating. The GAP aimed to restore independence and national sovereignty, implement a series of reforms (through less radical than those envisaged in the 1980 Programme) and call a general election. The FMLN and the purged government forces would combine to form the new army.

But hopes for a negotiated settlement faded in the ensuing months as the Salvadorean government became increasingly confident that it could defeat the guerillas. The counter-insurgency war was relaunched with renewed vigour after Duarte's election in a bid to remove the FMLN's civilian support — 'draining the sea to catch the fish'.[15] On 28 August 1984, troops headed by the Atlacatl brigade invaded

*Meeting of the Salvadorean women's organization, AMES, disrupted as A-37 bomber flies overhead*

Chalatenango near the village of Las Vueltas and surrounded some 400 peasants at the confluence of the Sumpul and Gualsinga rivers. The massacre which followed on 30 August left at least 50 civilians dead from the hamlets of El Tamarindo, Hacienditas and Leoneses. Fifty-one others were captured and eventually handed over to the International Red Cross. The box on page 234 is an account of the events; it makes plain the small number of armed people in the area, which would have been apparent to the Salvadorean armed forces from the surveillance flights over the area. The author herself lived in these villages in the early months of 1984, and many of the peasants whose stories appear in this book are from there. Despite the evidence from those who escaped the massacre and from journalists who managed subsequently to evade the army and reach the scene of the massacre, Elliott Abrams, now the Assistant Secretary of State for Inter-American Affairs, denied that it had ever happened (see box, page 236). President Duarte also denied the massacre had taken place, during a press conference shortly afterwards.

233

# The Gualsinga River Massacre

On 28 August 1984 a mortar shelling started against the inhabitants of El Tamarindo. This killed a 26-day-old girl when a mortar shell hit the house of Señora Irma Ayala. The people of the village realized that the army was threatening and the fear started. People organized themselves in various groups, according to their respective *cantón*, in order to escape from the area. These people are called *masa* by the guerilla; among these people there were between two and three militiamen with hand guns. While they were fleeing, three guerilla *combatientes* joined the people to help the civilians escape. There were about 600 civilians: women, elderly people and children who were the majority. The escape was organized in the direction of the town of Nueva Trinidad. People were also walking during the night. On August 29, they crossed the river Sumpul over a hanging bridge made of hammocks and thus entered *cantón* Jaguatalla. People were very tired and the first people were beginning to separate from the group and hide in the hills. During that day, the shooting at civilians continued, but the army was unable to do them major harm. Almost everybody managed during the night of 29 August to get to a curve of the Gualsinga river near the village of Los Cordova. They tried to hide in a brook of the Gualsinga river. About 7am on 30 August some people saw the first soldiers. Some of them thought at first that they were guerilla *combatientes* who were arriving to protect them. The place is surrounded by hills. At about 10am, they saw helicopters transporting the troops and they realized that it was the soldiers who were encircling them. People were trying to find better hiding places. At about 11.45am, the army started shooting at people. At that moment, panic started and people dispersed in all directions. One of the guerillas who was accompanying the people started shooting in order to break the circle and he opened a way through which about 80 people managed to escape. Some other people jumped into the Gualsinga river which at that point is very close to the mouth of the Sumpul river. Since the river was very high, some people drowned. Some others who managed to grab some tree trunks, managed to escape down the Gualsinga to the Sumpul river. The shooting by the army lasted until about 1pm. Afterwards, the troops started searching the area, discovering people who had been hiding. The majority of those who survived were in the area of Jaguatalla; some survivors from the place where the events took place and a few from the places through which the soldiers passed before the operation. A total of 51 people were captured by the army. They were taken to Chalatenango. The captured people were handed over three days later to the International Red Cross by the military authorities. Many people managed to survive by means of escaping. At least 50 people died; it was possible to identify 31 bodies. There was also an unknown number of disappeared people. On 3 September, there was also another military action in Hacienda Vieja, El Sitio, Nombre de Jesús. Some people stated that there were two civilians killed who were not identified, and one man killed in San Antonio La Cruz.

Here is a statement that Tutela Legal obtained from a survivor of the massacre at the Gualsinga River, Pascual Ayala:

*I was working at the river when we heard a noise and we bent and I told my son 'don't run, because a mortar is coming' . . . I started walking very slowly and after I went a little, another shell came and hit near the edge of the road. Then I did not stop anymore and came here. And I did not see the baby anymore. I was looking around and the baby was not there anymore. She was killed by a mortar weapon, it took her brains out: she had three wounds, she was 26 days old. She was my daughter. At that point we decided to leave because it was dangerous to stay there. We left in the direction of the Gualsinga river and we spent two days walking. And then there was the massacre and I lost my entire family there, I was left with only one son . . . Including my wife, there were five people killed in my family, my wife's name was Irma Ayala, and my children: Raúl Ayala, Gumercina Ayala, Angélica Ayala and Guadalupe Ayala. They are not alive anymore. I'll keep working. I am from the militia. I, too, almost lost my life in the river because I was trying to catch my oldest child while I was already carrying the youngest one, and I could not keep them and the big one went with the river. The others died killed by bullets, the three of them, in a place called Los Pozos, at the shore of the Gualsinga river . . . (When the shooting started) we jumped to cross it, I did not manage to cross it, because the river was dragging me, so I got out and I stayed between the hills. I was the only one armed, in the road only two*

▶

Women and children of El Tamarindo, photographed during author's visit in 1984

235

*'What happened is that the army had reports of a terrorist advance party in the area and decided to organize a surprise attack. Many civilians who were in the zone with the subversives fled north towards Honduras, and when they tried to cross the Sumpul river many were drowned, taken away by the strong current. The army helped them and saved 35 civilians . . .'*[16]

In October 1984, Colonel Sigifredo Ochoa was made commander of the Fourth Infantry Brigade in Chalatenango. His appointment seems to have been the signal for a systematic campaign to oust the guerillas and their supporters from the department. Large-scale army operations

---

*people had arms, but where the people were, there were no armed people. There were approximately 500 people there.*

Elliott Abrams denied that the Gualsinga River massacre (and another massacre at Los Llanitos) happened, in this exchange on national television:

**Ted Koppel** 'Secretary Abrams, why was neither of those incidents reported?' (In the State Department's country report on El Salvador).
**Secretary Abrams** 'Because neither of them happened. Because it is a tactic of the guerilla every time there is a battle and a significant number of people are killed to say that they're all victims of human rights abuses.'
**Aryeh Neier** 'That's why *The New York Times* . . .'
**Secretary Abrams** 'Ted, there's one very important point here.'
**Aryeh Neier** '. . . and *The Boston Globe* and *The Miami Herald* and *The Christian Science Monitor* and Reuters and all the other reporters who went to the scene and looked at what took place, they were simply being propagandists for the guerillas? Is that right?'
**Secretary Abrams** 'I'm telling you that there were no significant . . . there were no massacres in El Salvador in 1984.'

('Nightline', ABC Television, 13 February 1985)

After having investigated the events, we are able to conclude that:
1 The military operation against *cantones* El Tamarindo, Hacienditas and others was an indiscriminate attack on civilians.
2 The civilians, called *masa* by the guerillas, were forced to escape to the Gualsinga river, near the village Los Cordova, jurisdiction Nueva Trinidad, department of Chalatenango, very close to the mouth of Sumpul river.
3 In one of the brooks of the Gualsinga River people were massacred. The soldiers knew who they were killing. It was during the day; the shooting lasted long enough to establish that it was not a confrontation; despite the firing by one guerilla member who did it in order to break the circle, as a result of which some people managed to get out.
4 It was possible to establish the number of dead people at 50, of whom only 31 bodies were identified.
5 There is an undetermined number of disappeared people.[17]

into Chalatenango combined with intensive bombardment began in November 1984. By February 1985, Ochoa was boasting that he had recovered most of the villages in the western part of the department. 'Now', he said, 'there is only guerilla persistence in the eastern part, such as Arcatao, San José las Flores, Nombre de Jesús, San Antonio de la Cruz and Las Vueltas'.[18]

The next chapter will show how this is precisely the area where the civilian population developed its strongest organization in the form of local popular government, with health and education programmes to improve their living conditions. It is this civilian population which has been targetted by Ochoa in denoting zones of 'free-fire' in the area.

Ochoa outlined his plans for a 'military civic action programme' in Chalatenango to the press in February 1985. It is a modified version of the civic action plan attempted in San Vicente in 1983. He described how 'little by little we have come to learn how to fight in this war. We had an army trained for regular war, with commanders who didn't understand this problem. Today's commanders understand that this is a social, military, economic and political war.'[19] Ochoa's programme includes phases of military intervention, consolidation and communal development, aimed at establishing 'something like a military structure within a civilian milieu. That's what the communists do, who base their work on the organization of the masses, and we have to do the same.'[20]

The military side of the programme was to involve 1,000 troops with air support; night patrols and constant large-scale operations would be used to expel the guerillas accompanied by 'psychological operations' to counteract the 'conscientization work of the rebels'. The phase of consolidation would include the appointment of new civil authorities and the establishment of civil defence patrols. Finally, development would involve social programmes and job creation schemes aimed at undermining the local government structures which had developed in the area in collaboration with the guerillas.

Some of this programme is already underway in areas of Chalatenango now under army control. In La Palma, for instance, civil defence training programmes have begun. Salvadorean instructors, themselves trained by US advisers, give two-month training courses. At the same time large amounts of US 'humanitarian' aid funds are channelled to the area through USAID. The new AID programme envisages expenditure of US$26 million a year to El Salvador for the next three years in temporary job creation projects, health programmes, emergency food aid and relocation of displaced people. A further US$60 million will be given towards the food aid programmes. Since 1982, average annual US aid for similar projects has not been more than US$6.2 million.[21] The regional director for Catholic Relief Services, which has been asked by US AID to administer the programmes, has called the aid package a 'highly political programme

One day six planes came, and all my family had to hide against a wall of
the school they were in at the time. When a bomb hit the school they
all got buried. Seventeen people died altogether, including my wife,
my mother-in-law and my five children. I was sick for days, not out of
demoralization but because I was full of hate and anger. And now I am
going to fight on to the end.

for pacification'. The Salvadorean Bishops' Conference rejected an AID request in September 1984 to coordinate a programme of food distribution because of its 'disastrous political implications'.[22]

In May 1985, church communities in Chalatenango published a letter to Monseñor Rivera Damas about the attacks on the eastern part of the department, itemizing the burning of crops and houses and the murder of civilians during army incursions. A Salvadorean priest referred to this letter when he wrote to friends abroad about the impact of the civic-military action programmes of the Salvadorean military:

*'Refugee camps continue receiving people who come fleeing from the war fronts. Perhaps the bombardments have decreased, but mortar attacks and invasions continue, forcing the people to abandon the zones, so that the fish is left without the water. I believe that the letter of the communities of Chalatenango very clearly reflects what is happening. It is certain that deaths continue, but direct deaths have decreased. Now it is mainly invasions and mortar attacks which destroy the material goods of the people and make them prisoners so that they will consider it freedom if they leave the zone. The programme of the Civic Military Action is Machiavellian, because with a mask of protection and defence of the civilians they are increasing the level of poverty, repression, injustice. Duarte continues helping the coffee growers because he needs them . . . And he does this at the cost of the peasants. It is the very same soldiers who after having burnt, destroyed and broken everything which they have found in their way, who are in charge of distributing food, clothes and medicine to the people who they have just hurt. It is something planned, efficient, deceitful. The hunger of the people is continually being played with.*

*About the dialogue we know little . . . it is almost comical that one talks about the humanization of the war (if within a war there is room at all for something humane), when they are destroying the few things the civilian population has.'* (Letter 30 May 1985)

*Popular Assembly*

# 8
# PEASANTS AND POWER

## Popular Power

At times of revolutionary change, the organizations of the existing order collapse. Into the vacuum may step new bodies which reflect the revised distribution of power. These bodies, though they are often short-lived, are examples of 'popular power', when government and administration are taken over by the people who live and work in the area.

In El Salvador, however, popular power did not emerge at a moment of imminent victory. The PPLs (*Poder Popular Local*, literally Local Popular Power) emerged in the areas of FMLN control during 1982 as organs of local government to administer the newly 'liberated' areas. Had the January 1981 offensive proved successful, the PPLs might well have been an early stage in the formation of a Democratic Revolutionary Government at a time when a number of parties and political forces co-existed and competed for influence. But instead, they came into existence in the midst of the protracted war and mostly in areas of FMLN control where usually one organization and one social class predominated. The richer farmers had fled Chalatenango, for instance, as the guerillas took control of the area, and by 1982 it was inhabited mostly by poor peasant farmers and the guerillas of the FPL.

The development of the PPLs has therefore been conditioned by the circumstances of their birth. They exist in a war situation, administering territory which is continuously invaded or threatened with invasion and devastated by army campaigns of destruction and bombing. Not only is there no basic infrastructure in the area, but there is hardly a house left intact. Food has to be grown locally at great risk from bombing or strafing from passing planes or helicopters. All other supplies have to be brought into the zones in night sorties involving long and dangerous hikes through enemy territory.

The PPLs attained their highest level of development in north-eastern Chalatenango during the period of relative security from army invasion that existed between 1982 and 1984. The descriptions in this chapter are based on my observations towards the end of this period. Since then, intensive bombardment and renewed army offensives have disrupted much of the activity and forced many people to flee the area. Nevertheless, despite the adverse conditions, the PPLs have struggled to maintain, and where possible extend, the activities outlined in this chapter.

The PPLs are an experiment in popular democracy and political participation unique in the history of El Salvador. Their development in Chalatenango was not simply due to an advantageous military situation. The FPL had never seen the zones of control as mere military rearguards. Rather they saw them within a broader framework of political mobilization, and as a means by which the civilian population could guarantee their needs and organize their society independent of the military command of the FPL. The peasants' ability to respond to the opportunity and play an active role in shaping their own lives rested on their prior experience first in the Christian base communities and subsequently in the peasant union. Many of the PPL representatives in Chalatenango came from the peasant union, the UTC.

The primary task of the PPL is to administer and organize the population in the zone of control. But there are evidently broader political objectives at stake as well. Each PPL is democratically elected by the civilian population from among their own ranks. They represent the first opportunity for poor peasant farmers to organize their own communities and participate in their own government. Through the PPLs, the peasants have gained experience and confidence in their capacity to work collectively and solve their own problems.

Many peasants, like the revolutionary organizations, also see the PPLs as the embryo of future forms of popular local government in a liberated El Salvador, and not simply as a necessary means of solving the material problems arising from the war. One peasant leader explained that the peasants were learning, first to resolve simple problems such as how to get water, and then more complex issues such as making a legal code for the communities. When the intellectuals came to resume their role in government and administration, he said, the peasants would at least have some experience to enable them to articulate and defend their interests and the real gains they had made. There would therefore be a more balanced relationship between the peasants and other classes in the new society. As one peasant said:

**The reaction of the people to the PPL elections was very courageous, because they had never had the opportunity to choose freely their own government. How good it is to elect a president whom one knows personally. Not like before, when it was some unknown person who might turn up here, and we would know nothing about his life, his attitudes.** (Vidal)

242

# PPLs: Structure and Development

The PPLs took root because the political conceptions of the FPL coincided with the material needs of the peasants. The FPL promoted the development of the PPLs as an implementation of their ideas of popular power, as will be described later. But, for the majority of peasants, the PPLs were primarily a response to real and urgent needs:

We know that alone things are very difficult, but in groups you can achieve a lot. People recognized that every day the situation was getting worse; many people were dying of malnutrition, the food was very inadequate. The other thing was that many people are illiterate here, because the government has never bothered about them. It was only interested in bleeding the people dry . . . it didn't interest them that we learn to read and write. They wanted us ignorant so that we wouldn't refuse tasks. In this situation, we got organized and found how, through the organization of the people, we could make changes. Here in the controlled zones there are more possibilities than ever in the past. (Walter)

---

Many people from here fled to Honduras, because the repression affected everyone. But all the time, new people arrived from other regions, some forced out by repression and others sympathizing with our movement. And more and more the need emerged to set up some structure that would organize production for all these people. Then later, an organized health service was needed; we needed someone who would gather information on traditional medicine, give treatment, so that we decided to set up another secretariat, for health. As we grew, so did our youth; there hasn't been any interruption in the production of children. Children are everywhere. They're even born on the *guindas*. So, the children had to learn to read and write. We needed schools, and so on. Finally, at the end of 1982, the PPLs gained real legitimacy, because it's really the population which elects them. The fact of forming the PPL was simply due to it being the only form of organization which filled all the requirements of the people: it guaranteed production, supplied health services and the rule of law. (Tomás)

At the time of my visit each PPL was elected by and responsible to about 400-500 people, the population of a 'locality'. The entire area of Chalatenango under guerilla control was divided into three sub-zones. The testimonies in this chapter come from sub-zone one, where by 1984 there were seven PPLs and a sub-regional government.

The inhabitants of each locality were divided between three or four *bases* or hamlets, which corresponded broadly to the old administrative units, the *cantones*. The highest power in each locality was the popular assembly, a general meeting of the whole population. Between popular assemblies power rested with the *junta* or council of the PPL, made up of a president, a vice-president and secretaries for production and popular economy, for social affairs (health and education), for legal affairs, for political education and for defence. Candidates were proposed by each community and the *junta* was elected at assemblies of each *base* for six month terms. The *bases* would continue to meet in assemblies about every 15 days to discuss problems with the *junta*. Every eight days there would be a meeting of the general secretaries of the mass organizations in the locality who were represented on the *consejo* (council) of the PPL and whose task was to mobilize the population behind the decisions of the PPL.

The first experience of democracy was a challenge that the peasants faced with enthusiasm:

**You would think it was pretty difficult to understand all the tasks of administration of a place, especially for the peasants, many of them illiterate. But it really wasn't because the people knew what the needs were. We really know the function of each secretary. For the secretary of production and popular economy, we look for and elect a *compañero* who knows about farming, who himself uses a machete, a plough, who understands commerce. The *compañeros* involved in health need preparatory courses; the auxiliary health workers know how to manage a pharmacy and give talks on health. In education, there's usually a *compa* who can read, who has been to school until the fifth or sixth grade and has shown willingness to teach those who don't know. The same applies to self-defence. A *compa* is chosen from the militia who has shown he can guarantee successful retreats when the army invades. Those responsible for the PPLs have much to do. There are no grand and easy solutions, but slowly we are learning things.** (Quique)

The first sub-regional government for sub-zone one was elected in September 1983 for a six-month term, to coordinate the work of the seven PPLs in the sub-zone. At the same time, a programme of government and code of popular justice had been put to the vote and agreed. Its general objective was:

'*that the Popular Power becomes a true organ of government in the zone of control in the economic, political and social (spheres)'.*

Specifically, it aimed to:

'. . . *control and develop the popular economy and war production, improve the health and education of the population, involve the population in the different tasks of defence and combat, guarantee the full participation of the*

244

*population in the decisions of the* bases, *ensure the active participation of the Popular Power in the development and security of the Armed Forces of Popular Liberation, and decree laws which govern our new social life where there is peace, justice and progress.'*

The PPLs were not to be mechanisms simply for resolving the immediate problems of the population, but were also rooted within the general revolutionary perspectives of the war:

*'directing themselves to making concrete the aims of the revolution: the installation of the Democratic Revolutionary Government'.*

The PPLs were uneven in their level of development. Much seemed to depend on the degree of prior involvement in the peasant union. In some PPLs there was considerable mobilization of the community and the PPLs were well-established. In others, progress was much slower and passivity, particularly amongst women, was more evident. María, the president of the first sub-regional government, explained why one of the seven PPLs was less developed than the others, suggesting that much depended on the degree to which the peasants had been affected by the war and therefore had been forced to reconstruct their own communities through their own efforts.

**The first thing you value in this revolution is your life: when you're near losing it, nothing else matters. But next is the little house, the *piedrita de maíz* [stone for grinding corn], the plate for eating off. These things are really valued by us, they are a necessity, a means of existence. To abandon our homes has been one of the hardest things we have had to suffer. That area where the PPL is less developed, is also the area where the people have only had to move across a valley . . . (María)**

A European doctor, who spent some time working with the PPLs suggested something similar:

**One day, I was sent to a village about half an hour from the hospital where I was working. People had arrived in the village from the south of Chalatenango which had been very badly bombed. They came without food and settled in an abandoned village. There was a lot of malnutrition and disease. There were psychological problems too, everyone was very frightened from the bombing and had become apathetic. Some of the diseases could have been treated with better nutrition, but I couldn't give them that, nor was it any use giving pills, we just didn't have much to give.**

**I was invited to a meeting of the PPLs, they were discussing the particular problem of the village which didn't yet have a PPL as the people had only recently arrived. The meeting included all those responsible for social affairs, including health and education, for each locality of the sub-zone and the representative of the sub-**

## Structure of the PPLs

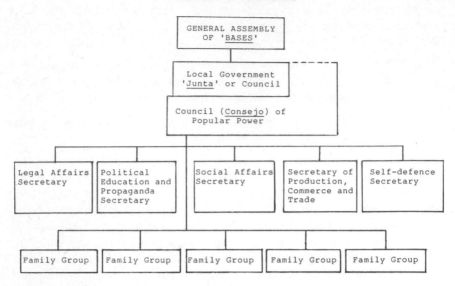

regional government. They asked me my opinion as to what to do in the village. Because of the problems of nutrition in the village, all the other villages had to put something together to give them. But we also knew that we would not be able to do that in the long term. The people had to do something to help themselves. We discussed it and came to the conclusion that the people had to be mobilized and their passive, waiting attitude had to be changed. We decided to send someone from the PPL to stay with them for a time and move them into action. We also talked about the possibility of training one of them as an auxilliary health worker, a *sanitario*, so that they wouldn't need outsiders to treat them. It took some discussions with the village before they agreed to appoint one. I didn't follow the thing very closely as I went somewhere else. But after a while I returned; I heard that they were not asking for food any longer, but they were asking for seeds to grow their own food. I think this was quite an advance, even though it took time.

He had been struck by the uneven development of the PPLs and had given some thought to the reasons:

I didn't research it, but I had some ideas. For one thing, the population in the area were not all native to it. Many had come from other parts of the country and had very different backgrounds. Not all had participated in the peasant organization. Those who had, felt the need to organize themselves and didn't look to easy solutions from above; they wanted to do things for themselves. In some villages, the people were very individualistic, and in others you have a really collective spirit. You could see in some villages a

246

*Sub-regional government of Chalatenango, 1984*

high proportion of the fields were collectively farmed, and in others very few. There were some notable advances, however, during the time I was there. There were far more fields collectively farmed in 1984 than the previous year.

Much depended on the capacity of the PPL to really mobilize people, encourage them to do things. In some PPLs they had weekly assemblies, and some of them were real discussions, in which many people take part and gave their views and the women talk in front of all the people. We used to encourage the auxiliary health workers to talk in these assemblies, to use the opportunity to do some preventive health care. But much depended on whether the PPL gave people the opportunity to speak. In other places you had PPLs with very good intentions, but in the assembly they would tend to hold a monologue just to explain things, and then there might be a discussion.

## The FPL and Popular Power

The FPL have played an important role in promoting the PPLs in the areas they control. They were able to do so precisely because many of the peasants in the area had already been forged by their previous experience into an active and combative base of support for their guerilla fighters, anxious to participate as much as possible in the revolutionary struggle.

*PPL election, 1983*

The PPLs were always seen by the FPL as an institution of government which would not be subject to control of the party. They were intended to be autonomous organs of the peasantry, whose emergence reflected the collapse of the political and military authority of the 'enemy', and the establishment of the power of the people. Close collaboration between the military command of the FPL and the PPLs was necessary but only to coordinate retreats and defence when the army invaded.

But the situation in which the PPLs emerged did not allow for the full realization of this aim. As there was no central government to coordinate the PPLs within a wider process of social transformation, the FPL *de facto* played an orienting role and its priorities inevitably influenced the development of the PPLs. This meant that political debates within the FPL and the tensions between the demands of the war and those of the revolutionary process, referred to in the previous chapter, did affect the work of the PPLs. There were debates, for instance, on how far the PPLs should try to implement far-reaching social changes in the midst of the war. While acknowledging the importance of the political process prior to victory, some argued that energies should nevertheless be concentrated on the war effort and winning that victory. Others did not want to see the political process

*PPL Junta of Chalatenango*

in any way subordinated to military pressures. The impact of these debates on health and education policy and efforts to change the role of women varied and will be discussed in the sections which follow. Debates over political and military priorities have intensified within the FPL in the course of the war. In addition to the constraints imposed by the circumstances of the PPLs' formation, it is evident that time is needed for a traditionally passive and uneducated peasantry to move from participatory roles to those of full control and leadership. But though in practice the space for autonomy was not always as evident as theory suggested, neither were the PPLs in any respect mere instruments of the guerillas. The FPL placed considerable emphasis on the political value of the PPLs in their own right as a means of preparing the people politically for a transition to socialism. They contrasted their view with the situation in territory controlled by the ERP, where the PPLs tended to be a means of mobilizing people for the war effort rather than for political preparation. There were many areas of decision-making in which the PPLs were clearly in charge and many problems were worked out by the peasants themselves. There was in any case, little technical expertise around, even amongst the guerillas, and the peasants often had no choice but to resolve difficulties themselves. The PPLs were seen by the peasants as their government, corresponding to their real needs, and they thus had a genuine base of support in the population independent of the FPL.

The following interview with a member of the FPL who was in Chalatenango during the early formation of the PPLs explains their origins from the perspective of the guerilla movement:

**We found ourselves in territory in which there was the civilian population, the militias and the guerillas. We realized that we had to deepen our revolutionary struggle and organize the population, to show them that, though the triumph hadn't come, nor had they lost the war. We had to find forms of organization which responded to the aspirations of the people to participate in the war. There was a vacuum in that sense; the people had been organized in the FTC, but with the new situation, when most of the young people had joined the guerillas, and others had joined the militia and everyone was talking about combat and military struggle, the masses were more or less stuck in the middle: 'well, and us, what do we do here? What is our role? Our role isn't just to go on *guindas*.' They had come out of the political struggle which had first taken the form of economic demands for land, loans, markets for their produce; they had experience of an organization. But now they were in lands controlled by the people. From whom could they ask lands now or better salaries on the plantations? We had to respond to this new situation, to find a structure which would enable them to defend themselves from the enemy offensives and to discover their own role in the revolutionary process.**

**Something else that we had to consider was the need to create real links between our zones and the rest of society. We cannot live isolated from the rest of society, because what we have in mind is the creation of a different society, a better society, not a backward, isolated one. We cannot deny, let's say, the advantages which the development of production have brought and which are outside the zone. Therefore we encouraged contact with people living outside the zone, buying and selling of goods for instance. We don't have medicines or the capacity to produce all the shoes the people need. We can't let our people go without shoes or clothes so we have to get them from outside the zone. We also said that our people can't just subsist, they have to trade. We must create popular shops within our zones. People must have a purchasing power, they must sell what they produce. The guerilla units buy some things and the other part is sold outside the zone. If people didn't have purchasing power, we felt they would lose the real meaning of a better life. We want to build socialism, but we can't build it in small areas; in the process of building socialism, commercial relations are essential. Then our society isn't just reduced to the territories under our**

250

*Another of the PPL Juntas of Chalatenango*

control. Our society is the whole country, where productive and commercial life is going on.

At first the people were organized into group of 15 families, small units which had their own internal leadership and could organize self-defence and supplies. But these soon became obsolete, that is, they ended up being incapable of responding to all the needs of the population. And once we had more effective control of the area, we were better able to cope with the enemy invasions and our military units could repel them more easily. Our families could then move around with great freedom and consider other problems confronting them. There had to be schools for the children, health provision, production cooperatives and workshops. It was important to try and resolve some of the production problems ourselves even in a small way, such as through shoe workshops. We have a river, so we could organize a fishing cooperative. It was important that the people have work to do, and are involved in production. By the end of 1981 we were beginning to build PPLs in each *cantón* or *base* as we called them; I left the area then, but we were already planning a PPL which would be an expression of the sub-region, and later one that would become the government of all the Front. The PPLs would then have a firm base in each of the little villages of the controlled territory, while maintaining links with the rest of society. The enemy wouldn't then be able to annihilate all the villages in the area, where there is a vibrant and very real economic, social, political and cultural life in permanent contact with the rest of the country.

Our military units have a great deal of respect for the PPLs; they always buy what they need from the PPLs and never try to get anything that is not authorized by the PPL. The PPLs developed around the need to build a new society, not around the military units. When it comes to decisions, it is the PPL which takes them.


## Production in the Controlled Zone

The organization of production, like all other aspects of life in the controlled zones, reflects the dual reality of war and revolution. On the one hand, there are the immediate demands of the war: the need to sustain the civilian population and the guerilla army in the face of the destruction caused by army offensives and aerial bombardment. On the other hand, there is the desire to begin the revolutionary transformation of land tenure and forms of production.

The realities of war constrained the extent to which change was possible: the material conditions did not exist for the establishment of

*Members of the FTC engaged in production for the guerilla army*

'The youngest members of the FTC went into the militias; they went on operations but when there's production work to do, they do that too. There are also the self-defence militias who man guard posts. We think military work should be combined with political work. Now there are some compañeros in the armed forces and some from the FTC in production, there's a combination. And people are very clear that they're participating in giving food to our troops. Those who are capable of fighting do so, but the others who can't can at least work to provide sustenance for our armed forces.' (Victor)

---

cooperatives on any systematic basis, or for a general land reform. The PPLs' approach at this stage was to encourage a more cooperative and collective spirit, which might in the future lay the foundations of more sweeping changes in the peasants' relation to the land. As one leader explained:

One of our objectives is to set up cooperatives: for instance, a fishing cooperative, to improve our daily diet. We would also like to set up agricultural cooperatives, so that the person who doesn't have a millimetre of land will have somewhere to cultivate. We try to educate the people to love the products of the land, and not regard the land as it is seen under capitalism — this is my hill, and that one too. But rather — this hill is producing this, the other, that.

253

*Workshop making boots out of car tyres and canvas. These boots will last about six months in the rough terrain*

**Everything has to be of service to all, producing for all. In some places the people are enthusiastic about working collectively, because they can be given seeds, herbicides, sickles. But because of the scarcity of materials, everyone has been told they can work individually as well.** (Jacob)

Three types of production exist under the PPL: centralized, collective, and family production. Centralized production is earmarked for the sustenance of the guerilla army. Collective production is for the benefit of the community as a whole. This work goes to support those who provide services for the community, such as the teacher or the paramedic in the popular clinic, and those who are unable to support themselves, such as the orphaned children or those too old to work. Generally, the able-bodied members of the community would give two or three days a week to collective

254

*Child selling food*

production. Family production is worked by and for the family unit, for its own consumption or sale.

There is no compulsion to work in any particular type of production, though the PPL encourages participation in centralized and collective production. One peasant spoke for many when he explained the attitude to production:

**Yes, I thought of going to Honduras and looking for land there, but I never followed it up, because at that stage things were taking clearer shape here. We were already beginning to get organized and no longer thought of leaving, but rather of working here politically. Now we are working collectively, sometimes two or three days a week, according to whether we have time. When we are very behind with our individual work, then we only work one day or so. Now that we have land here, both for individual and for collective work, we are working for everyone, and for our army too. The army can't work the land. Its work is fighting while we are working here with the machete to support them, so that they don't lack food. And in this way we are helping the war along, the army and us. (Tomás)**

The approach to the land question is similarly cautious. There is no

255

*Peasants crushing sugar cane look up as a Salvadorean Airforce jet makes a rocket attack on nearby village. Work continues . . .*

attempt to introduce new forms of land tenure. 'We are respectful of ownership of land', one peasant told me, 'provided that the person is not exploiting his brother. There will be no expropriation here, or collectivization.' Another peasant underlined the importance of introducing changes step-by-step:

**Yes, peasants like to have their own bit of land. Yet here in our *base* this mentality is being overcome, although it's a long process because the idea of private property is well-anchored in the people. One cannot do away with it quickly. That's why we are respecting private property. But we won't let the reins run loose, so that exploitative landowners emerge again. So, many cooperatives are still only in the planning stage. There is land here belonging to the owners who have left, or to others who have been killed. So there's no land problem now. We produce where the PPL tells us to. If it is the land of someone who has left, if they return it's still their land: we don't take any land away, but yes, we do work it. (Vidal)**

The poor peasants who now dominate guerilla-controlled Chalatenango are willing to collaborate with other sections of the peasantry:

**Many medium landowners objected to the idea that peasants**

should have access to the land. They supported the government, became members of ORDEN, became traitors. And when Chalate was liberated, they left the zone. But some people stayed who used to be medium landowners. Like this man in Los Amates, Abraham, a peasant who used to have about 80 *manzanas* and 40 cows. I talked to him, asking him how he felt about the situation, given that his house had been destroyed by the enemy. 'There are other houses around where I can live', he said. 'The enemy took my cows, but they left two of them, which is sufficient for me to live on, to have my glass of milk and to give some to other people or to sell it. I knew this had to happen.' There are middle peasants like this; and there are others who left, who didn't understand. So I proposed that they elect Abraham as the secretary of production. He was very pleased. (Quique)

The same man also spoke of the treatment of ORDEN sympathizers:

There were also peasants who didn't have anything who became enemies. But they did that because of the promises of ORDEN that they would receive arms, that they wouldn't be beaten. I told them that the land wouldn't be taken from them, but they would insist 'This is my land and I want my two *manzanas* to cultivate'. In fact, the people here have that. It's just that no-one can now exploit their own people like before. So peasants here, in the new zones under control, aspire to having their own house, and a small bit of land where they can live, and their fruit garden. And this we don't deny them; all of us have that.

The war is never far away, with government forces deliberately making production in the zones a target for destruction:

In the past, people grew sorghum and corn here, renting land at 250 *colones* a *manzana*. Much of the land belonged to the big estates, where a lot of different things were sown. Now it is different, because each PPL has access to land within its limits. The land is distributed and as there is plenty, a lot can be done. In some areas there are rice fields. The person in charge of production brings up the discussion in the assemblies of the *base* and groups are formed and commissions to organize the planting. There are still problems because of lack of seeds. And the bombardments affect us. For example, last year, the sorghum fields were dry and ready to harvest, but the incendiary bombs of the air force destroyed the irrigation canals, and set the fields on fire. When the enemy invades, they always destroy the grain reserves of the families, they burn our cornfields and sorghum fields and destroy our freshly planted vegetable beds. The PPL had to decree that all grain that can be kept should be hidden or buried. (Abel)

257

*Members of a fishing cooperative*

Nineteen eighty three was a great year for us. The enemy didn't have the military capacity to invade Chalate and destroy our production. All the other years we lived through hunger as the enemy came in and destroyed all the fields we had sown. But this year they didn't dare. Only in August 1983 did they manage to get to the mountains, but we caused them many casualties and seized their weapons. They went running off. So in 1983, we were able to harvest everything we planted over the two periods of May and August. That's why we aren't suffering hunger this year. We even have enough to sell. (Jacobo)

Within the constraints imposed by the war, the PPLs have attempted to foster other types of production, trade and commerce:

The fishing cooperative gives some of what they produce to feed the people in need and also to help the FPL. We also have craftsmen who have organized cottage industries. Here, we need many things, more than you can imagine. But the creativity of the people has achieved much. We produce shoes, sandals, soap, and knives, using the little material we have. For instance, the knives are made from discarded bullet cases. (Lito)

In this *base* there are two workshops; a tailor and a cobbler. In the

*A member of the popular militia of Chalatenango. The popular militia are local people, responsible for the defence of their village. They may also go on small-scale operations*

Lección 29      ¡¡Chalatenango heroico....

ii.zona de control revolucionario
Frente apolinario Serráno !!

1.-Leamos la palabra

frente

2.-Dividamos la palabra en golpes de voz

fren-te

3.-Encuadremos la sílaba a aprender

fren|te

4.-Leamos la familia silábica

fren-fron-fran-frun-frin

5.-Escribamos en el cuaderno la familia silábica

6.-Leamos la familia silábica

fran-fren-frin-fron-frun

7.-Escribamos en el cuaderno la familia silábica

8.-Leamos las palabras

frente - frontera - franja - fruncir -

9.-Formemos las palabras          Formemos nuevas palabras

fren
fron     te ——— frente
fran     cir
frun     ja      ra

frí    ga    do
fru    tar
fre    jol  ——— frijol
fra    ta
fro    ter   no

10.-Escribamos las palabras formadas

11.-Leamos y comentemos las oraciones

- el salvador....territorio en combate
- en las tierras de chalatenango heroico y
  liberado, sus hombres y mujeres organizan y
  dirigen ya la nueva sociedad.
- ¡viva chalatenango heroico...zona de control
  revolucionario..
- frente norte apolinário serrano

12.-Hagamos un dictado.

*From a page from the literacy manual used in Chalatenango*

'Lesson 29 Heroic Chalatenango! . . . zone of revolutionary control Apolinario Serráno front.' (see page 264)

260

next district there are three; a blacksmith, and two makers of containers for sorghum. The *compas* are also thinking of setting up a fishing co-op, the problem is material for nets. There is a sugar mill which all the PPLs use: fifteen days one, fifteen days the other. Everyone comes in their spare time to make sweets. One of our problems is that we cannot easily sell our products outside the zone as the enemy won't let us. So what we do is exchange products here in the zone. Sometimes we manage to sell our goods in the zones of dispute, and we even get into enemy zones and then we are able to bring all the things we need, we buy fertilizers, herbicides and medicines. Some basic things are sold through the *tienda popular* [popular shop], flour, sugar, some sweets and candles. The PPL adds ten per cent to the price and the profit is used to subsidize goods for those who are not able to make money through trade. (Carmen)

## 'Breaking our Silence' — Literacy and Education

Even before the PPLs were established, there was some attempt to hold classes in Chalatenango, mainly literacy courses, which encompassed children and adults, fighters and civilians. Education was not considered a luxury, but a vital part of the process of people taking control over their lives. Classes sprang up spontaneously. Though the teachers debated whether a full-scale literacy programme might not be premature, the demand from the population was firm: learning to read and write was one of their expectations of the revolution, a way to 'break our silence' they said. A teacher involved in developing the literacy manual tells this story:

I was in a guerilla camp and we were correcting the literacy manual. A very young comrade, who nevertheless had been an activist for ten years or so, kept looking over my shoulders, making me very nervous. I asked him if he knew how to read and write. 'No', he said, 'and that's why I'm waiting until you've finished so that you'll lend me the manual and I can learn to read'. 'But that's our only copy', I said, 'I can't lend it to you'. 'Yes, but I want to learn to read', he said. I was very struck by this incident.

A nun, who had once taught in a college in San Salvador, wrote this description of her work in Chalatenango in 1981, coordinating the early educational programmes:

I give classes and try to coordinate four centres in the same number of guerilla camps . . . The anxiety to learn is felt amongst adults who could not attend schools because of the disastrous socio-economic situation of the country. Now, despite the tremendous tasks that mothers and fathers have, they take time where they can

*Adult literacy class*

**to come to classes. They are very punctual and they don't want to lose a word, they don't want to go early. They really feel that desire to learn to read and write . . . While the government closes schools and kills teachers and students we open little schools, teach literacy to adults and children and also train a considerable number of peasant teachers.**

However, the early attempts had many difficulties. In 1981 and 1982, when the FMLN still did not have total control over the area, a gathering of people together for any length of time ran the risk of attack. There were also great problems with infrastructure and materials. Classes were often held without chalk, blackboards, pencils or notebooks. Sometimes classes would have to be held on riverbanks where it was possible to write on the wet sand. Or when chalk and blackboards were absent, the writing would be scratched on doors with stones. Most seriously, the early attempts were unsystematic, and based on traditional methods in which the peasant teacher might simply pass on what he or she had learnt from a rudimentary education under the old system. In some cases, such as Guazapa, small schools were established very quickly — 23 in 1982 — but they soon collapsed due to the lack of follow-up, clear methodology, and materials.

*Children in school, held under the trees in case of bombardment*

With the establishment of the PPLs, the teachers' group (members of the teachers' union ANDES) began to draw up plans for a systematic literacy campaign and post-literacy education which would be a permanent part of the programme of the new local governments. They wanted to strengthen the PPLs and the programme was worked out with them. The PPLs chose to stress three basic elements: 'Literacy is conscientization and action', 'We all learn from each other', 'We all have knowledge'. The teachers would be semi-literate peasants given some training in literacy teaching, using methods and a basic manual prepared by the ANDES group.

The ANDES group were very keen to avoid creating a separate class of professional teachers. In Nicaragua, the idea of the semi-literate teacher was born after the revolution. In El Salvador, this was to be an important principle established within the struggle itself. The idea was that people should learn in the process of teaching and that they should be encouraged to solve their own problems rather than looking to so-called experts. This was not an easy task, and the method had already encountered problems in experiments with adult classes in the refugee camps. On one occasion, adults had refused to attend a class taught by a sixteen-year-old semi-literate youth: they wanted a 'proper teacher'.

There were no clear models to follow in planning a programme suitable for a war situation: very different circumstances to the large-scale literacy programmes carried out in Cuba, Nicaragua and Grenada. The ANDES group wanted to use the methods of literacy teaching developed by the Brazilian, Paulo Freire, in which the educational process is used to deepen understanding of the reality in which people live and how that reality might be changed. In this educational method, teaching and learning are not separated from real life, but real life experiences become the basis for learning.

The ANDES group wished to adapt these ideas to the situation of the controlled zones. It was not enough to use the method to raise political awareness. They did not see the project simply as a way of 'using literacy as an excuse to "politicize" the masses, nor is it a question of teaching reading and writing in isolation'. Literacy had to respond, both to the real need of the population to learn to read and write as well as to the demands of the war and of the revolution. It had to combine both the educative task as such with the preparation of the people for the tasks of building their own government in a time of war.

The situation called for what the ANDES group described as 'a practical dialogue', in which literacy was related to activities needed to sustain life in the zones. The controlled zones only existed because of the war of liberation, and education and literacy programmes had to help to activate and motivate people to contribute to the struggle as well as to resolve their own needs. People would be encouraged, for example, to hold their literacy class once they had camouflaged their school to hide it from the planes, or dug a tunnel or air raid shelter.

Sometimes there were difficulties in combining technical aspects of the literacy programme with the political ones. If the literacy manual was too political people might not learn, but if it was purely technical it would not contribute to raising consciousness. The literacy manual was written using key words which had a direct meaning for the pupil. Syllabic families were taught using words that meant something to the people, for instance *Fren*te 'front', dere*cho*, 'right' and semi*lla* 'seed'. (See page 260.)

There was discussion also on how many subjects the programme was to cover. In Cuba and Nicaragua, people learnt to read before they could write. But in the war situation, the teachers believed that writing was equally important. People needed to be able to write to their relatives, to express and articulate their experiences on paper. But there was some disagreement on what kind of script to teach. Some argued that people should be taught to print letters first and that joined-up writing should be taught only during post-literacy. The team working within the zone argued that both print and joined-up should be taught at the same time, since adults wanted to learn how to write like everyone else does. No agreement was reached and it was decided to teach print but to carry out an experiment using both with

264

the first pilot project in Chalatenango.

There was much discussion also about whether maths should be included in the first campaign. Some teachers argued that maths should not be taught at the same time as literacy. But those working in the zones argued that numbers were present in every aspect of peasant life, not only in terms of production and economic questions, but also because of the war. For instance, they would hear on the guerilla radio how many arms the guerillas had captured, or how many bombs were dropped by the A-37 planes. In the end it was decided not to include maths for the pragmatic reason that the people who would teach literacy were themselves semi-literate peasants and they would probably withdraw from the campaign if asked to teach maths as well as two types of writing.

The planning group also gave attention to post-literacy education. They aimed to base this on people's perception of what they needed to know. Maths, for instance, was needed for production, and for understanding messages and codes. Geography interested people who wanted to know which countries supported their struggle. People didn't want to know about first aid, as they had already been forced to learn quite a lot through practical experience. Instead they wanted to know about parts of the human body. The teachers were at first disappointed, as this seemed rather academic, but they found that this desire arose out of people's experiences during the war. Some people wanted to know about bones because they had suffered fractures or had had to carry people with fractured bones. When escaping from the army by swimming across the Sumpul river in May 1982, one woman from Chalatenango had accidentally killed her daughter by holding her hand over the girl's mouth to stop her making a noise. She wanted to know more about respiratory systems in order to avoid such a terrible thing happening again. Another man had been tortured by being hit in the chest while a plastic bag was placed over his head. He wanted to know about breathing in order to withstand torture if it ever happened again. The teachers realized that they had to respond to such tragic personal experiences.

At first they had hoped to launch a literacy campaign throughout all the controlled zones. But they recognized that this was too ambitious, and instead they concentrated their resources on a pilot project in Chalatenango. The intention was to extend the programme later to other zones, under the slogan 'Chalatenango defeated ignorance. Let's struggle against ignorance in . . .' The project was started at the beginning of 1983. The PPLs created a coordinating team of three peasants and three teachers. The team was responsible for supporting the PPLs in the elaboration of the project which would begin with a literacy campaign for adults and children. Tragically, the first three teachers chosen for the team were killed by the army on their way to launching the project. In July, a new team was formed,

265

this time with six new teachers, and the project got under way in September in sub-zone one. At that time the team found that only 16 of 24 *bases* in sub-zone one had a school, usually no more than chairs and a blackboard under the trees where there was some camouflage from passing planes.

The PPLs chose from among those who had some ability to read and write, a number of peasants to form literacy brigades. The *brigadistas* were then given 15-day courses in teaching methods using the literacy manual specially designed for the project. The following is taken from an interview with the coordinator in the zones of control on how they set about organizing the literacy campaign in Chalatenango.

**There were particular problems here in Chalatenango, especially in the northern part, the most isolated area where there had been no schools before the war. There were very high levels of illiteracy, and that's where a great number of our guerilla troops come from. There's higher literacy in areas closer to San Salvador, like Guazapa, and where communications are better, such as San Vicente and Zacatecoluca.**

**At first, there was an emphasis on the children. The adults said: 'Well, if they are going to take over afterwards, they must learn'. Some were fatalistic, they would say that as they were going to die anyway, what's the point of learning to read, young people perhaps, but not them. But many others said they wanted to learn too and the PPLs put literacy into their programmes as a fundamental element. We saw that literacy had a great deal to do with the organization of the people: it was an activity of the PPLs in which all the people could participate. And for us, literacy is of very great importance in the life of the people and in the exercise of power. For the first time, there was popular government with a minimum programme which gained legitimacy as schools began to function. In the midst of the war they were setting them up while the enemy was closing them; for instance, the 'Alberto Masferrer' teacher-training institute has been turned into a barracks for the Atlacatl brigade. Even amongst the people who don't live in the zones this has had an impact.**

**We considered how we could attract people to the campaign and found that what absorbed them most was the war. So this was how we organized the campaign, as a war against illiteracy. The campaign was organized around literacy teams and volunteer brigades. We used slogans like 'death to illiteracy' and 'literacy, another weapon in the revolution' to motivate people. The base of the campaign was to be the locality. That's not the same as a *base;* there are PPLs with up to three *bases* with a population of up to 500 people. Our aim was a school for each PPL, that's as much as we**

266

could achieve.

At the head of each literacy team is the volunteer literacy worker. Next comes the least illiterate whose task is to carry out the literacy programme. All the volunteers came together in what was called a brigade led by the political education secretary of the PPLs. The programme contributed to the development of the PPLs because, through literacy, people could be brought into more tasks; it mobilizes the population. The PPL chooses who are to be the literacy teachers.

The preparation for a campaign takes three to four months. First we do a census. This had been done already in many parts of Chalate. Then the organizational units are set up, the national team of volunteers, and then the local literacy teams themselves. There are one or two volunteers assigned to the sub-zone to set up the teams and a training course of fifteen days is organized.

The project was in its early stages when I visited Chalatenango and was severely hampered by the war's demands on limited resources and personnel as well as by the escalation in bombing which began in 1984. Classes were still being held under the trees rather than in buildings, to reduce the risks of bombardment. Shortage of materials was a major problem, though international solidarity networks had begun to send supplies of notebooks, pencils and other teaching materials. There was no doubt about the wish to learn amongst adults and children and no-one missed the day's class.

# Health

Health care is the area of social life most distorted by the war. Establishing a war-time medical service was an essential and urgent task for the FMLN. There were some medical students and doctors in the political-military organizations but not in the numbers required for the war. Some North American and European doctors offered their services out of sympathy with the revolutionary movement or out of a desire to help the civilian population in the controlled zones.[1] Auxiliary health workers known as *sanitarios* were trained to supplement the medical team, and one would be attached to each platoon of the guerilla forces. Eventually a medical system was organized geared primarily to the needs of the war, with a system of mobile hospitals to accompany the guerilla troops and fixed hospitals for more complicated surgery and convalescence.

The patients we treat here are soldiers injured in combat. First the emergency cases go to the central hospital, then they come here to this hospital to recuperate, but these are only the less seriously injured. Here in the *base* there's also the popular clinics. The

267

difference between them is the sort of cases they treat. If, for example, the nurse in the clinic can't treat the case or doesn't know about it, it's passed on to this hospital.

I've worked as a nurse for four years. When I got involved in the revolutionary struggle, nursing was what I really wanted to do, because, well, it seemed the best way of helping the people. First I was working in the *bases* when the clandestine militias were in existence. Later they formed the guerilla army and I formed a health team. Then I was also involved in the fighting, but now I only work in the hospital. To tell you about the training I got: first there were study manuals, then we got the first course which is first aid, then to the second grade and the third where we learned about more serious injuries. We learned how to treat patients who had been hit by shrapnel, but we only learned how to do local anaesthetics. Thanks to the comrade doctors, I learned how to do limb amputations, like feet, hands and arms. Once, when the enemy was showering this terrible bombardment on us and we didn't have any doctors, with the help of another comrade, we managed to amputate the arm of a girl who had been hit in the shoulder. (Tato)

But though war needs took priority, there was a desperate need to provide health care for the civilian population in the zones of control. Access to medical care had been almost unknown for the peasants under government control:

In the past, there were clinics, but you had to pay. Those who didn't have the money died. In the clinics a consultation cost two *colones*. If you didn't have two *colones*, just die, brother. But we have our revolutionary doctors here now, who eat tortillas and beans just like us. No one pays them a penny, and they are doing everything they can.

Before, for the two *colones* you would get a consultation, but not the medicine. You paid your *colones* and they made up the prescription and then onto the pharmacy. But if you didn't have enough to go to the pharmacy or to buy the medicine they prescribed, you died all the same, only that you had paid the two *colones*. And in cases of emergency, it would cost ten or fifteen *colones* depending on the decision of the doctor. (Walter)

The rudiments of a health service were provided for each *base* by setting up popular clinics in the villages, under the auspices of the PPLs. Young peasants, usually girls, were trained in basic health care in the guerilla hospitals, and sent back to the villages to administer first aid and to treat some of the common illnesses, as well as run public health education campaigns on, for example, parasites or vitamins:

One difficulty is the lack of specialized personnel. We're making big efforts to train nurses. We're forced into this by the conditions of the war, we just can't train proper doctors. But anyway, we're managing. Take the case of Manuel. Manuel is a peasant who couldn't read or write. He had never been to school because he came from a poor family of eight brothers. When the National Guard murdered his parents and five of his brothers, he went to San Antonio la Cruz, his native village, to join the guerillas. In one of the camps he learnt how to treat the wounded, to diagnose some illnesses common to the region, like malaria. As a nurse he went with a group of peasants who were seeking refuge in Honduras. On the journey a pregnant woman began her labour pains. After several hours had passed and the child had still not been born, Manuel decided to do a caesarian to try to save the mother and child. 'I had never done one before, just seen it done', he said. 'Luckily they survived', he said, grinning. (Tato)

The popular clinics, about ten of which were functioning in sub-zone one in early 1984, were called on to deal with about 50 deliveries a month, according to one *sanitario*. However, the total number of births was larger, because many women, through ignorance or embarassment, would not come to the clinics.

One *sanitaria* estimated that her clinic was dealing with a total of up to 300 patients a month. The most common complaints were malaria, diarrhoea, coughs, headaches, skin infections, gastroenteritis, diseases connected with malnutrition, bites from vampire bats (which began to attack humans after the cattle on which they normally lived had been killed during army raids), and sometimes typhoid. The material resources for dealing with these cases were limited. Antibiotics, such as chloramphenicol and tetracycline, used in great quantities for treating the wounded, were in very short supply as were anti-malarial drugs. There was some recourse to traditional medicine, or make-shift solutions such as quinine or *copalillo* for malaria, *iquilite* root for spasms, the bark of the mango tree for coughs and of the willow tree for headaches. Food too was scarce, and the diet for patients inadequate; usually beans and *tortillas* supplemented occasionally by milk or fruit in season:

Here in this area there are no doctors, only auxiliary health workers, nurses, who are in charge of the clinics and organize the distribution of medicines amongst the clinics. Also, we have been able to help the people a little with herbal medicine. We have got hold of an apparatus to extract teeth, so that everyone who wants a tooth taken out can come when the nurse comes. Another way in which we are solving our health problems is through the production of honey, with its medicinal qualities. We have people here who practise medicine with honey. So that they may get their supply

*Nurse in the popular clinic*

(and all the family's too), honey is being given to the clinics directly for distribution. They are being told to use it only as medicine, because for other usage, like sweetening, there is molasses. (Lito)

The principle behind the popular clinics is the same as in education, that the people solve their own problems rather than rely on outside professionals:

First of all, I worked as a health adviser, then they put me in hospitals in the *bases* and then a team of health workers was formed in which I worked, and now I'm here in a popular clinic where I have responsibility for three other municipal clinics where other nurses work. I've been in the struggle for seven years and worked in different areas — the militias, the guerillas, propaganda — despite the fact that my real work is farming. I was a peasant when I went on my first health training course. Then I got to the second grade and what I learned I've taught others. Here in this municipality, we've taught seven people who are now working in the hospital or with fighting units as medical orderlies. Here in the clinic we treat all civilian cases, including complicated pregnancies, we also know how to extract teeth and how to treat light injuries. (Ulises)

The process was not without its dilemmas and difficulties, as a European doctor who worked with the popular clinics explained:

There had been a lot of enthusiasm about the popular clinics in the PPLs at the beginning, but after a while there was less emphasis on health care in the villages and people came to hospitals for consultations. People didn't always trust the young *sanitarios*, usually peasants from their villages who had been given some basic medical training in the hospitals. Then, many of them were taken out of the villages into the hospitals because we had so few of them and we needed the very good ones.

There were many discussions about what could be done about problems not directly related to the war. There were people who said, we are at war and we cannot deal with too many other problems, let's win the war first and then deal with other things like health care in the villages, literacy, the situation of women. Being there, I could understand that position much better than outsiders, where it is easy to say those people are wrong. But living the daily situation, you see the difficulties of maintaining the liberation movement and keeping the initiative. Not only does that mean the military units going from one point to the other, but they also have to be fed, they need boots, medical care. People are very busy doing all that, and therefore it's not strange if people say they can't do anything else. But finally the prevailing argument is, what is this war about? It is to improve the lives of the people, and we can't wait for that until we win the war. We have to do that simultaneously, which is very difficult, but we have to try.

Where we have created a relatively stable situation in some of the controlled areas there is a chance of doing something and some energy had to go into it. This was precisely why the PPLs emerged and to me they are the most significant decision after that of taking up arms. They are a most important form of democracy and participation. This does not mean that all decisions can be taken at a village level, that would be idealistic, but we have to find structures where those things very important to village life can be decided. The health system and the popular clinics are an important part of this. This is not only because we don't want people to come to the hospital, but because we want to develop a health service in which we don't have technicians and professionals giving something to the people: we want a system where people can participate and make decisions, feel responsible for their own health. I talked a lot to the PPLs about this and to the military commanders. Finally, it was decided to reactivate the popular clinics. I was very happy, I felt that all our discussions had been worthwhile and had had practical consequences.

There was still the question of how to do it. There were so many experiences in other parts of the world in primary health care, some through the World Health Organization. Some of them were very bad, things didn't really work, but we couldn't read about

271

them. I felt the need to exchange experiences with other liberation movements. But we just had to get started. We formed a team of three people, one male nurse, myself and one *sanitario*. The military health structure had agreed that we should work with the PPLs which was an important step as they also needed us. We felt it was very important to work within the PPL structure. This was also because we felt that health should not be isolated from other aspects of village development. So we contacted the people responsible for social affairs in the PPLs and met with them twice a week. Together we carried out a kind of survey to find out what the situation was, where there were *sanitarios*, how they worked, what the population felt about them. In some villages the PPL representative gave a very positive report, there was a lot of confidence between the *sanitarios* and the population and they didn't need much from us. There were other villages where there were no *sanitarios*. Others where the *sanitarios* didn't do much work and the people didn't trust them. There were also *sanitarios* with very different levels of knowledge. We found we needed to train more people and to give further training to those already in work.

We made surveys in the village not only through the PPL representative but also with the people in the village themselves. Many felt there were not enough medicines available; they were very influenced by pharmaceutical propaganda on the radio. Some people had been trying to make a library of traditional herbal remedies and to include such remedies in the teaching of the *sanitarios*. But it was not done very systematically. We found that only the very old people had knowledge, usually a remedy for everything. We doubted if that was really true.

One big problem was the *sanitarios* themselves, who felt they could work only if they had enough medicines. This attitude went very deep with people. They have the experience that if they take an aspirin for a headache, it goes away. You can't tell them that it doesn't help, it clearly does. Then you try and tell them that it does have other effects too, and you also have to look at what causes the headache. We try and tell them that we are lucky not to have too many medicines: people have to think of other methods. Sometimes we went to the villages to help the *sanitario* give consultations. But when there was a doctor present, everyone wanted to see the doctor. We had to tell them to go and see the *sanitario* first — you have to learn to be a bad doctor sometimes, but it's good in the long term! We had many discussions with the *sanitarios* about this and other problems; it was very slow. We organized a distribution of medicines in one place every two weeks and invited them to come, which was very difficult for them as they had to walk for over two hours to get there. But we had to talk to

272

them about the side effects of medicines and complications.

Things began to move through this work. But the PPLs often wanted quick results. Once they wanted to organize a campaign of latrine-building and they thought of organizing the whole thing in one week. But it was impossible. It was May and they also had to plant. There were very few technical people around to advise them. Usually the person in charge of the PPL for social affairs would consult with someone from the health command (*mando de sanidad*) of the FPL, but he or she was not a trained professional so they couldn't give technical advice. Everyone was very conscious that they had to find their own solutions, help themselves. There was a strong sense that everyone was equal and had to look for solutions to problems. Often they would come up with trying to get more medicines, and our team had to introduce new concepts. On this latrine programme for example, we explained that it wasn't necessary to build a lot of latrines in such a short period of time. Even if they did, people wouldn't necessarily use them. A latrine is not a pleasant place to go, people need to understand their importance, and that they must be kept clean otherwise they'll be a breeding ground for diseases. So we shouldn't look for quick results.

The doctor talked also of war-related medical problems:

In our medical work we saw an increase in psychosomatic problems, the beginnings of schizophrenia, and in physical terms, problems ranged from gastritis to gynaecological problems in women, such as irregular menstruation and increasing numbers of spontaneous abortions. I think these are the effects of long-term tension. Women continued to get pregnant. Very seldom were we asked to give something to prevent it. It was mainly fighters that wanted contraceptives, but I can't remember many village people doing so. But all the women were afraid for the babies during the *guindas*. Quite often, groups of civilians have been encircled by government troops and they have to break through it, normally during the night. They can only do it if they are not discovered by the enemy. It is incredible how close to the soldiers they have to walk. It is very dangerous if the babies cry. Sometimes we have to give them valium. Many are afraid of this situation as some women have accidentally suffocated their children trying to stop them crying out.

## Women

Women are represented on the council of the PPL through the mass organization, AMES (Association of Salvadorean Women). Founded in 1979, it was forced into clandestinity after 1980 and began work mainly among refugees and in the controlled zones. Much of its work involves mobilizing and motivating women to participate in different aspects of the war effort. AMES runs some bakery and fish cleaning cooperatives and sewing workshops. It encourages women to grow vegetables and prepare food for the hospitals and the guerilla army.

The efforts of AMES combined with the effects of war on the conditions of women's lives in the zones to bring many more women into political life. There are large numbers of widows and orphans in the zone and many women are forced to take over responsibilities previously carried out by their husbands. Many find themselves head of the household, and in some cases have to take responsibility for food production. The situation in general has forced many women to look away from the family toward the wider community:

**The women here have had to put up with most of the exploitation by the system. And the men here are mostly *macho*, so that women find themselves doubly exploited by the system and the *compañero*. So the integration into political life of women is not very easy, as we grew up with a mentality, given to us through generations, that woman is no more than a person to look after the house, raise the children. But with the revolution this stopped; women found that they could do the same things as men.**

**From late 1982 until mid-1983, I was general secretary of AMES in this sub-zone. AMES is an organization that has two aims: the liberation of women as such and the liberation of the people, within which women ought to participate as a living element of the people. We struggle so that our women do not get stuck with the role of housewife who looks after the children, but also that they integrate themselves into political life. A woman has to have the opportunity to be mayoress or president.**

**When AMES was founded it strongly supported the BPR, for which it was attacked. Around 1980 it went into exile as repression got heavier and it was weakened. But after 1982, we here inside El Salvador began to reactivate the work of AMES, the women's movement, because we need to have an organization that identifies us as women and revolutionaries. We realize that our demands as an organization are not a struggle against the other sex. On the contrary, it's our liberation and that of our *compañeros*, liberation from the *machismo* that the system has created. I feel that we are gaining a lot. (María)**

Even so, as far as I could observe, the majority of women in the controlled zone still tended to be involved primarily in tasks traditional to them even if these were now geared to the community rather than the home. The arduous and time-consuming activity of *tortilla*-making still absorbed the main part of the day for many women, though they might now be working together to produce food

*Women members of a sewing workshop*

for the guerilla army as it passed through their village:

I am doing work here in the *base* itself, because of the children which keep me here. For example, when the guerilla troops are here, I work in the kitchen the whole time. But I didn't accept the post of responsibility which they offered me because I knew that it involved going to meetings all day long, and I can't do this until the girls are grown up. It would be different if the organization helped me, but that's not the case, because they don't have the means to help everyone. When they have some corn, they give it to me, but that doesn't happen often.

Now life is different from before; because I didn't know even Las Penas, a *base* that's pretty near; before I only worked in the house, looking after the animals, the children, going to give the lunch to the *compas*. Now, I know things further away, although life is more difficult in other ways, such as the bombings. I began to participate in the struggle after my husband died in 1980, when we had to flee to the mountains. I felt desperate because he was no longer there, and because I was left with five small children. I went to the comrades and discussed with them whether I should leave. Some said yes, some no, because outside I would suffer more with my children. That's why I didn't leave.

But in spite of all the bombings and all that, the only thing we

*Women members of a fishing cooperative*

can do is go on fighting. AMES is a good organization in my eyes. It's an organization for us, the women, where we ought to work. For example, we make scones to send to the troops. Now we are grinding the maize together, three to five of us. We hand over forty per cent of what we make and keep sixty per cent. Of that we give thirty per cent to the guerilla forces and ten per cent to the local militia. This is how we all work at the moment and not only the women, those from the FTC too.

To get food for the children, I now go to the sugar cane field. I was given a bit of land from a comrade, but as I didn't have a machete, I asked the *compa* responsible for this, Lito, to get me one, and he arranged it for me. So I go out and cut sugar, and press it either in the sugar mill up there, or the one further down, make sweets and sell them or exchange them for some salt. Or when there is some meeting, I sell a soft drink which I make, and with the money I buy maize and salt which I get in the popular shop. (Norma)

The options available to the younger women were very much more varied than those of the mothers with children. In the absence of creche or nursery facilities, most women could not participate in activities which took them away from home. Efforts to recruit women for the popular militia ran into difficulties on this account. There was

*The peasants have written many songs about their struggle which are sung on battered old guitars during dances and meetings in the zone of control*

*'For you, suffering people*
*today I shall not cease to sing*
*and I shall remind you*
*that for you, there is no Christmas*
*until there is freedom.'*

some reluctance to organize such nursery facilities, since gathering children in large groups could be risky, though it was an issue some members of AMES in the zone wanted to explore more.

Younger peasant women, however, were able to participate in a wider range of roles. Many became *sanitarias* in the village clinics and hospitals. Others joined the guerilla army, often in support functions, for instance as radio operator, but there were increasing numbers of female combatants also.

**Among the projects we've set up are a pottery workshop and a soap-making workshop to satisfy our basic needs here. The pottery workshop makes crockery which is sent to places where our troops are.**

**We are organized as a group so that we can help ourselves. We also set up the finance for little farms with a few animals. Other work which AMES women do is in the popular clinics. We also train women so that they can give literacy classes to everyone in the zones of control. Women are also encouraged to join the militias, because they need to defend themselves against the enemy which kills women and children. We would also like to see women involved in making barricades and trenches.** (Juanita, zonal head of AMES)

It is not so unusual in a war situation for women to assume tasks they would not normally carry out. How this might be translated into more permanent changes in women's role and status is a rather more difficult question. There were many debates on whether it was appropriate to take up the specific problems of women and gender-relations in their widest sense in the midst of the war or whether the war effort should take precedence. Discussions also centred on whether AMES should be autonomous from the political-military organization, as was originally the intention, or subject to its priorities.

In many ways, the debates echo those in other fields, for instance how far scarce resources should be channelled into health care and the development of popular clinics for the civilian population when the demands of the war were so immediate and pressing. Although the women's issue is considerably more complex than this, it is yet another reflection of how the situation following the January 1981 offensive created a real tension between the pursuit of the war and the deepening of the political process.

AMES have always stressed that the basic struggle was that of the people and that women's vital interests, like those of men, lay in a victory of the liberation movement. Early in the war, as the statement below illustrates, emphasis was also given to the need to raise women's issues now and not await a victory of the FMLN/FDR, though in practice AMES' work in the zones tended to concentrate on encouraging women's participation in tasks connected with the war:

'*A woman's decision to become a politically conscious militant implies a much longer and more difficult process than that taken by a man. Obviously this does not signify that we have resolved our specific problem of "being women" nor that militancy can be a panacea which allows us to find our own identity. However, we think that the characteristic of a "revolutionary feminism" is that it is part of a project for the transformation of society. We also know that the liberation of women requires a level of collective consciousness which in turn is the product of new ideological development . . . even after the Democratic Revolutionary Government is constituted, we will have to continue to fight against the traditional attitudes of men and women. The bad traits of the system of exploitation and oppression will continue to exist for some time, mainly in those areas which concern women; it is impossible for them to disappear from one day to the next.*'[2]

AMES have stressed caution in introducing changes too quickly in view of the weight of tradition upon women, and in particular the influence of traditional Catholic teaching upon individuals. This would not be overcome rapidly and AMES believe they should be respectful of existing customs. This was the view of one member of AMES interviewed in Mexico City:

'*AMES has no official position on family planning or abortion. In part this is because of priorities: there are more urgent necessities for Salvadorean women, above all, an end to the civilian massacres, and national liberation. But it is also because AMES has a democratic and integrated concept of society. We wish to see a complete women's programme implemented, but first it is absolutely necessary to embark upon a huge amount of educational work. We cannot impose a programme from above without prior consultation or without consideration for the cultural traditions of the vast majority of the Salvadorean population. And while AMES has begun such educational work, especially among refugees and in the controlled zones, we cannot hope to make serious progress until the war has ended.*' [3]

AMES is caught up in the dilemma of many Third World women's organizations; how to guarantee that the struggle for wider social transformation brings material changes to women's lives. In some post-revolutionary societies, women find they continue to bear their traditional burden of domestic labour, sometimes in addition to new tasks in the productive sphere but without any change in their status in the community. How this problem is raised in the pre-revolutionary period will affect how seriously women's case is argued when resources are subsequently allocated and priorities chosen; some argue that if the question is not already firmly on the agenda, half the population may get left behind as the new society is built.

*Young women radio operators*

# The Popular Church

The church in Chalatenango paid dearly for its support for the peasant union. The following is a report presented on 12 February 1981 to a meeting of church people working in the Archdiocese of San Salvador:

*'After threats in October 1980, terror grew in the town [of Chalatenango]. People didn't come to church because of the presence of soldiers. The number of spies [orejas] has increased considerably, nuns can't visit families and the atmosphere of terror is such that people are afraid even to greet the nuns. Army searches are continuous and during them the people are robbed. Father Jaime Paredes could not return to Chalatenango because of the threats, there are only two priests left in the whole of Chalatenango . . . In San Antonio de los Ranchos the people are fleeing. They are bombarding the town from Chalatenango. The church, like that of San Miguel de Mercedes is destroyed.'*

Religious life is of central importance to the peasants in the controlled zones. The task of organizing it in the wake of the situation described above was undertaken by the National Council of the People's Church (CONIP), an organization founded in 1980 following the death of Archbishop Romero to coordinate the work of the grass roots communities. CONIP took a strong position on the question of Christian commitment to the struggle of the poor:

*'The Church must support, community-wise, the poor people's revolution. This does not mean that it should deny each Christian their political activity. On the contrary the "Church of the poor" considers it a Christian duty to be politically active in organizations which defend and fight for the rights of the impoverished without losing their Christian identity. It is out of faith that he must contribute to the humanization of the organizations. It is a missionary action without oppressive proselytism.'*[4]

Víctor Guillén, a Salvadorean peasant and church activist since 1975, talks of the importance of pastoral work in the controlled zones:

*'CONIP has always sought dialogue with the bishops and wants them to take seriously their role as pastors and to guide their flock. We ask them to be in the forefront of our struggle and to assume the risks that Bishop Romero did for his people. At this time in El Salvador the Christian communities in the guerilla-controlled zones are not receiving pastoral care from their bishops. Except for Bishop Rivera y Damas of San Salvador, the bishops seem unconcerned about the pastoral needs of these Christians living in the war zones. We ask that they take on the church's preferential option for the poor that was adopted so explicitly by the Latin American bishops at the Medellín and Puebla conferences. That means that they must be with the people in time of war — indeed, they must take the lead. The Gospel says that in time of danger, when the wolf comes, the shepherd cannot abandon his sheep.'*[5]

Much of the pastoral work in the zone is undertaken by peasant catechists, who live and work in the communities. They can hold services, always in the open air as all the churches in the area have been destroyed, and perform baptisms. In 1984, their work was coordinated by two priests, members of CONIP, who had opted to live in the zone of control. One of them was Rutilio Sánchez, who describes below the relationship of the priests and catechists to the PPLs in the guerilla-controlled Chalatenango:

**The catechists are integrated into the PPL, but they're not in it as the Church, but as normal citizens. On Sundays, the day of the popular assembly, we as CONIP discuss and evaluate what we have been doing towards making a new society. When the people judge what the PPL president has been doing, they don't do it on the basis of whether or not he's a Christian, but treat him as a brother in the community — that is our perspective. The catechists, of course,**

*A peasant farmer and his children stand inside their church, destroyed by the Salvadorean airforce*

have the power to call people together, this is recognized by the community. They are always having discussions with the comrades of the PPL about what should be done and the problems they've had during the week.

The priests and catechists play an important role in sustaining morale and hope in the face of the bombardments and invasions. Services usually contain a message of comfort from the Bible. Another priest describes the pastoral activities in the zone:

'Here our role as priests is to serve as a point of union and to elucidate problems. There is a programme of visits, the baptisms and baptismal talks are prepared — there's no party but everyone comes along to the meeting even though it's at night. The priest also visits the sick. He can explain certain problems, because the people have great confidence in him. The celebrator of the word and the catechist also have religious duties, but when the priest comes the people have greatest confidence. I have always felt that, being human, as weak as everyone in all senses, the priest's presence at difficult moments in the community helps people sense the divine presence. Personally, I feel very ashamed because I'm not divine nor so holy, but that's how it is. Suppose there's a bombardment, or an invasion. In these cases the presence of a priest lifts morale, they say "It's alright, the priest has come, he is going to give his blessing". Then their courage is reborn out of their weakness and they feel the confidence that can come from faith, that they shouldn't weaken, but must defend the children, be more disciplined, more fraternal, not abandon the wounded, they must protect the community things. Often our pastoral team will run down the columns of 200 or 300 people during the evacuation of the community, raising people's spirits, giving blessing or saying a prayer. That is effective in religous terms and psychological terms.

As a priest-pastor I have to visit the communities, give little courses in the Bible and theology, organize the catechists and the programme of religious activities. We give training to the catechists; Bible and liturgical training. The former is concerned with how Bible themes must be appropriate for the community . . . What we do at a pastoral level with biblical themes is to relate them to people's lives. Let's suppose that we read a passage where Moses had to leave his country. This is very real to the people, it happens here and they can draw conclusions from it. Not all the Bible is of equal use in that sense. What is basically used is the life of Jesus (the four Gospels) and the first five books of the Pentateuch. There is the book of Exodus, the formation of a people; Deuteronomy, on social laws, they say much about what we are; Genesis, what exists and why it exists within a fraternity in which we are all children of the same Father, etc . . .

Liturgical training is given on how the baptisms are celebrated and to clarify the value of the sacraments so that they don't remain just rituals. It is necessary to explain the important things; the value of matrimony, of the eucharist, what are the sacraments and the rites. We show how some of

*A popular church service by a lay preacher*

*these have been commercialized. We have advanced somewhat in this, but the custom of paying the priest is very deep-seated in humble and generous people. I have been with people who have kept ten or fifteen* colones *saved for three or four years as an offering to a saint and for the mass when the priest arrives.*

*A very important question is the relations amongst the people. Traditional vices against which we have to struggle are robbery, alcoholism, idleness, also slander, and divisions between communities. This has now changed. The first thing which has disappeared since 1981 is alcohol. It is absolutely forbidden to have alcohol here. There is no doubt that in our society most people like to drink, but from this you don't have to deduce that everyone is a drunkard. Those are the minority, the great majority agree that there should be no alcohol and have discovered that it's not the only way to enjoy oneself.*

*Another thing is theft. It doesn't exist like it used to. If there's any kind of theft, if you can really call it that, it's of food. For example, there is a plot of land which has been planted individually or collectively, and there is an invasion and everything is destroyed. Then the community and all those who own land recognize that they cannot keep everything themselves while others are suffering hunger. They cannot keep food or sell it or be selfish in that way. In such cases, there is usually an assembly, the landowner is called and the thing is discussed. And I don't think I've ever found that the*

285

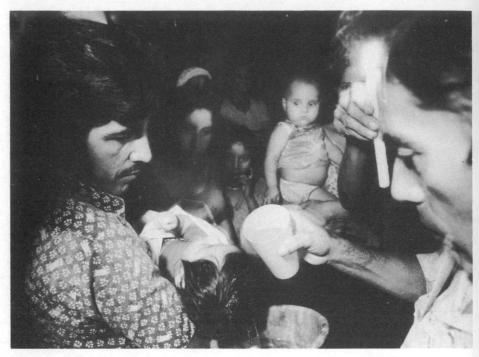

*Baptism in the zone of control*

*landowner minds, because he knows that by giving food to the community, he guarantees his own food in the future, and he also has the moral recognition of the community.'*[6]

## The Implications of the PPLs

The establishment of the PPLs in Chalatenango has clearly been the beginning of a political process with enormous implications for building a new kind of society in El Salvador. In areas where the UTC had already mobilized the population, the transformation has been remarkable, as peasants took over the running of their communities. PPL elections are deliberately held frequently in order to give as many people as possible the experience of administration. The PPLs have made the revolution a concrete reality, not something carried out on the peasants' behalf by others. The revolution has still brought much hardship and deprivation, but through the PPLs the peasants have begun to make real changes to their lives, as the testimonies in this chapter demonstrate. This explains why thousands stayed in the area rather than fled to the refugee camps during the 1982-84 period.

The future role of the PPLs in a new society has always been unclear: how, for instance, they would relate to central government;

*Building a new society*

or what would happen in those areas of the country where there had
been no peasant mobilization and no development of the PPLs. The
decision to pursue a negotiated settlement based on the proposal for a
Provisional Government of Broad Participation (GAP, see page 230)
has reduced the likelihood of the PPLs being the basis for local
organization in any future popular government. The FDR/FMLN
would be sharing power with a range of social forces, some of whom
would be far from sympathetic to the institutionalization of popular
power at any level of society. The people of the Salvadorean
countryside have, however, fought hard to gain those basic things that
people in richer countries take for granted. Whatever happens to the
PPLs, whether they survive the onslaught of the Salvadorean armed
forces or win a place in a future popular government, the experience of
building them has left a deep and lasting impression on the peasants
involved. Their opponents should see that they will not now return to
the old passivity. For them there is no way back to the past. The
women of AMES spoke for all sectors when they said:

*'We are a group with a specific condition and specific demands and we
cannnot wait for socialism and structural changes to solve our
problems tomorrow.'*[7]

*'The mortars won't get me. The day of the triumph I will simply die of joy!'*
(María)

# 9
# CONCLUSION

Whatever the outcome of the Salvadorean civil war, the basic dilemmas of the country's economy will remain: insufficient productive land unequally distributed in relation to a growing population and lack of alternative employment to absorb the large labour suplus. Figure 9.1 on page 290 illustrates this dilemma with a projection of landlessness by the year 1990. There are no easy solutions to this situation. Jorge Sol, a former Salvadorean economy minister, points out the fundamental issue:

'. . . the long-term structural problems of the country face all parties — the FMLN-FDR, the Duarte government and the Reagan administration. That long-term problem is the relation of population to resources. We Salvadorans are now more than five million; by the year 2000 we'll be ten million. When I was minister of economy, I always said El Salvador was not a viable country. Before the civil war, we had attained a certain equilibrium, at least on the surface. It was based on three elements: one, keeping the majority of the population working in conditions of serfdom; two, maintaining on that basis an intensive and profitable plantation agriculture (coffee, cotton and sugar); and three, having access to a relatively successful common market which allowed El Salvador to develop light industry. That was a precarious equilibrium, for a population of three and a half million. Now, it has been completely dislocated by the war. The plantation economy is collapsing, the common market is non-functional, the population is exploding. The most ambitious goal of the Kissinger Commission is to achieve zero economic growth by 1986.*

Whoever wins power in El Salvador will have to confront a mounting problem of destitution, misery and famine. The country as it stands is economically unviable. If we ever achieve peace, we will need a strong government — and I don't want to enter into academic discussions about socialism or Marxism-Leninism — that recognizes that the way to make the Salvadorean economy viable is to create a labor-intensive economy, based on widespread participation of the people, on cooperatives, on permanent employment, on what is nowadays called the area of social ownership. And private enterprise will never organize the economy in that way.'[1]

Some elements of a solution must lie in a redistribution of resources through agrarian reform. But what kind of reform and who will

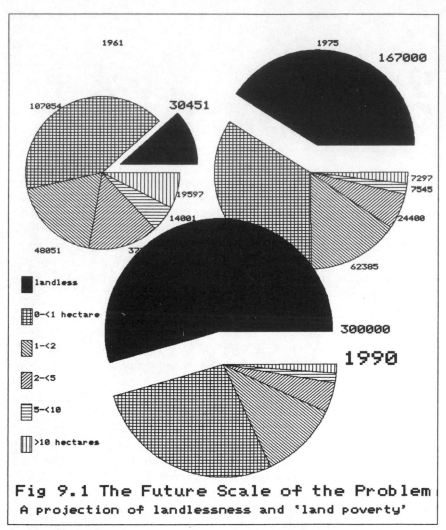

Fig 9.1 The Future Scale of the Problem
A projection of landlessness and 'land poverty'

Source: Projection Assumptions: Population Growth Rates from *Ministerio de Planificación* (1981) applied to rural households less migration projections (war-related disruptions not included). Increase split between landless and land poor in same proportions as for period 1961-1975 (see Figure 1.1)

benefit from it are controversial political issues. As Solón Barraclough points out:

'*Agrarian reform is primarily a political concept useful for describing rapid, profound changes in land tenure and associated power relationships in the direction of greater participation by smallholders, tenants, squatters and landless laborers in decision-making at all levels of society. It is especially concerned with those decisions affecting agricultural production, marketing, credit and the distribution of benefits. It implies a large-scale change in*

290

## Myths and Misconceptions

Like the coup of 15 October 1979, the land reform is shrouded in myths and misconceptions advanced by those whose political interests are thus served. Both conservatives, bitterly opposed to the land redistribution, and liberals, who see it as another unwelcome example of Yankee imperialism, charge that the Salvadoran program has a bold 'made in the USA' label stamped on it. In contrast, US officials have sought to portray their involvement as minimal. 'The land reform now being implemented in El Salvador is a program developed by the Salvadorans, not by the United States,' the State Department declared a few days after the program had been announced. 'We understand that the Salvadoran Government has received the advice of private agrarian reform experts from several countries including the United States. This technical assistance was arranged entirely by the Salvadorans. The United States Government was not involved in planning the programs.' This statement is disingenuous at best.

It is true that the basic provisions of Phase I and II were drafted by the Salvadorans — principally Enrique Alvarez and his aides before the first junta collapsed. But the United States was involved, and it provided more than mere 'technical' assistance. The American Institute for Free Labor Development's (AIFLD) man in El Salvador in early 1980 was Roy Prosterman, a law professor from the University of Washington. Prosterman, who speaks no Spanish, was asked by AIFLD to work on the Salvadoran program primarily because he had been a principal architect of the land reform program imposed by the United States in Vietnam. According to a 'United States Government Memorandum' three days before the land reform was announced in El Salvador, Prosterman met with junta member Colonel Gutiérrez 'and reached an agreement on two of Prosterman's proposed three changes to the agrarian reform law'. Then, the memorandum continued, 'Prosterman met with Archbishop Romero for two hours, went over the land reform, and the Archbishop said he would support the decree if the junta adopted it this week.'[3]

*agrarian structure, resulting in significantly greater access to land, essential inputs, services and markets by poor* campesino *groups at the expense of landlords, their allies and associates.'*[2]

Redistribution of land inevitably provokes resistance from large landowners and their allies. Indeed, effective agrarian reform has rarely been carried out without pressure from below and has often involved violent conflict. These features were present in March 1980 when an agrarian reform was decreed in El Salvador. It would not have been drawn up if peasant unrest had not threatened to engulf the country in civil war, and was immediately opposed by the landowners. It was put together in great haste with considerable US involvement and first implemented by a *junta* headed by Christian Democrat José Napoleón Duarte, under state of siege conditions.

# The 1980 Agrarian Reform: Conception . . .

On paper, the reform goes beyond all previous efforts to deal with the agrarian crisis in El Salvador. In practice, it is fraught with problems both in design and execution. In the short term the militarily-linked objective of the reform is to preempt FMLN/FDR demands for more radical measures, and win peasant support for the government.

There are a number of precedents in recent history for the use of small-farmer reform programmes for political purposes, as D. Dunham points out:

'. . . in American strategic thinking on counter-insurgency both in Asia and in Latin America civic and military aid policies were intertwined. The aim was, at best, to enable governments to win support from peasants through "welfare measures" while having at hand the institutionalized violence to maintain control. In this highly politicized context, programmes of reform or "small farmer development" could not simply be seen as the outcome of technical concerns with raising agricultural output and productivity or of vague, ethical demands for redistributive justice. The situation was far more complex than that. In countries where there was seen to be an actual or potential threat of "communist insurgency" (the Philippines, Vietnam, Thailand or Central America) the American government's aim was "internal security", and the experience that was gained in these "critical areas" was to influence its more general thinking on rural development . . . In the context of this double-edged strategy of reform and repression "small-farmer" policies (credit and input provision, agricultural prices, extension and welfare services) were introduced as part of the broader effort to create a cadre of peasants who were loyal to the government . . . In this, "small farmer" policies served political objectives and acquired a political as well as a technical rationale.'[4]

There is, however, also a longer-term political objective behind the agrarian reform. Both the US government and the Christian Democrat Party hope that the reform will lay the basis for lasting social stability in El Salvador. To consolidate its own political authority, the Christian Democrat Party needs to build a social base to counterbalance the power of the oligarchy and the FDR/FMLN and it hopes that collaboration with the Reagan administration will provide it with the means to do so. Many of the features of the agrarian reform, building a class of productive small farmers whether farming independently or in cooperatives, accord with the Party's traditional philosophy. It is important therefore to assess the reform from within its own rationale and whether it is in fact capable of establishing a more stable social order in El Salvador.

Details of the 1980 reform are given in the box on page 293 while the table on page 294 quantifies its aims, giving official targets for land

## The 1980 Land Reform

There are three parts to the land reform. Its idealized aims are set out as follows:

*'. . . agrarian reform shall be understood to mean the transformation of the country's agrarian structure and the incorporation of the rural population into the economic, social and political development of the nation, . . . based on a equitable distribution of land, an adequate credit system, and comprehensive assistance to the producers . . . '* (Article 2, Basic Law of Agrarian Reform, Decree 153, 6 March 1980)

**Phase I** of the reform allows for the expropriation, with compensation, of land holdings over 500 hectares to be given to peasant cooperatives formed by former permanent estate workers. These are mostly cattle ranches, together with some cotton and sugar estates. An estimated 15 per cent of the nation's agricultural land is involved and some 60,000 workers could benefit according to official targets. A right of reserve of up to 150 hectares (plus 20 per cent more if the landowner carries out improvements) enables the owner to retain some of his land. The land redistributed is to be administered as a joint venture with the government. The cost of the land and other capital investments provided by government agencies constitutes an agrarian reform debt to be repaid by the beneficiaries over a 20-30 year period (Decree 153).

**Phase II** affects land between 100 and 500 hectares. This would include the bulk of coffee estates and some sugar and cotton plantations. A quarter of Salvador's agricultural land is involved. The rights of reserve are the same as for Phase I. The average size of estate affected is about 200 hectares, of which 150 could be exempted. The 1983 constitution set the maximum individual landholding at 245 hectares. No attempt to implement this phase has been made, nor is any expected.

**Phase III** is set out in Decree 207 of 28 April 1980, known as the 'land to the tiller' programme. This grants title to those who both rent and work land up to seven hectares, for which they have to pay compensation to the former owner over a period of 30 years. The programme was to be implemented by the agency FINATA created in December 1980 and strongly promoted by USAID. Fourteen per cent of agricultural land is covered by this phase of the reform and an estimated 150,000 small tenant farmers could benefit. The average plot size implied by official targets is 0.75 hectares.

to be redistributed and numbers of farmers to benefit. We can analyse the ability of this reform to fulfil, within its own terms, the Christian Democrat (and US) aims. What has happened in practice will be dealt with below.

Phases I and III of the reform can theoretically reach some 50 per cent of Salvador's rural poor. Much of the land distributed under

## 1980 Land Reform: Salvadorean Government Targets

| Phase | I | II | III | Total |
|---|---|---|---|---|
| Property affected (ha) | 500+ | 100-500 | rented land under 7 ha | — |
| Number of Properties included | 328 | 1,739 | 30,000 | — |
| Area of land notionally included (ha) | 224,326 | 342,877* | 200,000 | 767,203 |
| Percentage of total farming land | 15 | 24 | 14 | 53 |
| Area left after reserve (ha) | 209,000 | 82,027† | 200,000 | 491,027 |
| Percentage of land available | 14 | 6 | 14 | 34 |
| Number of farmers to benefit | 60,000 | n.a. | 150,000 | 210,000 |
| Average size of plot implied per farmer | 3.5 | — | 0.75 | — |

Sources: US State Department, March 1983
   * Checchi and Company, 1981
   †Seminario Permanente sobre la Economía Nacional del Departamento de Economía, 'La fase II de la reforma agraria y el artículo 105 de la constitucíon política: mito y realidad'. *Boletín de Ciencias Económicas y Sociales*, Jan-Feb 1984.

Phase I is poor agricultural land and requires considerable capital investment and technical aid. Phase III is intended to benefit the largest number of peasants, giving permanent title to small tenant farmers. But, as this book has already indicated, most of these farmers work small plots on badly eroded and poor soils. Providing them with title will not solve the problem of productivity on this land. Although peasants can apply for up to seven hectares, even this would not guarantee a reasonable income without fertilizer, crop rotation, adequate marketing facilities and other technical assistance. In fact, if all those eligible received land they would receive only three quarters of a hectare each. The quality of land in El Salvador is as important as the size of a plot. But Phase III cannot provide sufficient good land to raise the living standards of even its intended beneficiaries. And, in reality, the government's possible achievements are more limited still. With a fast growing rural population this is at best an attempted static solution to a dynamic problem.

Does this reform meet the Christian Democrat/US aim of providing a stable social and political foundation in rural El Salvador? Further, even if it were fully implemented, would it meet the real needs of the people? All those unable to rent land are excluded (and in practice many more — see below). Those theoretically included would not receive enough land to raise productivity and living standards sufficiently to provide rural stability. They would still be 'land poor'. We can see that the real needs of the people cannot be met. Nor in these circumstances can a successful implementation be judged credible either for the Christian Democrats or the US.

Phase II of the reform directly affects the interests of the oligarchy, covering the major coffee and cotton producing estates. While this is of central importance for the control of economic power in El Salvador, it is of lesser significance as a plausible source of help for the small farmer. The coffee estates are largely unsuitable for other crops and the economy will continue to depend on foreign exchange earned in this sector. However, transfer of control of the surplus

---

**Five Years of Land Reform 1980-1985**

| Phase | I | III | Total |
|---|---|---|---|
| Claimed land distributed (ha) | 213,791 | 96,750 | 310,541 |
| Percentage of total farming land | 15 | 7 | 22 |
| Numbers of farmers claiming | 31,359 | 63,663 | 95,022 |
| Percentage of rural poor claiming (see notes) | 8 | 16 | 24 |
| Number of final titles issued | 22* | 5,456† | 5,478 |
| Percentage of rural poor granted title | 1.0 | 1.4 | 2.4 |

Source: President Duarte, January 1985
          *Checchi and Co., 1983
          †FINATA, 1983

Notes: 1. The rural poor are here defined as the landless and those possessing less than one hectare. Figures derived from the 1975 United Nations figures (305,000) and Salvadorean government population projections (just under a 30% increase in ten years). War related dislocation not included.

2. President Duarte's claims are disputed. USAID's Inspector General found in 1984 that only 25,000 Phase III beneficiaries were in actual possession. 20,000 had been evicted or had abandoned their plots. A further 15,000 were inaccessible for verification for security reasons.

produced here, from the hands of the oligarchy to the majority, is of vital importance to El Salvador's future. Given the rights of reserve built into the original proposal, this would never have been seriously threatened. The 1983 constitution, which raised the maximum individual holding to 245 hectares, has probably removed any minimal impact even were the reform implemented.


## . . . and Implementation

The results of the land reform are set out in the table below. The figures given there do not adequately reflect the size of its failure. The data given by Salvadorean government agencies is incomplete and misleading, while that of USAID is scarcely more reliable. For example, the latter's estimates of the number of properties expropriated under Phase I have ranged from 360 in May 1983 to 194 in January 1984. USAID's Inspector General found the situation '. . . illustrative of the degree of confusion which we found so pervasively present in the data and baseline information concerning the agrarian reform program'.[5] Further, the data cannot convey the inadequacy of giving title to people farming marginal land with totally insufficient resources.

Perhaps the most glaring omission of the reform in this respect, is its failure to offer anything to the landless. It is difficult to see how any reform which does not tackle this ever-increasing problem of the Salvadorean economy (see Figure 9.1) could possibly bring lasting social peace to the country. The intended beneficiaries are mostly estate workers and small tenant farmers. Much of the land distributed under Phase I is poor agricultural land, and with insufficient credit and technical assistance many of the cooperatives set up under its provisions have collapsed. A team representing USAID's Inspector General visited 16 Phase I cooperatives in May-October 1983 and found them to be financially unviable. They had huge capital debts, no working capital, and weak management. Forty-three per cent of land was non-productive and most of the rest of very poor quality. The average application to FINATA under the Phase III scheme, as of 1983, was for a plot less than 1.6 hectares, insufficient to support a peasant family or attract credit on a commercial basis.[6]

Phase II has in fact never been implemented. It should have included a further 25 per cent of agricultural land in the reform, most of it from the highly productive agro-export sector. Its expropriation would have doubled the amount of land owned by ISTA (the Salvadorean Institute for Agrarian Transformation). Now that the minimum right of reserve is 245 hectares, the land owners could retain their best land even if Phase II were ever implemented.

## Circumvention, Corruption and Repression

San Cayetano was expropriated from Regaldo and converted to a peasant cooperative as part of Phase I of the government's land redistribution program. . . . the milking sheds were barren. Anticipating implementation of the land reform program, Regaldo had slaughtered most of his beef herd and driven the rest to Guatemala, where he also took his farm machinery. Most other large landowners circumvented the new law, at least in part, in the same manner. A few miles from San Cayetano, at the 1,675 acre San Rafael el Porvenir cooperative, only three pieces of farm machinery were parked under the corrugated tin roof of the machinery shed. Five small tractors, two combines, four trucks, and 1,200 head of cattle had been sold by the prior owner before the government acted.[7]

Many of those older (ISTA) farms were purchased at inflated prices under schemes that yielded kickbacks to former government officials, sources say. The farms, which must repay the Government for the land purchases, are recording losses because the land can't produce enough to cover the inflated debt burdens. On one such farm, not very far from El Aguacate, the government manager says living conditions actually have declined, because of the farm's operating losses. In addition to repaying the impossible debt burden, the peasants must pay for 'protection' from the local *Hacienda* police, perhaps the most feared element of the Salvadorean security forces. The police on this farm recently helped soldiers kill seven local peasants — including a mentally retarded man returning from a fishing trip — after guerillas ambushed an army convoy. 'The people say that under the old owner life was better,' the manager says, 'but life was bad then, and it's bad now. It's impossible to say which is worse.'[8]

At San Francisco Guajoyo, the largest original UCS cooperative, the assassins arrived at about three-thirty in the morning, while the 160 families were sleeping. They were dressed in military uniforms; a small armored personnel carrier was brought along in case things got out of hand. The men went from door to door, rounding up peasants whose names were on a list. ISTA employees showed their identification. To no avail. Fourteen peasants were shot, as the other members of the cooperative were forced to watch. Junta members Morales Ehrlich and Colonel Gutiérrez told AID officials that the perpetrators of the massacre were guerillas who had dressed in army uniforms and stolen the small tank. But one person had survived. When Leonel Gómez, the ISTA deputy director, and an aid official found him in the Santa Ana hospital, they spirited him away, knowing that survivors are often hunted down and killed in their hospital beds. He was laid on a mattress in the back of a pickup truck, with the AID man holding his plasma bottle. The survivor provided the details: the killings had been carried out by the National

▶

Guard. Concerned AID officials visited Guajoyo after the incident. A few days later, according to a classified 'Memorandum to the File', the Guard returned and killed more peasants.

El Peñón, San Francisco Guajoyo, Santa Catalina weren't random or isolated incidents. They were part of a pattern. According to an AIFLD memorandum, 184 peasants, government employees, and others associated with the land reform were 'killed violently' during the eight months after the reforms were enacted. Gómez, who tracked the repression for ISTA, testified before the House Subcommittee on Inter-American Affairs that between March and December 1980, 240 leaders of cooperatives were killed. AIFLD and Gómez blamed the government for most of the killings.[9]

While the oligarchy retains political power, it is highly unlikely that Phase II will ever be put into operation. But, in fact, the 1980 reform cannot of itself solve El Salvador's agrarian problem. It may only give short-term benefits to the sector of the peasantry which is pro-government and whose allegiance can be affirmed by the grant of a land title either individually or within a cooperative.

The fact that the reform has from its inception been accompanied by extreme brutality against the rural population is not an unavoidable result of the activities of extremist groups as it is frequently presented. It is because the reform is designed to identify and reward those peasants loyal to the government. Civilian peasant supporters of the guerilla forces and often those uncommitted to any side are treated as combatants, targets for torture and murder.

The unwillingness of the US and the Salvadorean government to challenge the political and economic power of the landed oligarchy has enabled the wealthy elite to mobilize its allies in the armed forces and security forces against even the pro-government beneficiaries of the reform. The political will to implement serious reform has been lacking, while the aim of defeating the guerilla movement and its civilian base has been pursued relentlessly. Evidence even from US government-sponsored studies of agrarian reform point not only to the climate of insecurity which has surrounded it, but to completely inadequate financial and technical assistance, lack of educational and training programmes, bureaucratic delays caused by under-financed government agencies, legal complexities, dishonest administration and outright corruption.

The reform has further divided the peasantry of El Salvador. The organizations which have benefited are all heavily influenced by the Christian Democrat Party and US labour organizations, though even the UCS is reported to have little voice within the administration of the agrarian reform process (see box on page 300). The FTC has been forced underground and its members have been amongst the most prominent victims of army and death squad violence. This is how an FTC member in Chatalenango saw the agrarian reform:

For us, an authentic agrarian reform would be one that would not be just a political manoeuvre but one which really got down to the issues. We think that the agrarian reform carried out by the present regime has been a political move rather than a truly effective and concrete measure which could benefit the farm labourers.

The Salvadorean government and the US president have realized that the peasantry here is engaged in a struggle for the land. They have also realized that all their efforts to impede this struggle for land have been unsuccessful. The repression launched against the peasant organizations has been very hard and this has damaged not only the image of the government but also that of the Armed Forces, nationally and internationally. So the regime had to do what the US asked it to do and implement the reform.

The *haciendas* are being taken over by the military so that it can say to the peasants that the army is on the side of the people, of the peasants. But the agricultural workers had already formed a platform of demands, which were flatly rejected. Before the army took over the *hacienda*, La Colima, to distribute its lands according to their plans, it had already been occupied by the peasants. This was done to highlight the fact that the land reform didn't really have any benefits for the workers and to demand that the plans for the reform were at least carried out without violence. Then the army took the land and said that it was going to distribute it to the peasants. But which peasants? They believed that they had the support of the unorganized peasants and those in ORDEN. First of all the army took those people and settled them on the *haciendas*, claiming that it had redistributed the land to the peasants. Now you can see the results of all this: the situation of the peasants hasn't improved, it has actually worsened. Many peasants realized that what the FTC had told them is true. The land reform is a deceitful way to make them conform and to try to gain political advantage which would provide a better image for the regime.

The crucial issue for us is whether they will implement the second phase of the reform. The third phase affects the interests of the rich and even the medium peasant, but the implementation of the second phase affects directly the interests of the oligarchs and the ruling class. And it's there that we believe that the reform has to hit.

When we talk of an authentic land reform, it means a reform of the land but also accompanied by technological improvement and education. We know that our territory is very small and so land

## AIFLD's Alter Ego

'AIFLD, which was expelled from El Salvador in 1973 but returned after the coup in 1979, has demonstrated in other ways that it is more concerned about US policy than about the interests of Salvadorean peasants. It tried to subvert the land reform program that was being considered by the first junta. AIFLD was opposed to taking land from all the largest landowners, arguing instead that only one or two farms be expropriated and converted into peasant cooperatives, 'as pilot projects,' said Leonel Gómez, deputy director of ISTA at the time. The AIFLD representatives also tried to persuade José Rodolfo Viera not to take the job as head of ISTA, offering him a postition with AIFLD at $1,000 a month. But after consulting Archbishop Romero, Viera, a peasant with only three years formal schooling, became the ISTA director. At that point AIFLD rented him a suite at the Sheraton, 'for no reason at all,' said Gómez. 'They were just trying to buy him. But they couldn't.'

AIFLD did, however, effectively become the largest Salvadorean peasant union, known by its Spanish initials as the UCS, and the Democratic Popular Unity (UPD), an umbrella organization for four labor groups. Peasant unions were banned from 1932 until the late 1960s, when the government set up the UCS with assistance from AIFLD. It was about that time that Mike Hammer first worked in El Salvador. When AIFLD became involved with the UCS again in 1980, it paid some 400 UCS members salaries of $160 a month — a hefty amount for a peasant — to work as promoters, going into the countryside to explain the law and seek new members. Each peasant paid 25 centavos (about 60 cents) a month to be a member of the UCS; the rest of the organisation's annual budget of nearly $2 million came from AIFLD. The UCS has become little more than an alter ego for AIFLD and the US policy.

During one crucial period when President Reagan had to certify that progress was being made in the land reform program in order to continue military aid to El Salvador, the UCS complained in a letter to Duarte that 'the failure of the agrarian reform process is an immediate and imminent danger.' Just three days after that negative letter had been made public, in a front-page story by Karen De Young in *The Washington Post*, AIFLD released another letter purportedly written by UCS leaders, this time praising the Duarte goverment's efforts on behalf of peasants. This letter was the basis of a front-page story in *The New York Times* under the headline 'Salvador Peasants Praise Land Policy'.

The letter was dated January 25 and purportedly written in El Salvador. AIFLD made it public with a press release on January 28. But mail does not arrive from El Salvador in three days, and the name of one of the UCS leaders, Samuel Maldonado, who supposedly signed the letter, was misspelled. In fact, the letter was written by AIFLD in Washington.

AIFLD has used the UCS and its leaders on other occasions, flying them to Washington to testify before congressional committees sceptical about continuing aid to El Salvador. But AIFLD leaders have never allowed them to say publicly what they voice in private, such as their support for negotiations to end the war.'[10]

*The sub-regional government of Chalatenango 1984.*

**reform isn't easy. It would need to go hand in hand with these definite improvements in technology, coupled with an improvement in social provision for the peasants. To this end, we support the idea of cooperatives but those which work on the basis of educating, raising consciousness; and not like the present reform where they are trying to divide the people, to make them self-seeking and believe that they are going to be rich, so that they don't look after the needs of others.** (René)

The independent cooperative movement which was first launched by the Catholic Church in the 1950s has also been excluded from the land reform. In 1982 a number of cooperative associations that wished to remain independent of the Christian Democrat party and US government influence came together in a national confederation of cooperative associations, COACES. It has tried to defend the rights of workers on the cooperatives and lobbied for a new cooperative law

## Mobilization and participation

'In the long run, agrarian structures in Central America will inevitably change regardless of what policies current governments pursue. Such policies are, however, crucially important for influencing the terms of participation in the societies of the small producers and farm workers who make up the vast majority of the rural population. Without question, past "agrarian reforms" in Central America have been diversions for most of these rural poor. Such reforms were either subverted or the government promulgating them was overthrown by a military coup. Real reforms . . . are indispensable, however, if the poor are to enjoy a minimum of human dignity, rights and satisfaction of their basic needs. Agrarian transformation and reform is a prerequisite for democratic national development geared to meet popular needs and aspirations and not economic growth primarily benefitting small wealthy elites, their stooges and their foreign allies. The question is not one of land tenure reform or fiscal incentives, colonization, etc, but of mobilizing all these mechanisms and many more to support effective agrarian reforms. Such reforms, however, require genuine political participation by these same potential beneficiaries. They cannot just be handed down from above or from abroad. Such participation is now being achieved through more conventional democratic processes in Costa Rica. It is difficult to imagine how effective peasant and worker organization and participation could be achieved in El Salvador or Guatemala without major social and political transformations in the whole society taking place first. In societies such as these, elections are often meaningless exercises.'[11]

more relevant to their needs than that of 1969 and for financial and technical assistance for its beleaguered cooperatives. In 1984 and 1985 it organized a number of demonstrations involving some ten thousand peasants — a remarkable feat in the repressive climate of El Salvador — but it still awaits the new law.

But even the project of benefitting selected groups of peasants has come up against the limits of a reform which fails to tackle the political power of the wealthy elite and which fears independent peasant organization. Those organizations which have expected to benefit from the reform have grown restless at its failures and angry at the repression, which despite their loyalty, the government has been unable to prevent. One observer who visited the department of Sonsonate in 1985, one of the western departments where the left has traditionally been weak since 1932 and which has been less affected by the war, found deep frustrations amongst the peasants. The president of the National Association of Salvadorean Indians (ANIS), traditionally supported by AIFLD, told her: 'We worked tirelessly to elect Napoleón Duarte, we risked our lives to do it, and when he was elected (in May 1984) people thought everything would change. But we are still waiting for justice.'

# Promised Land

Unfulfilled promises and continued misery have led many rural as well as urban workers to protest. 1984 and 1985 have seen the first resurgence of strike activity, marches and demonstrations since 1980. Much of this has been spontaneous and has involved workers linked to organizations across the political spectrum, including the Christian Democrats' own affiliates. The government has been trapped by the need to appease its social base and its inability to meet their material needs while wealth and power remain with the oligarchy. In a situation of deepening economic crisis, it has usually preferred to appease the agro-exporters rather than risk further decline. As a result, it has often resorted to repression as the only way to control the labour movement.

The war created the land reform but also prevents its effective implementation. I have, however, shown its inadequacy even if it could be carried out. The land affected by Phase III of the reform is on the very margin of productivity and there are no free resources which could provide a buffer. This goes some way to explain the brutality of repression in El Salvador. Without a far-reaching solution to the agrarian question, repression will be the only option for any future Salvadorean government. In the conditions of El Salvador, a strategy which only benefits a minority of the population will necessarily demand the repression of the excluded majority — in other words, a system of government founded upon murder.

The arguments presented in this book lead to the conclusion that only an agrarian reform carried out within a broad process of radical social transformation can possibly pave the way for lasting peace and development in El Salvador. Compromise solutions based on alliances with sectors of the existing ruling class cannot solve the problems which first led to the Salvadorean civil war. Privilege and the repressive force which sustains it can have no place if genuine solutions are sought to the problems of El Salvador's poor majority. A far-reaching agrarian reform will have to tackle ownership of wealth and production throughout Salvadorean society, and the poor majority must participate in its design and implementation in order to guarantee that it meets their needs. Any negotiated settlement which excludes the people whose lives are described in this book is not a solution.

El Salvador's history of popular mobilization provides a positive basis for the building of a new and just social order. Many third world societies embarking on programmes of socialist transition have tried, but been unable, to foster the emergence of a peasantry which is no longer passive and manipulated, but is capable of active involvement in the building of a new society. The peasants of Chalatenango showed that it can happen. They point the way to a more humane society.

Their aspirations for a better life are those of all El Salvador's working people, and it is appropriate to conclude with their words:

We saw in other poor people what we were suffering. When we went looking for work, we saw the poverty in which some people were living in their little farms with all their children, everything wet inside, without enough to support their families. And seeing all that, your heart felt pretty soft, wishing for a solution to these problems. When you are poor, you think of other poor people, so that you see many things. But the landowners don't look upon us as their own people, they only use us when they need us to do their work. We saw that it is necessary to unite in struggle for the good of all, so that one day we can all be free and that we might live a more happy life as human beings, as brothers, as sons of God. All of us must achieve this, not just a few. (Tomás)

---

The objective of the struggle is to achieve a social life in which all of us have the same value, the workers as much as the educated. That the student does not look on the peasant as though he were of less value, that we all consider each other as we really are, that we all live as brothers, that there not be any divisions. Until now we haven't had a government that truly responded to the interests of our people. Now the government is only concerned with the interests of the upper classes. They depend on our labour for survival, but we have learned through the struggle that we can quite happily live without them. One day there will be a government of workers and peasants which will look after the interests of the people. (Quique)

# Notes

## Chapter 1

1. Browning 1971: 16
2. Wolf 1959: 176
3. White 1973: 29
4. In Browning 1971: 76
5. *Ibid*.: 134
6. Durham 1979: 40
7. Browning 1971: 78
8. *Ibid*.: 91-92
9. British Parliamentary Human Rights Group Delegation to El Salvador, Dec. 1978: 12
10. In Browning 1971: 173
11. Munro 1978: 149
12. Wilson 1978: 197
13. Durham 1979: 56
14. Wilson 1978: 198
15. Smith 1945: 371-372
16. Anderson 1971: 10
17. Durham 1979: 32
18. Colindres 1977: 49
19. Colindres 1976: 466
20. PROCCARA 1971: 58
21. Browning 1971: 255-256
22. Cabarrús 1983: 68
23. Browning 1971: 260
24. Simon 1982: 19
25. Deere & Diskin 1984: 20
26. PROCCARA 1971: 117
27. Deere & Diskin 1984: 25
28. *Ibid*.: 28
29. *Ibid*.: 31
30. Ruiz 1976: 161
31. Durham 1979: 56-57
32. White 1973: 185
33. Russell 1984: 85
34. Downing 1977: 13
35. Castillo 1980: 152
36. Cabarrús 1983: 138
37. Deere & Diskin 1984: 32
38. *Ibid*.: 33
39. Downing 1978: 15
40. Samaniego 1980: 132
41. Downing 1978: 53
42. OAS 1974: 145
43. Marroquín 1977: 144-145
44. Browning 1971: 275
45. *Ibid*.: 281
46. Montes 1980: 288
47. Ungo 1976: 457
48. Downing 1978: 19
49. Slutzky 1972
50. Aubey 1969: 275-276
51. Dunkerley 1985: 53
52. Samaniego 1980: 138
53. Burke 1976: 481
54. Deere & Diskin 1984: 8
55. *Ibid*.: 41-42

## Chapter 2

1. Durham 1979: 34
2. Barón Castro 1982: 151
3. Browning 1971: 162
4. Flores V. 1979: 52
5. OAS 1974: 93
6. El Salvador, Ministerio de Planificación 1975: 49
7. El Salvador, Banco Hipotecario 1974: Cuadro VI-6
8. Monteforte 1972: 95
9. Russell 1984: 81
10. Larde & Jacir 1980: 18-19
11. Huizer 1972: 25-26
12. Flores V. 1979: Cuadros II-1 & 2
13. *Ibid*.: Cuadro III-4

14. PROCCARA 1971: 77
15. Castro 1976: 171
16. *Ibid.*: 172
17. In Larde & Jacir 1980: 236
18. Guerra 1976: 205
19. Castro 1976: 181
20. Cabarrús 1983: 125
21. White 1973: 140
22. In Thomson 1986
23. Larde & Jacir 1980: 112-136
24. *Ibid.*: 59
25. Cabarrús 1983: 89
26. White 1973: 149
27. ILO 1954: 10-17

## Chapter 3

1. Argueta 1983: 60-62
2. Miguel Mármol, in Dalton 1972: 343
3. Keogh 1981: 14
4. *Ibid.*: 15
5. Anderson 1971: 38-39
6. *Ibid.*: 136
7. *Ibid.*: 131
8. In McClintock 1985: 112
9. Heckhorn 1983: 53
10. In McClintock 1985: 118
11. *Ibid.*: 122
12. *Ibid.*: 125
13. White 1973: 209
14. McClintock 1985: 197
15. Nairn 1984: 21
16. *Ibid.*: 23
17. McClintock 1985: 208
18. Pyes 1983
19. *Ibid.*
20. Guerra 1976: 210
21. *Ibid.*: 221-222
22. Pearce 1982: 45
23. In Montes 1980: 271-273
24. *Ibid.*: 273
25. Forché & Wheaton 1980: 8
26. *Ibid.*: 10
27. Montgomery 1982: 123
28. Bonner 1984: 193
29. Webre 1979: 62
30. *Ibid.*: 67
31. Guerra 1976: 232-237
32. *Ibid.*: 237

## Chapter 4

1. Moore 1973: 453
2. Wolf 1975: 272
3. Huizer 1973: 159
4. Keogh 1981: 57
5. Berryman 1984: 104
6. UCA 1982: 39
7. Richard 1982: 70-71
8. Rivera 1977: 809
9. Berryman 1984: 105
10. Montgomery 1982: 103
11. *Ibid.*: 103
12. Brockman 1982: 18
13. UCA 1978: 67
14. *Ibid.*: 80
15. Cabarrús 1983: 160
16. UCA 1978: 84
17. *Ibid.*: 87
18. White 1973: 213
19. Harnecker 1983: 146
20. Comandante Marcial 1982: 15
21. *Ibid.*: 34
22. *Ibid.*: 34
23. Menéndez Rodríguez 1980: 52
24. Comandante Marcial 1982: 40
25. Gilly 1965
26. Comandante Marcial 1982: 76
27. Harnecker 1983: 145
28. *Ibid.*: 148
29. Publicaciones de la Revolución Salvadoreña
30. Resistencia Nacional: 29
31. *Ibid.*: 61
32. PRS 1977
33. Cabarrús 1983: 162

## Chapter 5

1. Cabarrús 1983: 184-185
2. Cabarrús 1983 & Montes, 1980
3. Cabarrús 1983: 184
4. *Ibid.*: 183
5. *Ibid.*: 186-197
6. *Ibid.*: 197
7. In Brockman 1982: 179
8. In Alegría 1983: 88-91
9. Cabarrús 1983: 252
10. *Ibid.*: 262
11. *Ibid.*: 246

# Chapter 6

1. Cabarrús 1983: 244
2. Alas 1982: 175
3. McClintock 1985: 175
4. Brockman 1982: 3
5. Cabarrús 1983: 267
6. Brockman 1982: 4
7. Berryman 1984: 124
8. UCA 1978: 108
9. US House of Representatives 1977: 86
10. Erdozaín 1981: 32
11. Armstrong & Shenk 1982: 92
12. LAB 1979: 40
13. Menjívar 1979: 116
14. Samayoa & Galván 1979: 596
15. *Ibid.*: 598
16. McClintock 1985: 194
17. Brockman 1982: 103
18. Arzobispado de San Salvador 1978
19. FTC Boletin Internacional 1979
20. Anaya 1980: 105
21. LAB 1979: 43-44
22. Brockman 1982: 176
23. Romero 1980: 199-201
24. Romero 1978: 763
25. FECCAS-UTC 1978: 776
26. Prensa Latina, 7 March 1980
27. *Combate Popular* 1979

# Chapter 7

1. Bonner 1984: 165
2. *Ibid.*: 205
3. Harnecker 1983: 156
4. Comandancia General del FMLN 1984
5. Pearce 1982: 260
6. In Stetler 1970: 175-176
7. FPL 1980: 21
8. Rigoberto 1982: 104-105
9. *Proceso*, 11 February 1985

10. In Americas Watch 1985: 25
11. *Proceso*, 11 February 1985
12. *Central American Bulletin* (Berkeley), April 1985
13. *Washington Post*, 17 August 1984
14. *Washington Post*, 23 October 1984
15. *Proceso*, 11 February 1985
16. *ECA*, September 1984
17. Americas Watch 1985: 12-13
18. *Proceso*, 28 January 1985
19. *Ibid.*
20. *Ibid.*
21. *Ibid.*
22. *Ibid.*

# Chapter 8

1. e.g. Clements 1984
2. AMES 1981
3. Thomson 1986
4. CELADEC. Cuadernos de Estudio No. 23
5. Guillén 1983: 11
6. CRIE 1984: Nos. 153-4
7. AMES 1981

# Chapter 9

1. Sol 1985: 32
2. Barraclough 1984: 5
3. Bonner 1984: 190
4. Dunham 1983: 9-11
5. Thome 1984: 8
6. *Ibid.*: 19
7. Bonner 1984: 187
8. Frazier, *Wall Street Journal*, 15 January 1982
9. Bonner 1984: 200
10. *Ibid.*: 193-194
11. Barraclough 1984: 10-11

# List of Abbreviations

| | |
|---|---|
| ABC | Administración de Bienestar Campesino/Administration of Peasant Welfare |
| AID | US Agency for International Development (USAID) |
| AIFLD | American Institute for Free Labor Development |
| AFL-CIO | American Federation of Labor – Congress of Industrial Organizations |
| AGEUS | Asociación General de Estudiantes Universitarios Salvadoreños/General Association of Salvadorean University Students |
| AMES | Asociación de Mujeres de El Salvador/Association of Salvadorean Women |
| ANDES | Asociación Nacional de Educadores Salvadoreños/National Association of Salvadorean Teachers |
| ANEP | Asociación Nacional de la Empresa Privada/National Association of Private Enterprise |
| ANIS | Asociación Nacional Indigenista Salvadoreña/National Association of Salvadorean Indians |
| ANSESAL | Agencia Nacional de Seguridad Salvadoreña/Salvadorean National Security Agency |
| ARENA | Alianza Republicana Nacionalista/Nationalist Republican Alliance |
| ATACES | Asociación de Trabajadores Asalariados del Campo de El Salvador/Association of Salvadorean Farm Workers |
| BFA | Banco de Fomento Agropecuario/Agricultural Development Bank |
| BPR | Bloque Popular Revolucionario/Popular Revolutionary Bloc |
| CEDES | Conferencia Episcopal de El Salvador/Salvadorean Bishops' Conference |
| CESPROP | Centro de Estudios y Promoción Popular/Centre of Social Studies and Popular Promotion |
| CGS | Confederación General de Sindicatos/General Confederation of Trade Unions |
| CIA | US Central Intelligence Agency |
| CLASC | Central Latinoamericana de Sindicatos Cristianos/Latin American Confederation of Christian Trade Unions |
| CLAT | Central Latinoamericana de Trabajadores/Latin American Workers' Congress |
| COACES | Confederación de Asociaciones de Cooperativas de El Salvador/Confederation of Cooperative Associations |

| | |
|---|---|
| CONIP | Coordinadora Nacional de la Iglesia Popular/National Council of the People's Church |
| COOR | Comité Obrero de Orientación Revolucionaria/Workers' Committee of Revolutionary Orientation |
| CRM | Coordinadora Revolucionaria de Masas/Revolutionary Coordination of the Masses |
| CUTS | Confederación Unitaria de Trabajadores Salvadoreños/United Confederation of Salvadorean Workers |
| DRU | Dirección Revolucionaria Unificada/Unified Revolutionary Directorate |
| EPL | Ejército Popular de Liberación/Popular Liberation Army |
| ERP | Ejército Revolucionario del Pueblo/People's Revolutionary Army |
| FAL | Fuerzas Armadas de Liberación/Armed Liberation Forces |
| FAPU | Frente de Acción Popular Unificada/United Popular Action Front |
| FARN | Fuerzas Armadas de Resistencia Nacional/Armed Forces of National Resistance |
| FARO | Frente de Agricultores de la Región Oriental/Eastern Region Farmers' Front |
| FDN | Frente Democrático Nacional/National Democratic Front |
| FDR | Frente Democrático Revolucionario/Democratic Revolutionary Front |
| FDS | Frente Democrático Salvadoreño/Salvadorean Democratic Front |
| FECCAS | Federación Cristiana de Campesinos Salvadoreños/Christian Federation of Salvadorean Peasants |
| FENASTRAS | Federación National Sindical de Trabajodores Salvadoreños/National Trade Union Federation of Salvadorean Workers |
| FINATA | Financiera Nacional de Tierras Agrícolas/Salvadorean National Financial Institute for Agricultural Land |
| FMLN | Frente Farabundo Martí para la Liberación Nacional/Farabundo Martí National Liberation Front |
| FPL | Fuerzas Populares de Liberación/Popular Liberation Forces |
| FRTS | Federación Regional de Trabajadores de El Salvador/Regional Federation of Salvadorean Workers |
| FTC | Federación de Trabajadores del Campo/Rural Workers' Federation |
| FUERSA | Frente Unido de Estudiantes Revolucionarios Salvador Allende/Salvador Allende United Front of Revolutionary Students |
| FUNPROCOOP | Fundación Promotora de Cooperativas/Foundation for the Promotion of Cooperatives |
| FUSS | Federación Unitaria Sindical Salvadoreña/Salvadorean Unitary Trade Union Federation |
| GAP | Gobierno de Amplia Participación/Government of Broad Participation |

| | |
|---|---|
| IAF | Interamerican Foundation |
| ICR | Instituto de Colonización Regional/Regional Colonization Institute |
| ILO | International Labour Office/Oficina Internacional del Trabajo |
| INCAP | Instituto de Nutrición para Centroamérica y Panamá/ Nutrition Institute of Central America and Panama |
| INSAFOCOOP | Instituto Salvadoreño de Fomento Cooperativo/ Salvadorean Institute for the Development of Cooperatives |
| IRA | Instituto Regulador de Abastecimientos/Institute for the Regulation of Supplies |
| ISTA | Instituto Salvadoreño de Transformación Agraria/ Salvadorean Institute of Agrarian Transformation |
| LL | Ligas de Liberación/Liberation Leagues |
| LP-28 | Ligas Populares "28 de febrero"/"28th February" Popular Leagues |
| MEGA | Mejoramiento Ganadero/(a program for) the improvement of the cattle industry |
| MERS | Movimiento Estudiantil Revolucionario de Secundario/National Revolutionary Movement of Secondary Students |
| MNR | Movimiento Nacional Revolucionario/National Revolutionary Movement |
| MLP | Movimiento de Liberación Popular/Popular Liberation Movement |
| MPL | Milicias Populares de Liberación/Popular Liberation Militias |
| OAS | Organization of American States/Organización de Estados Americanos |
| ORDEN | Organización Democrática Nacionalista/Democratic Nationalist Organization |
| ORT | Organización Revolucionaria de Trabajadores/ Revolutionary Workers' Organization |
| PAR | Partido de Acción Renovadora/Party of Renovative Action |
| PCN | Partido de Conciliación Nacional/National Conciliation Party |
| PCS | Partido Comunista Salvadoreño/Salvadorean Communist Party |
| PDC | Partido Demócrata Cristiano/Christian Democrat Party |
| PPL | Poder Popular Local/Local Popular Power |
| PROCCARA | Programa de Capacitación Campesina para la Reforma Agraria/Peasant Training Programme for Agrarian Reform |
| PRS | Partido de la Revolución Salvadoreña/Salvadorean Revolutionary Party |
| PRTC | Partido Revolucionario de los Trabajadores Centro- americanos/Central American Workers' Revolutionary Party |

| | |
|---|---|
| RN | Resistencia Nacional/National Resistance |
| SNI | Servicio Nacional de Inteligencia/National Intelligence Service |
| SRI | Socorro Rojo Internacional/International Red Aid |
| STECEL | Sindicato de Trabajadores de la Empresa Comisión Ejecutiva Hidroeléctrica de Río Lempa/Rio Lempa Electrical Company Workers' Trade Union |
| STUC | Sindicato de la Unión de Trabajadores de la Construcción/ Union of Construction Workers |
| UCA | Universidad Centroamericana "José Simeón Cañas"/ "José Simeón Cañas" Central American University |
| UCS | Unión Comunal Salvadoreña/Salvadorean Communal Union |
| UDN | Unión Democrática Nacionalista/Democratic Nationalist Union |
| UGB | Unión Guerrera Blanca/White Warrior's Union |
| UNO | Unión Nacional Opositora/National Opposition Union |
| UNOC | Unión Nacional de Obreros Cristianos/Union of Christian Workers |
| UPD | Unión Popular Democrática/Popular Democratic Unity |
| UPT | Unión de Pobladores de Tugurios/Union of Shanty-town Dwellers |
| UR-19 | Universitarios Revolucionario 19 de Julio/19th July Revolutionary Students |
| UTC | Unión de Trabajadores del Campo/Union of Rural Workers |

# Bibliography

Alas, Higinio. *El Salvador: Por qué la Insurrección?* Secretariado Permanente de la Comisión para la Defensa de los Derechos Humanos en Centroamérica, Costa Rica, 1982.

Alegría, Claribel & D.J. Flakoll. *No Me Agarran Viva: La Mujer Salvadoreña en Lucha*, Era, Mexico D.F., 1983.

Americas Watch. *Draining the Sea . . . Sixth Supplement to the Report on Human Rights in El Salvador*. New York & Washington D.C., 1985.

Americas Watch. *Protection of the Weak and Unarmed: The Dispute over Counting Human Rights in El Salvador*. New York, 1984.

Americas Watch & the American Civil Liberties Union (ACLU). *Report on Human Rights in El Salvador*. Vintage, New York, 1982.

AMES. *Participación de la Mujer en las Organizaciones Sociales y Políticas. Reflexiones de las Mujeres*. Mimeo, Nov. 1981.

Anaya, Eugenio. "Crónica del Mes de Enero 1980", *ECA*, Jan.-Feb.

Anderson, Thomas P. *Matanza*. University of Nebraska Press, Lincoln, 1971.

Argueta, Manlio. *One Day of Life*. Chatto & Windus, London, 1983.

Arias Gómez, Jorge. *Farabundo Martí*. EDUCA, San José, 1972

Armstrong, Robert & Janet Shenk. *El Salvador: The Face of Revolution*. Pluto Press, London, 1982.

Arzobispado de San Salvador. "Los Sucesos de San Pedro Perulapán", *ECA*, pp.223-247, April 1978.

Aubrey, Robert T. "Entrepreneurial Formation in El Salvador", *Explorations in Entrepreneurial History*, pp.268-285, Spring-Summer, 1969.

Barón Castro, Rodolfo. *La Población de El Salvador*. UCA Editores, San Salvador, 1978.

Barraclough, Solón. *Agrarian Reform in Central America: Diversion or Necessity?* Edited version of a talk prepared for an ODC and SAIS Conference on "Alternative Economic Strategies for Central America and the Implications for US Policy", Washington, D.C., May 15-16, 1984.

Berryman, Philip. *The Religious Roots of Rebellion. Christians in the Central American Revolutions*. SCM Press, London, 1984.

Bonner, Raymond. "Gains from Salvador Land Distribution Disputed", *New York Times*, 8 April, 1982.

Bonner, Raymond. *Weakness and Deceit*. Times Books, New York, 1984.

British Parliamentary Delegation. *Human Rights in El Salvador*. Report, December 1978.

Brockman, James R. *The World Remains: A Life of Oscar Romero*. Orbis, Maryknoll, N.Y., 1982.

Browning, David. "Agrarian Reform in El Salvador", *Journal of Latin*

*American Studies*, pp.399-426, Cambridge, 1983.

Browning, David. *El Salvador: Landscape and Society*. Clarendon Press, Oxford, 1971.

Burke, Melvin. "El Sistema de Plantación y la Proletarización del Trabajo Agrícola en El Salvador", *ECA*, pp.473-83, Sep.-Oct. 1976.

Cabarrús, Carlos Rafael. *Génesis de una Revolución*. Ediciones de la Casa Chata, Mexico D.F., 1983.

Cáceres Prendes, Jorge. "Radicalización Política y Pastoral Popular en El Salvador: 1969-1979", *Estudios Sociales Centroamericanos*, pp.93-153, Sept-Dec. 1982.

Campos, Tomás R. "La Iglesia y las Organizaciones Populares en El Salvador", *ECA*, pp.692-702, Sept. 1978.

Carpio, Salvador Cayetano. In *La Guerra Popular en El Salvador*. Ediciones de la Paz, Mexico D.F., 1982.

Carpio, Salvador Cayetano. *La Huelga General Obrera de Abril 1967*. Imprenta Elena, San José, Costa Rica 1968.

Carpio, Salvador Cayetano. *Secuestro y Capucha*, EDUCA, San José, Costa Rica, 1979.

Carranza, S. "'Aguilares.' Una Experiencia de Evangelización Rural, Septiembre de 1972 — Agosto de 1974", *ECA*, pp.838-854, Oct.-Nov. 1977.

Castillo Rivas, Donald. *Acumulación de Capital y Empresas Transnacionales en Centroamérica*. Siglo XXI, Mexico D.F., 1980.

Castro, Pablo. *La Participación del Estado en la Penetración Capitalista de un Departmento Atrasado de El Salvador: El Caso de Chalatenango (1950-1975)*. Thesis. Universidad de Costa Rica, San José, 1976.

*CEPAL, FAO, OIT, IICA, SIECA, OCT, OEA. Tenencia de la Tierra y Desarrollo Rural en Centroamérica*. EDUCA, San José, 1973.

Centro Agronómico Tropical de Investigación y Enseñanza (CATIE). *Caracterización Ambiental y de los Principales Sistemas de Cultivo en Fincas Pequeñas. Tejutla, El Salvador*. Departamento de Producción Vegetal, Costa Rica, 1984.

Centro Regional de Informaciones Ecuménicas (CRIE). "La Vida en Las Zonas Controladas por el FMLN", *CRIE*, Nos. 153-4, Jul. 3 & 17, 1984.

Checchi and Company. *Agrarian Reform in El Salvador*. Prepared for USAID, Washington, D.C., 1981 & 1983.

Clements, Charles. *Witness to War*. Bantam, New York, 1984.

Colindres, Eduardo. *Fundamentos Económicos de la Burguesía Salvadoreña*. UCA, San Salvador, 1977.

Colindres, Eduardo. "La Tenencia de la Tierra en El Salvador", *ECA* Editores pp.463-472. Sept.-Oct. 1976

Comandancia General del FMLN. — *Situación Revolucionaria y Escalada Intervencionista en la Guerra Salvadoreña*. Mimeo, 1984.

Comandante Marcial (Salvador Cayetano Carpio). *La Lucha de Clases, Motor del Desarrollo de la Guerra Popular de Liberación*. Enero 32, Mexico, 1982.

Comandante Rigoberto. In *La Guerra Popular en El Salvador*. Ediciones de la Paz, Mexico D.F., 1982.

Committee of Professional Health Workers. *El Salvador: War and Health. The Consequences of the War on the Health of the Salvadorean People*. COMIN, 1984.

Dada Hirezi, Héctor. *La Economía de El Salvador y la Integración Centroamericana*. UCA, San Salvador, 1978.

Dalton, Roque. *Miguel Mármol*. EDUCA, San José, 1972.

Deere, Carmen & Martin Diskin. *Rural Poverty in El Salvador*. World Employment Program Research Paper # 64. International Labor Organization, Geneva, 1984.

Doljanin, Nicolás. *Chalatenango: La Guerra Descalza*. El Día, Mexico D.F., 1982.

Dorner, Peter & Rodolfo Quiros. "Institutional Dualism in Central America's Agricultural Development", *Journal of Latin American Studies*, pp.217-232, Cambridge, 1973.

Downing, T.J. *Agricultural Modernization in El Salvador*. Centre of Latin American Studies, Cambridge University, 1978.

Downing, T.J. *Water Resources in Development Planning: Case Study Central America*. Working Paper 192. University of Leeds, 1977.

Dunham, David. *Rural Development as Counter-Insurgency: Notes on the Political Dimensions of "Small-Farmer" Policies*. Mimeo, Institute of Social Studies, The Hague, 1983.

Dunkerley, James. *The Long War*. Verso, London, 1985.

Durham, William. *Scarcity and Survival in Central America*. Stanford University Press, Stanford, 1979.

ECA. *"Las Masacres de Cabañas y Chalatenango"*, Sept. 1984.

El Salvador. *Atlas Económico de El Salvador*. Banco Hipotecario, 1974.

El Salvador. *Indicadores Económicos*. Ministerio de Planificación y Coordinación, San Salvador, 1975.

El Salvador. *Indicadores Económicas y Sociales*. Ministerio de Planificación, San Salvador, Jul.-Dec. 1981.

El Salvador. *El Salvador en Gráficas*. Dirección de Estadísticas y Censos, San Salvador, 1975.

Erdozaín, Plácido. *Archbishop Romero*. Orbis, Maryknoll, N.Y., 1981.

FAPU. "La Clase Obrera Combatiente", *Pueblo*, El Salvador, Dec. 1977.

FECCAS. *Carta de Principios*. El Salvador, 1975.

FECCAS-UTC a los Cristianos de El Salvador y Centroamérica, *ECA*, Sept. pp.776-778, 1978.

Flores, Marina. *Dieta Adecuada de Costo Mínimo para El Salvador*. Institute of Nutrition of Central America and Panama, Guatemala, 1969.

Flores Alvarado, Humberto. *Centroamérica: Empleo y Desempleo Rural*. PROCCARA, Honduras, 1976.

Flores Valdivieso, Julio César. *Población, Desarrollo Rural y Migraciones Internas en El Salvador: Departmento de Chalatenango (1961-71)*. Thesis. UCA, San Salvador, 1979.

Forché, Carolyn & Philip Wheaton. *History and Motivations of US Involvement in the Control of the Peasant Movement in El Salvador. The Role of AIFLD in the Agrarian Reform Process 1970-1980*. EPICA, Washington, 1980.

FPL. "La Revolución Avanza", *Campo Rebelde*, May 1978.

FPL. "La Estrategia Revolucionaria hacia Centroamérica", *El Rebelde*, El Salvador, Sept. 1977.

FPL. *Revolutionary Strategy in El Salvador*. Tricontinental Society, London, 1980.

FPL. *El Salvador: The Development of the People's Struggle*. Tricontinental

Society, London, 1980.

FTC. *Perspectiva Histórica de Movimiento Campesino Revolucionario en El Salvador* Enero 32, Mexico, 1979.

FTC. Los Trabajadores del Campo y La Reforma Agraria en El Salvador.

FTC. "Criminal Represión contra los Trabajadores del Campo en Cinquera", *Boletín Internacional*, April 1979.

Gilly, Adolfo. "Vietnam: A War of the Masses and the Socialist Revolution", *Monthly Review*, Dec. 1965.

Guerra, Walter. *Las Asociaciones Comunitarias en el Area Rural de El Salvador en la Década 1960-1970*. Serie Tesis de Grado No.4 Universidad de El Salvador, San Salvador, 1976.

Guidos Véjar, Rafael. *El Ascenso del Militarismo en El Salvador*. UCA Editores, San Salvador, 1980.

Guillén, José Víctor. "El Salvador: Christian Communities Active in the Free Zones". In *A New Way of Being Church*. Latinamerica Press, Lima, 1984.

Harnecker, Marta. *Pueblo en Armas*. Universidad Autónoma de Guerrero, Guerrero, Mexico, 1983.

Heckhorn, Manfred. *Die Enkel des Jaguar: El Salvador Einblicke in Kleines Land*. Rotbuch, Berlin, 1983.

Hernández, Alfonso. *León de Piedra (Testimonios de la Lucha de Clases en El Salvador)*. San Salvador, 1981.

Huizer, Gerrit. *Peasant Rebellion in Latin America*. Penguin, London, 1973.

Huizer, Gerrit. *The Revolutionary Potential of Peasants in Latin America*. Lexington Books, Massachusetts, 1972.

Huizer, Gerrit. "A Community Development Experience in a Central American Village. Some Reflections and Observations", *América Indígena*, pp.221-231, July 1964.

Huizer, Gerrit. "Resistencia al Cambio" como una Potencial para la Acción Radical Campesina: Foster y Erasmus", *América Indígena*, Ap., 1970.

ILO. *Informe al Gobierno de El Salvador sobre los Asalariados Agrícolas*. Geneva, 1954.

ILO-PREALC. *Situación y Perspectiva del Empleo en El Salvador*. Santiago, Chile, 1977.

Keogh, Dermot. *Romero: El Salvador's Martyr*. Dominican Publications, Dublin, 1981.

Latin America Bureau. *El Salvador under General Romero*. London, 1979.

Landsberger, Henry (ed). *Latin American Peasant Movements*. Cornell University Press, 1969.

Larde Laud, Anabella & Ana Evelyn Jacir Siman. *Una Forma de Producción Campesina en la Formación Social Salvadoreña*. Thesis. Universidad Centroamericana, San Salvador, 1980.

Lehoucq, Edward. *Reform with Repression: The Land Reform in El Salvador*, Institute for the Study of Human Issues. Occasional Papers in Social Change, Nos.5-6. Philadelphia, 1982.

Lemoine, Maurice. *Los Compañeros. Martyr, luttes et Espérances d'un Peuple. El Salvador*. Encre, Paris, 1982.

Luxton, R. *Mayan Dream Walk*. Hutchinson, London, 1981.

McClintock, Michael. *The American Connection. State Terror and Popular Resistance in El Salvador*. Vol. I Zed Press, London, 1985.

MacLeod, Murdo. *Spanish Central America*. University of California Press, Berkeley & Los Angeles, 1973.

Marroquín, Alejandro. "Estudio sobre la Crisis de los Años Treinta en El Salvador", pp.113-190, in *America Latina en los Años Treinta*. Universidad Autónoma de México, Mexico D.F., 1977.

May; Jacques & Donna L. McLellan. *The Ecology of Malnutrition in Mexico and Central America*. Hafner, New York, 1972.

Menédez Rodríguez, Mario. *El Salvador: Una Auténtica Guerra Civil*. EDUCA, San José, 1980.

Menjívar, Rafael. *Acumulación Originaria y Desarrollo del Capitalismo en El Salvador*. EDUCA, San Jose, 1980.

Menjívar, Rafael. *El Salvador: El Eslabón más Pequeño*. EDUCA, San José, 1981.

Menjívar, Rafael. *Formación y Lucha del Proletariado Industrial Salvadoreño*. UCA Editores, San Salvador, 1979.

Monteforte Toledo, Mario. *Centro América. Subdesarrollo y Dependencia*. Universidad Nacional Autónoma de México, Mexico D.F., 1972.

Montes, Segundo. *El Agro Salvadoreño (1973-1980)*. UCA Editores, San Salvador, 1980.

Montgomery, Tommie Sue. *Revolution in El Salvador. Origin and Evolution*. Westview Press, Boulder, 1982.

Moore, Barrington. *Social Origins of Dictatorship and Democracy*. Penguin, London, 1973.

Munro, Dana G. "El Salvador" in *El Salvador de 1840 a 1935*, pp.115-149. UCA Editores, San Salvador, 1978.

Nairn, Allan. "Behind the Death Squads", *Progressive*, pp.20-29, May 1984.

OAS. *El Salvador: Zonificación Agrícola*. Fase I. Washington, DC, 1974

Pearce, Jenny. *Under the Eagle*. LAB, London, 1982.

Pons, Gabriel. *Ecología Humana en Centroamérica*. OAS, El Salvador, 1977.

Porras Mendieta, Nemesio. *Estructura Económica de El Salvador*. PROCCARA-INA, Honduras, 1976.

PROCCARA. *El Salvador: Características Generales de la Utilización y Distribución de la Tierra.*, 1971.

PRS. *El Salvador: Una Perspectiva Revolucionaria. Octubre 1977. Comisión de Propaganda de la Revolución Salvadoreña.*

Publicaciones de la Revolución Salvadoreña. *El Salvador: Entrevista con el Comandante Juan Ramón Medrano del Ejército Revolucionario del Pueblo, ERP, miembro del FMLN, sobre el Desarrollo Político-militar de la Zona de Morazán.*

Pyes, Craig. "Salvadorean Rightists: The Deadly Patriots". Reprinted from a series in the *Albuquerque Journal*, December 18-22, 1983.

Resistencia Nacional. *Por la Causa Proletaria.*

Richard, Pablo & Guillermo Meléndez (eds). *La Iglesia de los Pobres en América Central*. DEI Editores, San José, 1982.

Romero, Oscar A. "Cese la Represión!". IEPALA, Madrid, Spain, 1980.

Romero, Oscar A. "La Iglesia y Las Organizaciones Políticas Populares. Tercera Carta Pastoral y Primera de Monseñor Arturo Rivera Damas". *ECA*. pp. 760-773, Sept. 1978.

Rivera Damas, Arturo. "Labor Pastoral de la Arquidiócesis de San Salvador Especialmente de las Comunidades Eclesiales de Base en su Proyección a la Justicia", *ECA*, pp.805-814, Oct.-Nov. 1977.

Ruiz, Santiago. "La Modernización Agrícola en El Salvador", *ECA*, pp.153-166, April 1976.

Russell, Philip. *El Salvador in Crisis*. Colorado River Press, Austin, Texas, 1984.

Samaniego, Carlos. "Movimiento Campesino o Lucha del Proletariado Rural en El Salvador", *Estudios Sociales Centroamericanos*, pp.125-144, Jan.-Apr. 1980.

Samayoa, S. & Galvan, G. "El Movimiento Obrero en El Salvador: Resurgimiento o agitación?" *ECA* No. 369-370, 1979.

Secretariado Cristiano de Solidaridad "Mons. Oscar Arnulfo Romero". *La Iglesia Salvadoreña Lucha, Reflexiona y Canta*, 1983.

Sevilla, Manuel. *La Concentración Económica en El Salvador*. INIES/CRIES, Managua, 1985.

Shanin, Teodor (ed). *Peasants and Peasant Societies*. Penguin, London, 1975.

Simon, Laurence & James C. Stephens, Jr. *El Salvador Land Reform. Impact Audit. 1980-1981. 1982 Supplement*. Oxfam America, Boston, 1982.

Slutzky, Daniel & Ester. "El Salvador: Estructura de la Explotación Cafetalera", *Estudios Sociales Centroamericanos*, pp.101-125, May-Aug. 1972.

Smith, Richard A. "El Salvador Diversifies Export Crops but Lags in Food Production", *Foreign Agriculture*, Oct. 1965.

Smith, T. Lynn. "Notes on Population and Rural Social Organizations in El Salvador", *Rural Sociology*, pp.359-379, Dec. 1945.

Sobrino, Jon. *Romero: Martyr for Liberation*. CIIR, London, 1982.

Sol, Ricardo. *Para Entender El Salvador*. DEI, San José, 1980.

Sol, Jorge. "El Salvador: Can the Duarte Experiment Work?" *NACLA*, pp.24-25 & 32, Jan.-Feb., 1985.

Stetler, Russell (ed). *The Military Art of People's War. Selected Writings of General Vo Nguyen Giap*. Monthly Review Press, New York & London, 1970.

Thome, Josef. *Agrarian Reform in El Salvador*. Briefing Paper to "Alternative Economic Strategies for Central America", Washington D.C., 1984.

Thomson, Marilyn. *Women of El Salvador. The Price of Freedom*. Zed Press, London, 1986.

Thompson, John Eric. *The Rise and Fall of the Mayan Civilization*. University of Oklahoma, Norman, 1966.

UCA. *Rutilio Grande. Mártir de la Evangelización Rural en El Salvador*. UCA Editores, San Salvador, 1978.

Ungo, Guillermo Manuel. "Consideraciones Jurídico/políticas sobre la Transformación Agraria". *ECA*, pp.451-462, Sept.-Oct. 1976.

US. House of Representatives, *The Recent Presidential Elections in El Salvador: Implications for US Foreign Policy. Hearings before the Sub-committees on International Organizations and on Inter-American Affairs of the Committee on Internal Relations*. March 9 & 17, 1977.

Valverde, Víctor et al. "Life Styles and Nutritional Status of Children from Different Ecological Areas of El Salvador", *Ecology of Food and Nutrition*, pp.167-177, 1980.

Villalobos, Joaquín. *Acerca de la Situación Militar en El Salvador*. 1983.

Villalobos, Joaquín. *Por Qué Lucha el FMLN?*. Ediciones Radio Venceremos, 1983.

Webre, Stephen. *José Napoleón Duarte and the Christian Democratic Part in Salvadorean Politics, 1960-1972*, L.S.U. Press, Baton Rouge, 1979.

Wheaton, Philip. *Agrarian Reform in El Salvador: A program of Rural Pacification*. EPICA, Washington D.C., 1980.

White, Alistair. *El Salvador*. Praeger, New York, 1973.

Wilson, Everett Alan. "La Crisis de la Integración Nacional en El Salvador" in *El Salvador de 1840 a 1935*. UCA Editores, San Salvador, 1978.

Winson, A. *Class Structure and Agrarian Transition in Central America*, Latin American Perspectives, Issue 19, Fall 1978.

Wolf, Eric. *Peasant Wars of the Twentieth Century*. Faber, London, 1973.

Wolf, Eric. *Sons of the Shaking Earth*. University of Chicago Press, Chicago & London, 1959.

Wolf, Eric. "On Peasant Rebellions", in *Peasants and Peasant Societies*, pp.264-274. Penguin, London, 1975.

World Bank/IBRD. *El Salvador: Demographic Issues and Prospects*. Latin America and the Caribbean Regional Office, Washington D.C., 1979.

## Other Publications

BPR *Combate Popular* 1977-78
   *Boletín Internacional* 1979-80
FAPU *Pueblo* (Organo de divulgación politíca del Frente de Acción Popular Unificada)
   *Pueblo Boletín Internacional*
FPL *Estrella Roja* — Organo ideológico 1975-
   *El Rebelde* 1975-
   *Campo Rebelde* 1976-
Justicia y Paz 1973-74
   *Boletín de las Comunidades Rurales Cristianas* 1975-
Radio Farabundo Martí — Recortes de las transmisiones 1983-

# Index

322

Sánchez, Juan Ramón, 132
Sánchez, Rutilio, 112, 171, 282
Sandinistas, 187
Sandino, 84
Serrano, Apolinario 'Polín', 143, 153-5, 157
Social Christian movement, 97, 99; youth 130
Social Democrat Party, 116
*Socorro Jurídico*, 227
Sol, Jorge, 289
Soviet Union, 126
SRI, 84
STECEL, 174, 185, 195
STUC, 94
Survil, Bernard, 169

Tobar, Father Benito, 112
Torres, Andrés, 138, 155, 161
Treasury Police, 87, 168, 176, 181, 297
*Tutela Legal*, 227

UCA, 114-5, 120, 135, 187
UCS, v, 82, 94-7, 142-3, 183, 297-8
UDN, 123
UGB, 171
UNDP, 26, 30, 42
Ungo, Guillermo, 187, 190
United States, 2-4, 7, 9, 32, 34-5, 41, 88, 91-2, 97-8, 134, 187-8, 193, 202-3, 208, 224, 229, 292-3, 295, 298-9, 300-1; Administration, 200; advisers, 237; Congress, 193, 231; Congressional hearings, 170; military aid, 231; Public Safety Programme, 89; State Department, 89, 193, 291, 294

UNO, 151, 166
UNOC, 99-100
UPD, 300
UPT, 136
UR-19, 136
Urquilla, Sebastian, 131
USAID, 35, 39, 59, 88-9, 93-7, 237, 293, 295-6
UTC, vi, 62, 109, 117-8, 136, 138, 141-9, 150, 152-5, 157-9, 161, 164-6, 170, 172-3, 175-6, 179, 183-4, 186, 204, 242, 286

Vásquez, Serafín, 168
Vásquez, Transito, 176
Vatican II, 93, 109-11, 113
Venezuela, 15
Ventura, Father Miguel, 132
Viera, José Rodolfo, 97, 300
Vietnam, 126, 202, 207, 291-2
Villalobos, Joaquín, 130, 199, 200

Wainwright, Juan Pablo, 84
*Washington Post, The*, 300
White, Alastair, 75, 87, 123
Wolf, Eric, 107-8
Worker-Peasant Alliance, 171
World Bank, 51
World Health Organization, 271

YSAX, archdiocesan radio station, 114, 170-1

Zapolitán scheme, 36